Political Economy of Latin America

International Papers in Political Economy Series

Series Editors: Philip Arestis and Malcolm Sawyer

This is the third volume of the new series of *International Papers in Political Economy (IPPE)*. The new series will consist of an annual volume with four to five papers on a single theme. The objective of the *IPPE* will continue to be the publication of papers dealing with important topics within the broad framework of Political Economy.

The original series of *International Papers in Political Economy* started in 1993 and has been published in the form of three issues a year with each issue containing a single extensive paper. Information on the old series and back copies can be obtained from Professor Malcolm Sawyer at the University of Leeds (e-mail: mcs@lubs.leeds.ac.uk)

Titles include:

Philip Arestis and Malcolm Sawyer *(editors)*
ALTERNATIVE PERSPECTIVES ON ECONOMIC POLICIES IN THE EUROPEAN UNION

FINANCIAL LIBERALIZATION
Beyond Orthodox Concerns.

POLITICAL ECONOMY OF LATIN AMERICA
Recent Economic Performance

International Papers in Political Economy
Series Standing Order ISBN 1-4039-9936-8

You can receive future titles in this series as they are published by placing a standing order. Please contact your bookseller or, in case of difficulty, write to us at the address below with your name and address, the title of the series and one of the ISBNs quoted above.

Customer Services Department, Macmillan Distribution Ltd, Houndmills, Basingstoke, Hampshire RG21 6XS, England

Political Economy of Latin America

Recent Economic Performance

Edited by

Philip Arestis and Malcolm Sawyer

First published 2007 by
PALGRAVE MACMILLAN
Houndmills, Basingstoke, Hampshire RG21 6XS and
175 Fifth Avenue, New York, N.Y. 10010
Companies and representatives throughout the world

PALGRAVE MACMILLAN is the global academic imprint of the Palgrave
Macmillan division of St. Martin's Press, LLC and of Palgrave Macmillan Ltd.
Macmillan® is a registered trademark in the United States, United Kingdom
and other countries. Palgrave is a registered trademark in the European Union
and other countries.

ISBN-13: 978-0-230-54703-2   hardback
ISBN-10: 0-230-54703-6   hardback

This book is printed on paper suitable for recycling and made from fully managed
and sustained forest sources. Logging, pulping and manufacturing processes are
expected to conform to the environmental regulations of the country of origin.

A catalogue record for this book is available from the British Library.

A catalog record for this book is available from the Library of Congress.

10   9   8   7   6   5   4   3   2   1
16   15   14   13   12   11   10   09   08   07

Printed and bound in Great Britain by
Antony Rowe Ltd, Chippenham and Eastbourne

Contents

List of Tables

List of Figures

Preface

This is the third volume of the new series of *International Papers in Political Economy* (*IPPE*). The new series will consist of an annual volume with a number of papers on a single theme. The objective of the *IPPE* will continue to be the publication of papers dealing with important topics within the broad framework of Political Economy.

The original series of *International Papers in Political Economy* started in 1993 and has been published in the form of three issues a year with each issue containing a single extensive paper. Information on the old series and back copies can be obtained from Professor Malcolm Sawyer at the University of Leeds (e-mail: mcs@lubs.leeds.ac.uk).

The theme of this third volume of six papers is the political economy of a number of Latin American countries in the aftermath of the introduction of liberalization policies in this part of the world, but concentrating on recent economic performance.

1

Neoliberalism, Democracy and Economic Policy in Latin America[1]

Alfredo Saad-Filho, Francesca Iannini and Elizabeth Jean Molinari
Department of Development Studies SOAS, University of London

Abstract

This chapter reviews the economic, social and political changes associated with the transition from import-substituting industrialization (ISI) to neoliberalism in Argentina and Brazil. It shows that, despite the significant differences in the economic performance of their ISI regimes, and the distinct social compositions and political forms associated with that system of accumulation, the transitions to neoliberalism in Argentina and Brazil have commonalities across several levels. This chapter explores three of these levels: the role of inflation stabilization, the relationship between the democratic transition and the economic transition to neoliberalism, and the tensions and displacements which currently limit the new liberal system of accumulation in both countries.

Keywords: Latin America, Brazil, Argentina, Democracy, Neoliberalism.

JEL Classification: O11, O54.

1.1 Introduction

The political economy of Latin America has changed significantly over the course of the last generation. Three important changes are especially evident. Firstly, the political system of a growing number of countries has become remarkably open as well as generally stable for more than twenty years. In the past, most countries were relatively closed as well as being politically unstable, undergoing sharp swings between relatively pluralistic and socially inclusive phases and harsh authoritarian rule. Secondly, their economies have been transformed. Between the early 1930s and the mid- to late 1970s, several Latin

American countries significantly expanded their manufacturing capacity through a strategy of import-substituting industrialization (ISI). Today, however, most countries have become relatively low-growth economies firmly tied to the neoliberal world order, and a significant degree of deindustrialization has been observed in the recent past. Most institutions associated with ISI have been dismantled, and their social structures and occupational patterns have been, correspondingly, transformed in a neoliberal direction. Thirdly, Latin America was, for several decades, typically a high inflation region. Today, high inflation has been eliminated almost everywhere.

These systemic shifts have been explained in different ways. Mainstream economists usually claim that ISI is an intrinsically inefficient accumulation strategy, which was imposed by populist administrations currying favour with minority constituencies at the expense of the general good (and at the expense of faster long-term growth; see Bresser-Pereira, 1991 and Dornbusch and Edwards, 1991). 'Populist' developmental states ran large fiscal deficits due to excessive welfare expenditures, ill-considered subsidy schemes, corruption, unrealistic wages in the public sector and the reckless expansion of deficit-prone state-owned enterprises (SOEs). Neoliberal economic reforms were essential, and they were implemented when the political circumstances permitted. This interpretation sees no relationship between the political transition to democracy and the economic transition to neoliberalism. The former is understood to depend on the balance of forces in society, and the latter on the (belated) realization that 'There Is No Alternative' to neoliberalism. Finally, these economists claim that the disappointing economic performance of most Latin American countries in the recent period has been due primarily to remaining economic rigidities (especially in the labour market), regulatory uncertainty, and external turbulence. In contrast, structuralist economists and *dependentistas* generally argue that poor economic performance, under both ISI and neoliberalism, is due primarily to the inefficiency of market processes in these countries, distributive conflicts and external transfers, especially following the debt crisis (see, for example, Fanelli, 2003 and Palma, 1998). More recently, trade and capital account liberalization are also considered to have contributed to the drainage of domestic resources, and added to the fragility of the balance of payments in both countries.

This chapter offers an alternative interpretation of the recent changes in the political economy of Latin America through a close examination of the cases of Argentina and Brazil. This interpretation is based on the relationship between the economic transition from ISI to neoliberalism, and the political transition from military rule to democracy in both countries. The chapter has six sections. This introduction is the first. The second briefly surveys the period of rapid growth under ISI in Argentina and Brazil and its exhaustion in the early 1980s. The third reviews the economic and political strategies of the military regimes in both countries, and their processes of transitions to democracy. The fourth examines the political economy of the democratic regimes

in Argentina and Brazil. The fifth considers the relationship between inflation stabilization and the neoliberal transition. The sixth concludes this
chapter with a brief examination of the limitations and potential fragilities of
the new liberal consensus (the hegemonic combination between neoliberal
economic policies with political democracy) in Argentina and Brazil.

1.2 The political economy of rapid growth

ISI is an accumulation strategy that focuses on the expansion of the share of
manufacturing industry in GDP, with a view to using captive domestic markets
and the available resources to replace imports, generate employment, internal-
ize new ('modern') technologies and cultural values, and alleviate structural
pressures on the balance of payments (see Bruton, 1998; Hirschman, 1968).

Urbanization and manufacturing sector development through ISI are, to
some extent, the spontaneous outcome of rising incomes and economic diversification under primary export-led growth. A tight balance of payments constraint (usually under a fixed exchange rate regime) can accelerate moves
towards ISI, for example, through the reduction of import capacity because
of declining terms of trade, crop failures or the unavailability of imports as a
result of foreign wars. Alternatively, ISI can also be stimulated by the imposition of tariff barriers by local governments, with a view to insulating the
domestic market to favour local producers (which may be either national or
foreign-based). Although the two world wars and the 1929 crisis played an
important role in the success of ISI in Latin America, adverse external shocks are
insufficient conditions for manufacturing growth. For example, these shocks
can provide incentives for the expansion of output only when spare manufacturing capacity is already available. Such outcomes depend on a preceding
period of export growth (or, alternatively, foreign loans or foreign investment).
Sizable domestic markets also create incentives for the domestic production
of manufactured goods, a factor that explains why ISI was normally more
successful in large economies than in small ones.

Experience shows that a successful process of ISI requires not only activist
trade policies but also extensive government direction in the allocation of
resources, along with other modalities of intervention in the markets for inputs
and labour power, and the provision of finance and infrastructure. Incentives
are normally required by transnational companies, domestic firms and SOEs
to produce manufactured goods locally, and the impact of any incentives is
maximized when they are supported by expansionary macroeconomic policies. The deployment of these interventionist policies was normally part of a
deliberate strategy to diversify the economy and reduce its vulnerability to
external shocks, which were perceived to represent an inherent weakness of the
primary-export-led model (see Thorp, 1992).

The development of domestic manufacturing capacity under ISI generally
follows a sequence of increasingly complex economic activities (see Tables 1.1

Table 1.1   Argentina: domestic industrial output, selected sectors, 1950–69 (%)

	1950–54	1955–59	1960–64	1965–69
Foodstuffs and beverages	24.6	22.5	20.4	18.8
Textiles and leather	23.4	19.9	15.2	13.4
Chemicals	13.0	14.1	15.9	17.5
Machinery and equipment	17.0	21.9	28.5	30.0
Other	22.0	21.6	20.0	20.3

Source: Katz and Kosacoff (2000, p. 289).

Table 1.2   Brazil: distribution of value added in manufacturing industry, 1919–59

	1919	1939	1949	1959
Consumer goods	80.2	69.7	61.9	46.6
Textiles	24.4	22.0	19.7	12.0
Clothing	7.3	4.8	4.3	3.6
Food	32.9	23.6	20.6	16.4
Other	15.6	19.3	17.3	14.6
Consumer durables	1.8	2.5	2.5	5.0
Intermediate goods	16.5	22.9	30.4	37.3
Metallurgy	3.8	7.6	9.4	11.8
Non-metallic minerals	2.8	4.3	6.5	6.1
Chemical	0.8	4.2	4.7	8.3
Wood	5.7	3.2	4.2	3.2
Other	3.4	3.6	5.6	7.9
Capital goods	1.5	4.9	5.2	11.1
Mechanical	0.1	1.3	2.1	3.4
Electrical	0.0	0.3	0.8	1.0
Transport equipment	1.4	3.3	2.2	6.7

Source: Abreu, Bevilacqua and Pinho (2000, p. 163).

and 1.2 and Figure 1.1). Domestic manufacturing production usually starts from the internalization of the production of non-durable consumer goods (cigarettes, beverages, cotton textiles, shoes, petrol, kerosene, and so on). The expansion of these industries is often followed by the production of consumer durables (e.g., household appliances and automobile assembly), as well as intermediate goods (auto parts, simple chemical and pharmaceutical products, cement, and so on). In Argentina and Brazil, the process of import substitution went further, to include the production of basic inputs and capital goods (steel, industrial machinery and electric motors, heavy and chemical industries, and large infrastructural projects). In Brazil, domestic production eventually included technologically complex goods like electronic machinery, turbines for hydroelectric dams, shipbuilding and aircraft design and assembly.

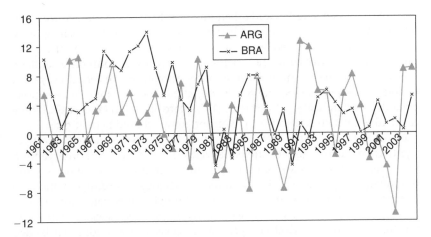

Figure 1.1 Argentina and Brazil: GDP growth (% per annum)
Source: World Development Indicators.

In both countries, under mature ISI, a 'macroeconomic division of labour' was established in which domestic capital tended to produce non-durable consumer goods and capital goods, while transnational companies normally produced durable consumer goods. State-owned enterprises provided subsidized infrastructure and basic goods and services, and state-owned banks supplied long-term credit for industrial development.

Politically, ISI in Argentina and Brazil was based essentially on a corporatist and populist model institutionalized, respectively, by General Juan D. Perón and Getúlio D. Vargas. Although their policies were often heavily authoritarian, these administrations also contributed to the enlargement and institutionalization of the civil and political rights of the working class, and transformed the industrial workers, in particular, into a political as well as economic agent. In Argentina, Perón's perception of the potentially revolutionary character of the working class, coupled with its importance within the Peronist alliance, led to the 1949 reform of the Constitution, which was overtly inspired by the distributive ideal of 'social justice'. These reforms introduced relatively sophisticated social policies and a welfare state in the country, aiming to co-opt the urban working class to support the accumulation strategy sponsored by the Argentine state (Weisman, 1987).

Similarly in Brazil, Vargas governed as a dictator after 1938. During this period he reformed labour law (closely following Mussolini's *Carta del Lavoro*), supported the organization of hundreds of trade unions, and introduced a rudimentary form of social provision for the urban workers and civil servants (Skidmore, 1973).

The uneasy coexistence between populism, nationalism and statism under ISI was primarily due to the intense conflicts of interest within the elite (for example, between agrarian and urban interests, between manufacturing capital and finance, and so on), and between the elite and other social groups, especially the marginalized but increasingly militant workers, and the urban middle classes. Stripped of their rich complexity, these conflicts essentially centred around the extent to which resources should be transferred away from the primary export sector, and where they should be allocated – for example, towards urban industry, infrastructure or welfare provision (and, within these alternatives, which sub-sectors, regions or groups should benefit most).

It was widely accepted that, in order to achieve developmental objectives (synthesized in the goal of industrialization), extensive state intervention was required at several levels. Economic interventionism was supported, and not infrequently disguised, by a nationalist ideology according to which the 'nation as a whole' would progress only through industrialization. In this developmentalist discourse, lack of industrialization was associated with backwardness and the political and economic power of the traditional landed elites, to be overcome through state action towards economic 'progress'. The relationship between nationalism, statism and developmentalism tended to become especially evident when private capital lacked the capacity or interest to invest in strategic areas such as oil, steel, electricity generation or transport links. In cases such as these, provision would often depend on extensive state intervention, either through the nationalization of the industry and its development through a state monopoly, or through the offer of subsidies or other incentives for private capital to address these supply constraints. The resolution of the conflicts of interest associated with the expansion of production in these key areas was never unproblematic. Conflicting popular demands, state initiatives and sectoral pressures were played out in the media, in educational and research institutions, in state institutions and on the streets, sometimes violently, and the outcomes were contingent on timing, circumstances and the constellation of forces mobilized on each side.[2]

The precise form of the relationship between nationalism, mass pressures and state economic interventionism depended to a large extent on the social and political relationships within the elite. They include, especially, the degree of elite consensus around developmentalist policy strategies and the capacity and interest of the state to impose developmental outcomes without the mobilization of the urban masses, particularly the emerging middle and working classes. Strong political currents took shape in this period in close association with the interests at stake in the process of industrialization. In Argentina, the Justicialist (Perónist) party was formed in 1945, and it remained closely associated at least in political mythology with ISI until the late 1980s. In Brazil, Vargas founded two political parties in 1945 as part of his effort to build a wide support base for his developmentalist policies: the Brazilian Labour Party (a left-wing organization based primarily on the organized workers) and the Social Democratic Party (a centre-left party with extensive links to the landed elite and the urban middle classes).

The intense conflicts around state ideology and priorities during this period, and around the form of implementation of the state's developmental goals, made resource allocation through fiscal policy a highly complex and contentious issue. The frequent conflation between economic and political objectives (for example, economic growth or the consolidation of political support for narrow interest groups), and between short-term and long-term initiatives (for example, social welfare or infrastructure provision) made the choice of state priorities very difficult, thus fuelling social conflicts and inflation. The growing paralysis of the state institutions, rising levels of social strife, the radicalization of the political parties associated with Perón and Vargas (which was partly a reflection of the growing influence of the far left), and the deterioration of the macroeconomic indicators in both countries contributed to the collapse of democracy in Argentina in 1966 and, more dramatically, in 1976, and in Brazil after 1964. In both countries, these military coups were a response to a hegemonic impasse (O'Donnell, 1982), which appeared as a 'a static equilibrium . . . [in which] no group, neither the conservatives nor the progressives, has the strength for victory, and [in which] the conservative group needs a master' (Gramsci, 1971, p. 451). Military intervention cut through the existing social divisions, and imposed national solutions which differed greatly in character.

1.3   From militarism to democracy

This section shows that the collapse of militarism in Argentina and Brazil was triggered by its loss of legitimacy, owing to a combination of two factors. On the one hand, a profound economic crisis, which the military regimes were unable to address. Indicators of the crisis included the accumulation of foreign (and domestic public) debt, the stagnation of incomes and economic growth, the rise of working-class struggles and, especially, high inflation, which synthesized the underlying economic tensions. On the other hand, a deep political crisis brought about by the rise of a democratic mass movement which could not be repressed. Political contestation to military rule encompassed a wide range of modalities of mass struggle, among them criticisms of widespread corruption, economic mismanagement and lack of democracy and accountability in the political system, trade union activity, and mass mobilization for economic and political democracy. At this stage, a significant change took place within the elites in both countries:[3] for the first time since, at least, the late 1920s, a consensus developed around political democracy.[4] This elite consensus was the outcome of external pressures as well as domestic developments, and it facilitated the democratic transition in Argentina and Brazil because it defused the potential conflicts that may have arisen around the change of political regime.

1.3.1   The bumpy Argentine road to new liberalism . . .

The military coup of March 1976 unleashed in Argentina a wide-ranging *Proceso de Reorganización Nacional* (process of national reorganization). The *Proceso* included an attempt to eliminate the radical left through the targeted killing of thousands of militants, to dismantle the organized working class, and to reform society in order to transform the country into a bastion of 'Western Christian values'. The economic programme of the dictatorship was inspired by monetarism, which seemed to offer a tool for dismantling ISI and for introducing a new system of accumulation based on primary product exports and services, supported by closer integration with the world economy through financial, trade and capital account liberalization.[5] It was expected that the 'market' would operate as the main disciplining mechanism in the economic sphere (supported by military power where necessary) against both inefficient entrepreneurs and the 'undisciplined' working class which had been created under ISI (see Smith, 1989; Schvarzer, 1981). The privatization programme, for example, afforded contractors a wide variety of benefits such as markets, tax advantages, guaranteed payments and easy credit from the state-owned Banco de la Nación, creating powerful (foreign and local) interests which, years later, would play a central role in the promotion and implementation of neoliberal policies.

After six years of military rule, the junta's objective of rapid growth with macroeconomic stability resulted, instead, in a deep economic and financial crisis, accelerating inflation and profound economic uncertainty (Díaz-Alejandro, 1985; see Figure 1.1 and Table 1.3). This outcome was exacerbated by the asymmetric impact of the recession across the economy. Whilst the liberalization of markets caused a 26 per cent decline in manufacturing output between 1975 and 1980 (Smith, 1985), a small group of large national firms, linked principally to the agrarian sector, profited enormously by establishing oligopolistic control over large swathes of the Argentine economy. In the meantime, after years of state terror, persecutions and drastic declines in real wages, the working class gradually rediscovered its political voice (Tedesco, 1999). Testament to this were the 621 strikes in the period 1980–81, compared to only 417 in the four preceding years (Munck, 1985, p. 67).

In its troubled twilight, the military government confronted a reinvigorated and renewed civil society expressing demands not only for political democracy, but also for an economic strategy favouring broader national interests, including employment generation and the reduction of external economic vulnerability. In an attempt to regain legitimacy by appealing to nationalistic feelings, the military regime gambled everything on the invasion of the Falkland (Malvinas) Islands in April 1982. The ensuing defeat not only demoralized the military regime politically; it also isolated the country from its erstwhile allies. By the end of 1982, with the external debt having reached US\$40 billion, Argentina was on the verge of insolvency (Smith, 1991). The transfer of power to civilians had become inevitable, and it was completed in October 1983, when Raúl Alfonsín (leader of the urban middle class Unión Cívica Radical) became Argentina's new democratically elected president.

The transition to democracy was carried out in the context of a structurally weakened popular sector, the result of both deindustrialization and repression,

Table 1.3   Inflation, GDP deflator (% per annum)

	Argentina	Brazil		Argentina	Brazil
1970	6	17	1988	388	651
1971	31	20	1989	3,058	1,323
1972	64	19	1990	2,077	2,509
1973	66	23	1991	133	415
1974	31	35	1992	12	969
1975	198	34	1993	−1	1,997
1976	438	48	1994	3	2,239
1977	159	46	1995	3	78
1978	161	41	1996	0	17
1979	147	56	1997	0	8
1980	91	87	1998	−2	5
1981	106	107	1999	−2	5
1982	208	105	2000	1	10
1983	382	140	2001	−1	7
1984	607	213	2002	31	10
1985	626	232	2003	11	15
1986	74	145	2004	9	8
1987	127	204			

Source: World Development Indicators.

weak political parties and powerful interest groups. One of the political implications of the military regime's destructive industrial policy was the terminal
decline of the industrial working class, as well as the weakening of the small
and medium-sized enterprises, which were the other main component of the
political alliance supporting ISI. For example, approximately 30 per cent of
worker-hours were lost through unemployment across the manufacturing
sector between 1976 and 1981, largely as a result of market liberalization, the
overvaluation of the currency and the inability of domestic industry to compete with cheaper imports (Peralta-Ramos and Weisman, 1987).

It is often claimed that the above conditions were unfavourable to the establishment of a stable democratic regime (see, for example, Peralta-Ramos and
Waisman, 1987). However, experience has shown that this interpretation is
incorrect. It would be more accurate to argue that the structural weakening
of the working class and its urban allies *supported* the emerging consensus for
political democracy. The democratic transition legitimized the Argentine state,
while the elite's political control over the transition was facilitated by the
profound disarticulation of the working class brought about by the military
regime. These developments helped to defuse the potential conflicts around
the political transition, and to secure the reproduction of the inequality and
social exclusion engineered by the military regime, which became its lasting
legacy. In other words, the long-term significance of the democratic transition lies in the fact that it *facilitated* the reproduction of the unequal social

relations imposed by the *Proceso*. The election of President Alfonsín drew on the enthusiasm and democratic expectations of the vast majority of the population, who were encouraged by utopian assertions such as *'con la democracia se come, se cura y se educa'* ('with democracy we eat, we cure and we educate', quoted in Mainwairing, 1995, p. 122). Alfonsín, however, did little to challenge the social and economic legacy of military rule.

The scope for radical social and economic transformation was severely restricted by Alfonsín's inheritance of an economy on the verge of collapse (see Table 1.3 and Figures 1.1 and 1.2, and Azpiazú, 1998, Canitrot and Sigal, 1995 and Carranza, 1997). Capital flight had reached an estimated US$22.4 billion, nearly half the foreign debt stock (Dornbusch, 1989, p. 8). Initially, the government implemented expansionary policies that seemed more in tune with a revitalized process of ISI than with the new economic constraints facing Argentina, especially its foreign debt commitments and depleted industrial base (see Basualdo, 2001; Tedesco, 1999, p. 89). These included an attempt to relaunch a national development project, by which the government sought to resolve the economic crisis through a *concertación nacional* (national consensus) including the government, business leaders and trade unions. An effort to stabilize the rate of inflation (which exceeded 600 per cent in 1984) through the implementation of heterodox measures collapsed (see below), partly owing to pressure from the Perónist trade unions. Unsurprisingly, the promised 5 per cent annual GDP growth rate also failed to materialize. Instead, the economy contracted 7.2 per cent between 1983 and 1985. Heterodox measures were abandoned in 1987, with a profoundly damaging effect on the government's credibility. Between 1986 and 1988 real wages declined by 18.4 per cent in the private sector and 15.1 per cent in the public sector (Tedesco, 1999, p. 150). By the end of

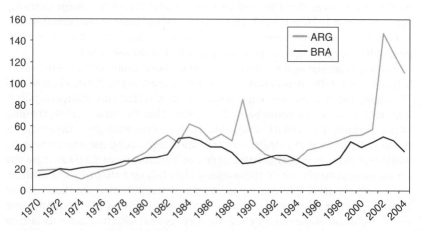

Figure 1.2   Total external debt/GDP ratio (%)
Source: World Development Indicators.

his presidency, Alfonsín faced food riots, the distrust of the bourgeoisie and the withdrawal of support from both the IMF and the World Bank.

The loss of legitimacy of the Alfonsín administration compromised the stability of democracy. Under conditions of hyperinflation and impending economic collapse, a new consensus emerged among the Argentine elite. Workers' struggles for economic participation were interpreted as a visceral rejection of economic liberalism, which was widely identified with the military regime. In this context, Alfonsín's hesitant economic record reinforced a growing sense that harsh neoliberal reforms – under a democratic political system – were needed to overcome the economic impasse and to reinstate capital's hegemony and profitability, while restoring social discipline.

1.3.2 . . . and the smoother Brazilian road

The defining feature of the Brazilian military regime, in power between 1964 and 1985, was its attempt to preserve social exclusion through a combination of economic growth and varying levels of political repression. The power of the regime declined gradually after 1974, due both to the political exhaustion of the government's heavy-handed approach towards dissent, and the economic exhaustion of the regime's 'growth miracle'. The country's foreign debt started escalating rapidly after the first oil shock, inflation simultaneously rose towards 40 per cent, and it reached 100 per cent in the early years of the next decade. The second oil shock, in 1979–80, triggered a deep economic crisis and the first GDP contraction since 1929. The economy stopped responding to the government's policies, and the military regime slowly ran out of options.

Democracy in Brazil did not emerge on the ruins of the institutions left behind by the dictatorship, as was the case in Argentina. Instead, the military commanders of the regime, allied with the country's conservative elites, were also the political commanders of the transition (see Markoff and Baretta, 1990, p. 431 and Weffort, 1989, p. 339). The Brazilian democratic movement emerged gradually in the mid-1970s. On the economic arena, large-scale industrial action, centred primarily in the manufacturing poles established under ISI and in the lower ranks of the civil service, extracted from the military regime higher wages and improved economic conditions for the workers. At the same time, censorship was abolished, the campaign for political amnesty achieved success, and the exiles returned. Finally, in 1983–84 elite and popular organizations and political parties staged a gigantic campaign for direct presidential elections. The campaign saw over ten million people take to the streets across the country, with a clear set of democratic demands that showed the desire for political reforms and extensive socioeconomic change (Alves, 1988, p. 51).

The economic crisis of the 1980s, the exhaustion of the military regime and the growth of the democratic movement and the political left triggered a historically significant political shift in the country. Elite concern over the potential radicalization of society and, especially, the escalation of demands for economic and political democracy (or the redistribution of economic and political power) led key political leaders to initiate negotiations with the military for a managed transfer of power. Elite attitudes shifted towards democracy because of a conviction, in the first instance, that the rise of the democratic movement could not be easily contained by force, and that any attempt to do so could be severely destabilizing. In addition to this, a majority among the elite realized that, although political democracy would dilute their political power, democracy *could* be compatible with the reproduction of the elite's economic power.[6] Finally, the elite increasingly rejected 'excessive' state intervention in the economy, which was perceived to be associated with the military regime. Their desire for economic liberalization and – in some quarters – the creation of an internal mass market, would benefit from the political reintegration of the formal sector workers, which required a democratic transformation of society (Markoff and Baretta, 1990, p. 429).

This strategy was successful. A constitutional amendment for the direct election of the president was narrowly defeated in Congress in April 1984, and a national consensus was formed in support of the moderate governor Tancredo Neves. Neves was duly elected president by a large majority in the dictatorship's own electoral college. The mass demonstrations for democracy, that had been disbanded, were briefly revived in support of Neves's candidacy. Unfortunately Tancredo Neves fell ill only hours before his inauguration, and died without taking office. Vice-president-elect José Sarney, until recently a key supporter of the military regime, became president of Brazil. Sarney's administration convened a Constituent Assembly in 1986, and direct presidential elections only took place in 1989.

The absence in the early years of the new democracy of comprehensive economic policies to reduce Brazil's massive socioeconomic inequalities reveals the unwillingness of the elite consensus in charge of the 'New Republic' towards any redistribution of resources that might have compromised the basic structures of governance or altered the concentration of wealth in the country. Brazil has some of the highest levels of inequality in the world. In 2002, it was estimated that the income of the poorest 20 per cent of the population would have to be multiplied by 33 to reach the income of the richest 20 per cent. By comparison, in the US it would have to be multiplied 'only' by a factor of 8 (Rose, 2006, p. 280). In the lead-up to the transition, popular organizations were conceded the opportunity to make proposals directly to the new Constituent Assembly. Two significant economic proposals were made concerning land reform and labour reforms to implement a 40-hour week and greater job security. The Assembly unsurprisingly rejected these proposals (Alves, 1988, p. 50). Their rejection was a stark illustration of where the lines were drawn for democratic accountability in the new regime.

The exclusion of significant alternative voices from meaningful participation in the democratic settlement and the dampening of their influence upon the democratic political institutions was achieved in two ways: *directly,* through (often implicit) threats of a return of military rule should social protests become too vociferous; and *indirectly*, through the economic pressures generated by the long-lasting economic crisis which, since the late 1970s, had resulted in declining growth rates and increasingly unmanageable levels of inflation (see Table 1.3 and Figure 1.1).

The substance of the elite pact that hijacked the democratic movement and sidelined the political left was very simple. In exchange for political freedom, the redistribution of economic power was ruled out. This shift was supported by the changes in the composition of the elite which had taken place since the mid-1970s. These changes were due to the transformations of the economy brought about both by the extended period of growth under the military, and by the crippling crisis of the 1970s and 1980s. The new elite included a younger and more outward-looking cohort of financiers and industrial leaders, and a more entrepreneurial brand of landowners.

The political transition established the most democratic and stable regime in the history of the Brazilian Republic. For more than twenty years there has been no press censorship, no political parties or movements of any significance have been declared illegal, and civil rights are formally guaranteed to a greater extent than in many 'old' democracies. For the first time since the late nineteenth century the military no longer interfere systematically in the political sphere, while the political influence of the Catholic Church has been drastically curtailed.[7] Finally, right-wing ideology has been utterly demoralized, and no influential organization claims to be either 'conservative' or on the 'right' (however right-wing their policies and practices may be). The stability of democracy can be explained not only by domestic political developments. It is also due to the fact that the greater political legitimacy of the democratic state can make it *less* permeable to popular pressure, and reduce the influence of the majority over state policy (see section 4).

The democratic transition satisfied most of the 'political' demands of the left, but only by disconnecting them from the 'economic' demands of the majority. Civil rights, free elections and political pluralism were achieved, but economic redistribution, the nationalization of strategically important firms and the non-payment of the foreign debt, for example, that were an inseparable part of the programme of the left, were never seriously considered by the centrist coalition in power. Matters would become even worse in the late 1980s, as the Brazilian elite gradually convinced itself that only a neoliberal economic strategy would permit the recovery of growth, the reproduction of the existing patterns of inequality, and the preservation of democracy (Saad-Filho and Morais, 2002). The Brazilian left was derailed by the democratic transition. Rather than continuing to lead mass campaigns for the radical transformation of the economy and society, the left was compelled to submit to the electoral calendar and operate within the 'bourgeois' institutions that it had previously denounced. Implementation of left-wing policies now required a democratic mandate that could be obtained only if the left-wing parties submitted themselves to the conventional logic of campaign finance, coalition-building, piecemeal reforms, endless negotiations with a myriad of interest groups and the imperatives of 'efficiency' and 'delivery' in local government. These limitations have tempered the left's enthusiasm for direct action and confrontations with the state.

1.4   The political economy of democracy

The minimalist (formal or procedural) definition of democracy associated with Schumpeter (1976) and Dahl (1971) is typified in the political regime that took shape in both Argentina and Brazil. Procedural democracy includes the protection of basic civil and political rights (freedoms of speech, of the press and of political organization, the franchise for a large section of the population, and so on), free elections for the legislature and the executive, civilian government and civilian control over the armed forces. Whilst the political freedoms granted were unquestionably significant, the democratic 'wave' (Huntington, 1993, p. 3) that swept across Latin America during the 1980s did not significantly transform the region's social and economic structures (Borón, 2006).

The scope of democracy has been limited to the political sphere, and identified with elementary civil rights and unfree competition in the political market, where government positions can, essentially, be purchased with cash. In Argentina and Brazil, citizens are regularly bombarded with propaganda and crude spin-doctoring, invited to cast their votes, and then go home. They are not supposed to influence policy-making or participate in policy implementation other than through compliance with the decisions of their elected representatives. This political arrangement – dubbed 'democracy lite' (see Markoff, 1997) – has greatly limited citizen input into the formulation and implementation of economic policy. This is clearly demonstrated by the recent election, in both countries, of politicians professing a critique of neoliberalism but who, in government, replicate (with minor variations) the economic policies which they had previously vowed to abandon – Carlos Menem and Néstor Kirchner in Argentina, and Luís Inácio Lula da Silva in Brazil are clear examples.

The relationship between political democracy and neoliberal economic policies in Argentina and Brazil is both functional and historical. As a political form, procedural democracy can be associated with any system of accumulation. Put differently, in the abstract political democracy has no intrinsic economic content and, therefore, no specific class content either, and democratic regimes can be associated with a wide variety of political coalitions. In this sense, political democracy is similar to nationalism, which also lacks a necessary correspondence with other political or economic forms.

The democratic transitions in Argentina and Brazil were exemplars in this respect. The class content of these transitions was initially heavily contested. The early mobilizations for democracy had a strongly left-wing flavour, and brought together demands for political as well as economic democracy.

However, when the transition was eventually accomplished it had acquired a centrist character with strong elite influence being preserved in the public administration. Eventually, with the neoliberal transition the influence of the poor majority on the political system declined even further, and demands for economic democracy (rather than simply public welfare programmes) retreated from every dimension of public discourse.

This transformation in the social content of democracy is symptomatic of a political transition which, in both countries, was the product of contradictory pressures: on the one hand, for political freedom and the democratization of economic power and, on the other hand, for the renewal of elite domination. In Argentina and Brazil, the democratic transition was successful because of the mass mobilization against the dictatorship, but it was completed through a strategic deal in which political freedom was exchanged for the continuing concentration of economic power, and military repression was replaced by new modes of political hegemony.

This strategic shift was grounded on domestic contingencies, but it was also due to the realization by the elite, in Argentina and Brazil, that dictatorships are fundamentally unreliable. They can successfully deploy extreme brutality in order to exterminate revolutionary movements and keep the country aligned with the West, but dictatorships also control the institutional tools permitting the mobilization, by non-market means, of vast resources for their own ends. These can include corruption or otherwise undesirable goals, as well as developmental objectives. In the case of the latter, even though state-led developmental strategies often fail dramatically, they can also succeed, as was shown by the examples of China, Taiwan, South Korea and the Soviet Union (in spite of the significant differences between these cases). Furthermore, little can be done institutionally to rein in or counterbalance the preferences of the top layers of the regime.

Dictatorships also tend to face large and cohesive opposition movements, often unified as a condition of survival, and which can become dangerously attached to a left-wing agenda. These opposition movements tend to harbour a 'grand' alternative vision for society, including political democracy and the redistribution of income and wealth. Political resistance and the potential growth of the opposition can limit the ability of the dictatorships to impose the repression required in order to implement neoliberal economic policies, unless the regime uses terrorist methods, as was the case in Argentina, Chile and Uruguay in the 1970s. In contrast, political democracy is convenient for the elite because the elaboration and implementation of economic policy in democratic societies requires a degree of consensus that stimulates (and requires) accommodation and political compromises, and which fosters the growth (and, frequently, the simultaneous fragmentation) of centrist political forces. For these reasons democratic societies tend to be politically fractured even when the political arena is dominated by large centrist parties – which are often little more than unwieldy coalitions or political fronts. These political formations are normally unable to offer consistent alternatives to the influence of the moneyed interests over the state. At the same time, resistance against neoliberal policies in democratic societies also tends to be fragmented, because *all* social movements tend to be fractured. In other words, democracy favours the multiplication of sectoral interest groups with narrow horizons and no 'grand' vision for the society.

Finally, elite groups in both countries acknowledged that the rise of the democratic movement could not be contained by force. Instead, it was preferable to accommodate it in order to preserve the stability of the power relations in society; otherwise, the political crisis could degenerate into a crisis of economic and social relations, in which the reproduction of the elite could be thrown into question. The elites in Argentina and Brazil became gradually convinced that, although democracy would inevitably disperse their political power by admitting new actors and pressure groups into the political scene, it would also encourage the continuing concentration of economic power. Democracy thus became an appealing political system to those in power only when they were confident that the interests they considered vital could be insulated from democratic accountability. This is because a democratic state would be able to implement policies in the interests of the economically powerful minority with little risk of loss of legitimacy. The *paradox of democracy* in Argentina and Brazil consists precisely in this: the enhanced legitimacy of the democratic regime, due to its *inclusionary* political rights, permits the deployment of repressive forces (institutional, political and military) that can ignore the interests of the majority and impose *exclusionary* economic policies more easily than most dictatorships. In these circumstances, the democratic state tends to become hostile towards the majority, precisely when conventional political theory indicates that it should be more responsive to pressures from below. In fact, after several decades of attempting to subvert democratic governments and shore up dictatorships across the globe, the US government and most local elites in poorer countries have realized that democratic states can follow diktats from Washington and impose policies inimical to economic democracy and the general populace more easily and reliably than most dictatorships.[8]

The disjuncture between political and economic democracy is predicated on the separation between the economic and political spheres in capitalist societies (Wood, 1981). This separation allows the allocation of economic resources to be controlled not through the jurisdiction of the state, but by the forces of competition. Given this basic separation, the universal civil and political rights granted under liberal democracy cannot be considered, in and of themselves, as tools of empowerment that can transform society, since civic equality does not directly affect class inequality. This separation permits the relocation of issues that are at the heart of the substantive interpretation of democracy which is shared by the majority – such as material welfare and distribution of resources – from the political to the economic sphere. This can lead to elections in which voting is restricted to inconsequential matters, which often hinge on irrelevant personality differences or pointless 'scandals' which are pumped up by the press with tedious regularity. Furthermore, the traditional notions of individual rights and freedoms drawing on Adam Smith's invisible hand and von Hayek's theories of social organization atomize society by disempowering and undermining the institutions geared to the protection of collective goods and rights. The market becomes, according to the orthodoxy, deeply intertwined with the idea of democracy, the achievement of human freedom and the efficient allocation of resources (Friedman, 1962). The subordination of democratic values to the imperatives of accumulation is, therefore, constitutive of the hegemonic notion of liberal democracy, while the potential breadth of democracy in Argentina and Brazil has been drastically limited by the exclusionary social relations in these countries (Borón, 2006, p. 32).

Since a large number of collective institutions, such as trade unions, state-owned enterprises and developmental state agencies were set up under ISI, their disarticulation or extinction was not only part of a 'democratic' celebration of the virtues of individualism, but a process of regeneration of elite hegemony through 'freeing' the market from the remnants of the old system of accumulation. The restoration of formal institutions of democracy – such as competitive elections and citizens' political rights – was evidently an important achievement for the popular sectors. However, the construction of neoliberalism in Argentina and Brazil would have been impossible without a hegemonic discourse that reduced democracy to a mere formality, and turned it into a political regime that aims at 'freeing' society of politics by attacking the perceived hyper-politicization of the 'state-centred matrix' built under ISI. The latter is blamed for the old, inefficient and inflation-prone system displaced by new liberalism (see Cavarozzi, 1994, p. 128; and Galafassi, 2004).

1.5 Inflation stabilization and the neoliberal transition

In Argentina and Brazil, the transition towards neoliberalism was completed under the guise of orthodox inflation stabilization programmes. Ostensibly in order to eliminate high inflation, these stabilization programmes imposed a set of long-run policy changes that dismantled the remnants of ISI and completed the economic transition to neoliberalism. It soon became clear that democratic regimes were able to impose unpopular economic policies which, in many cases, were beyond the political capability of the preceding military regimes. This modality of economic transition was the outcome of a new elite consensus which gradually emerged in the mid- and late 1980s, around the necessity of neoliberal economic policies in order to improve economic performance, stabilize the democratic regime, and secure the compatibility between political democracy and the continuing reproduction of social inequality. This consensus captured the state by democratic means through the presidential elections of Carlos Menem and Fernando Collor, in 1989.

1.5.1   The slide towards hyperinflation

The Latin American crisis of the early 1980s was triggered by the combination between the slowdown in the international economy which accompanied the disintegration of the Bretton Woods System, and the intrinsic limitations of ISI in the region. The onset of the crisis was postponed by the rapid accumulation of foreign debt, which was facilitated by the new international financial architecture emerging since the mid-1960s. The crisis finally erupted when the US imposed punitively high interest rates on borrowers around the world, as part of its own neoliberal transition (see Campbell, 2005; Duménil and Lévy, 2005; Harvey, 2005, 2006; and Panitch and Gindin, 2004, 2005).

The effects of the debt crisis in Latin America were nothing short of devastating. In 1972, the total foreign debt of the region was US\$31.3 billion, and it exceeded 33 per cent of GDP only in Nicaragua, Peru and Bolivia.[9] In the late 1980s, the debt reached US\$430 billion, and it exceeded 33 per cent of GDP in every single country in the region. The growth of the debt stock and higher international interest rates inflated interest payments from around 1 per cent of GDP, in 1972, to an average of 5.4 per cent of GDP in 1983. The Latin American foreign debt reached US\$750 billion at the turn of the millennium, and interest payments still exceed 2.5 per cent of GDP almost everywhere. In almost every country in the region, economic growth stalled, wages plummeted and inflation skyrocketed in the wake of the debt crisis.

The debt crisis was closely associated with rising inflation. Among the causes of inflation were deep distributive conflicts which reflected both the limitations of ISI (see section 1.2) and pressures emerging from recent international developments. In particular, rising transfers amid the debt crisis led to lower (and occasionally negative) GDP growth rates, and reduced the scope for accommodating the conflicting income demands of different social groups. A second important factor was the nationalization of the private foreign debt that occurred across the region. In order to service this debt, governments needed to purchase large quantities of hard currency from the private sector. These purchases were partly monetized (and potentially directly inflationary) and partly sterilized (which increased the costs of servicing the domestic public debt, in parallel with the growth of the external debt service). The ensuing fiscal crises triggered another round of inflation or, alternatively, reinforced the depressive tendencies of the economy. Finally, in this unstable environment, domestic firms tended to increase their degree of indexation, linking prices either to the dollar (especially in Argentina) or to the rate of inflation or the value of public sector bonds (in Brazil). Indexation makes inflation rigid downwards for three reasons. First, it means that firms and workers have adopted simple pricing rules which perpetuate past inflation by simply projecting it into the future. Secondly, in order to protect their profits firms often increased their mark-up when inflation was rising, or was expected to rise. Thirdly, indexation made the economy prone to step-wise increases in inflation after adverse supply shocks (Amadeo, 1994).

The acceleration of inflation created a tendency for the reduction of the intervals between price and wage increases. This had a clearly regressive distributive effect, because some agents were better able than others to protect their real income. Moreover, it has been abundantly shown in the literature that the shorter the adjustment period the higher the rate of inertial inflation, the more rigid it becomes, and the more sensitive it is to adverse shocks. In the early and mid-1980s, the Argentine and Brazilian economies became increasingly disorganized as inflation rose steadily. This disorganization introduced substantial uncertainty into economic calculation which, in all likelihood, contributed to the decline in the savings and investment rates in both economies (see below).

Inertial inflation sharply increased the cost of contractionary monetary and fiscal policies, because higher interest rates or lower government expenditures tended to have little effect on firms' pricing strategies or workers' wage demands. Attempts at inflation stabilization during this period went through three stages. First, orthodox monetary policies (in Argentina, this phase lasted between 1982 and mid-1985 and, in Brazil, between 1981 and early 1986). However, these contractionary policies could lead to *higher* prices rather than lower, if firms tried to maintain their gross profits in spite of their declining sales and higher financial costs. Second, the 'heterodox shocks' (in Argentina, between 1985 and 1987 and, in Brazil, between 1986 and 1987). By the mid-1980s, it was generally accepted in Argentina and Brazil that conventional fiscal and monetary policies were ineffective against inertial inflation, and that disinflation would require the co-ordinated de-indexation of prices and wages (see Dornbusch 1993; Dornbusch and Simonsen, 1983). Most economists realized that, in a highly indexed economy, demand restrictions would be of limited value in controlling inflation. Furthermore, when inflation stabilizes at the three-digit level, demand control cannot eliminate inflation without considerable costs in terms of higher unemployment, lost output, and political conflict. Since it was difficult to reduce inflation gradually, the obvious alternative was to look for a strategy of rapid transition to a low-inflation regime, in which de-indexation would necessarily play a prominent role (Saad-Filho and Mollo, 2002).

This strategy, as it evolved in Argentina and Brazil, included three key elements: an unanticipated freeze of prices and wages at their average real level for the previous period, e.g., one year; the abolition of indexation through a compulsory change in the existing contracts; and a currency change, to eliminate the surplus zeroes in the devalued money and, more importantly, to validate the changes in contracts being imposed by the government.

The heterodox shocks were initially highly successful. This is hardly surprising, since inflation will necessarily tend to zero as long as the price and wage freeze can be sustained. However, it was impossible to devise a strategy to exit the price freeze in an orderly manner, and to sustain the low inflation regime over time. This was largely for two reasons. First, the imposition of a sudden price freeze transforms short-term imbalances in relative prices, which are created daily by inflation, into permanent differences. The freeze prevents the correction of the short-term imbalances in the relative price system (for example, between those prices frozen at their peak in dollar terms, if they had been raised the day before the shock, and those frozen at the bottom, if they were due to change the day after the shock). While tolerable for a limited period, these imbalances led, over time, to the withdrawal from the market of artificially cheap products. Some of these products would be reintroduced later at higher prices, under new names or with cosmetic changes entitling them to be called 'new', in which case they would be exempt from the freeze. The price freeze was also unsustainable in the case of seasonal goods, especially agricultural products and meat, in which case supply oscillations can trigger substantial fluctuations in prices.[10] In addition to this, import difficulties because of trade restrictions or the scarcity of hard currency helped the companies operating in the domestic market to bypass the price ceilings imposed by the government. The heterodox shocks, and the continuing disputes for income under these circumstances, led to arbitrary shifts in economic returns, the breakdown of supply chains, bankruptcies, illegal trading, economic disorganization and, eventually, the collapse of the stabilization programmes.

The second reason for the instability of the heterodox shocks is related to the relative ease with which wages can be frozen at their average real level. All that is required for this is a willing accountant armed with a nominal wage series and a table of price indices. Yet the same strategy was not feasible for the market price of commodities. In the end, wages were frozen at their average, while prices were frozen at their peak, leading to workers' complaints that real wages were being compressed in the transition to the new regime. Consequently, real wages in Argentina and Brazil tended to decline between the mid-1980s and the mid-1990s both because of inflation, and because of the heterodox stabilization programmes. At a deeper level, however, the failure of the heterodox shocks was due to their inability to address the causes of inflation (primarily distributive conflicts, external shocks and inconsistent monetary and fiscal policies) while focusing, instead, on its propagation mechanism (indexation) (Saad-Filho and Mollo, 2002).

The failure of the heterodox programmes in both countries contributed to the disorganization of relative prices, increased inflationary expectations and, at the same time, reduced the social tolerance to high inflation in Argentina and Brazil. The failure of these programmes also sharpened the tensions associated with high inflation, especially the distributive conflicts involving key worker categories, employers and the state. In Argentina, these conflicts triggered a process of hyperinflation, and the extensive dollarization of the economy.

In Brazil, conflicts were less pronounced, inflation increased more slowly, and the government followed an effective policy of permanently high interest rates and high liquidity of central bank and Treasury securities. They provided a liquid store of value (in effect, a parallel currency) which contained the flight from currency into commodities (hyperinflation) or into other reserve assets (dollarization). However, this was an unreliable policy strategy against potentially runaway inflation, and it had sharply negative distributive implications.

1.5.2 Inflation stabilization and the neoliberal transition

The intensity and persistence of high inflation and the economic crisis in Argentina and Brazil made it relatively easy to accept that the system of accumulation based on ISI had collapsed, and should be replaced by neoliberalism. This viewpoint was stridently promoted by the US government, the IMF and the World Bank and also by important sections of the local elites.

The combination between external pressures and domestic tensions, including the economic crisis and the failure of the heterodox stabilization programmes, eroded the influence of the (then dominant) structuralist school and reinforced the notion that the so-called 'national project' centred on ISI was exhausted beyond repair. This claim was doubly misleading. On the one hand, ISI was socially unfair, intrinsically limited and structurally fragile (as was shown in section 1.2), but the crisis of the 1980s was only partly due to its shortcomings: it was also partly imposed by external developments. On the other hand, neoliberalism has been unable either to address most failings of ISI, or to match the growth performance of the previous period.

Argentine inflation approached 5,000 per cent in mid-1989. At this stage, it ceased to be primarily an expression of a distributive conflict between forces of equal strength. Instead, it became a mechanism through which the country's economic elite sought to impose their control over economic resources and the political system (see Acuña and Smith, 1994; Bonnet, 2006). The hyperinflation had a drastic effect on the distribution of income. Although inequality had increased steadily since the mid-1970s, the hyperinflation triggered a significant transfer of income from labour to capital, with large increases in poverty and inequality. Indeed, while sections of the elite were speculating on the foreign exchange market, real wages were depreciating by the hour (falling 37 per cent below their 1980 level by the end of the decade, see Altimir, Beccaria and Gonzalez Rosada, 2002). Looting became widespread, even under strong repression. The lasting consequence of hyperinflation was the submission of a traumatized working class, which accepted, or even welcomed, neoliberal reforms which imposed new mechanisms of social subordination under the guise of inflation stabilization measures.

Argentina's economic situation obviously required significant policy changes, which gave President Menem the legitimacy required for a *volte-face* on his electoral promises of a *salariazo* (massive increase in salaries) and a productive revolution. However, crucial to Menem's ability to introduce neoliberal economic policies through an inflation stabilization programme was not only the legitimacy conferred by democracy, but also his Peronist party's historical ties with the organized working class and the popular sector. Labour-based parties can have a comparative advantage in implementing policies that might result in the deterioration of the living conditions of their own constituencies because, as representatives of the popular sector, they enjoy their trust (Murillo, 2000).

It was not until the 1991 convertibility plan that the full extent of neoliberal reforms, and the consequent reconfiguration of class relations, were imposed in Argentina. The plan included a legally binding exchange rate of 1:1 between the peso and the US dollar, free convertibility between these currencies, extensive deregulation of the economy, fiscal reforms, trade liberalization, flexibilization of the labour market, centralization of the pension contributions with the state (instead of the trade unions), and the profound reform of the pension system. The convertibility plan signalled not only the adoption of orthodox stabilization measures, but the deepening of market-oriented reforms originally attempted by the military regime, of which minister of the economy Domingo Cavallo was a member.[11] Crucially, in the context of a new mode of insertion in the world economy, convertibility meant that the state lost the ability to use exchange rates in order to rectify imbalances between domestic and world prices through competitive devaluations. This implied that Argentina's competitiveness on the world market, which heavily influences the profitability of investment and the level and composition of the foreign capital inflows, became dependent primarily on changes in nominal wages and labour productivity. Convertibility created a continuous downward pressure on wages and a simultaneous pressure for the intensification of labour, which was supported by the labour market reforms and the rising unemployment rate in the country.

Brazil's *real* plan, imposed in 1994, was also not simply an inflation stabilization programme. It included policies which consolidated the neoliberal transition in the country, among them financial, trade and capital account liberalization, the privatization or closure of state-owned productive and financial enterprises, fiscal and labour market reforms, de-indexation, the overvaluation of the currency, and the closure of several state agencies and departments.

These policies were not entirely new. For example, privatizations and trade, capital account and financial liberalization were introduced in the early 1990s, and the systematic reduction of state policy-making capacity started in the 1980s. The *real* plan was innovative only in so far as it deployed these policies methodically, as part of an ambitious attempt to eliminate two foes of the neoliberal order simultaneously – high inflation and the relics of a presumably exhausted process of ISI.

The new policy regime lifted real wages by 15 per cent in dollar terms in the mid-1990s. This wage increase, the accelerated liberalization of imports, and the resumption of credit transformed the possibilities of consumption.

The country was transfixed by the appearance of previously unavailable consumer goods, at affordable prices, and available on credit. Import liberalization and inflation stabilization ensured F.H. Cardoso's presidential election in 1994, and his re-election in 1998. Cardoso presented his government as the harbinger of 'modernization' and the standard-bearer of the 'new globalised economy'.

The examples of Argentina and Brazil indicate that one of the peculiarities of the neoliberal transition in these countries is that it was often justified obliquely, by reference to the imperatives of inflation control. The reforms were, correspondingly, often disguised as 'technical' anti-inflationary measures. This conflation was facilitated by the specific form of the collapse of the previous system of accumulation, in which fiscal, financial and industrial crises often surfaced through runaway inflation. The imperative of inflation stabilization blurred the extent and the long-term consequences of the neoliberal transition. Unable to win the battle of ideas, and suffering from a persistent legitimacy deficit in societies where the neoliberal reforms were rightly perceived to be intrinsically undemocratic, the neoliberal elite consensus found it necessary to conceal its agenda in order to impose its policy preferences more easily.

In Argentina and Brazil, financial, trade and capital account liberalization, the wholesale privatization or closure of state-owned productive and financial firms, and profound fiscal and labour market reforms along neoliberal lines were imposed allegedly because they were essential for short-term macroeconomic stabilization and the resumption of economic growth. At the same time, most remaining institutions that had provided industrial policy co-ordination under ISI were dismantled, and regulations constraining foreign investment were abandoned.

Five policies played key roles in inflation control as well as in the neoliberal transition in Argentina and Brazil. First, *import liberalization*. ISI requires strong import restrictions in order to give local firms (including TNCs operating in the country) control of the domestic market. However, firms protected from foreign competition tend to have market power. They enjoy more freedom to raise prices, and more flexibility to accommodate wage demands, which increases the economy's vulnerability to cost-push inflation. Trade liberalization helps to control inflation because foreign competition limits the prices that domestic firms can charge. It also limits the workers' wage demands, since pay increases could make local firms uncompetitive. At a further remove, neoliberals claim that trade liberalization forces local firms to compete against 'best practice' foreign producers, which should help to increase productivity across the economy. Finally, unsuccessful local producers will close down, and their capital and labour will presumably be deployed more productively elsewhere.

Secondly, *exchange rate overvaluation*. Overvaluation artificially reduces the local currency price of imports, enhancing the impact of trade liberalization on inflation and competitivity. The combination between trade liberalization, currency overvaluation, high domestic interest rates and capital account liberalization was a fail-safe strategy to reduce inflation and lock in the neoliberal reforms simultaneously. Cheap imports were allowed in, while high interest rates, foreign loans, mass privatizations and TNC takeovers of domestic firms brought the foreign capital that paid for these imports. Inflation tumbled while consumers gorged on flashy automobiles, computers and DVDs, and happily splashed out on artificially cheap foreign holidays. Although the combination of import liberalization and exchange rate overvaluation is highly effective against inflation, and can be very popular with consumers, it can have a devastating impact on the balance of payments and on local industry and employment.

Argentine imports shot up from US$6.8 billion to US$19.3 billion between 1990 and 1992, and Brazilian imports increased from US$28.0 billion to US$63.3 billion between 1992 and 1995. Consumer goods imports increased from US$242 million to US$5.0 billion in Argentina between 1985 and 1998; during the same period, they increased from US$606 million to US$8.2 billion in Brazil. The foreign travel deficit increased, in that interval, from US$671 million to US$4.2 billion in Argentina, and from US$441 million to US$5.7 billion in Brazil (see Figures 1.3 and 1.4).

Cheap imports harmed local industry. In Argentina and Brazil, the proportion of manufacturing value added on GDP reached, respectively, 31 and 29 per cent in 1989. By 2001, these ratios had declined to 17 and 14 per cent. Industrial sector employment also fell, especially in Argentina, where it declined from 33 to 25 per cent of the labour force between 1991 and 1996. In Brazil, more than one million industrial jobs were lost between 1989 and 1997. During the neoliberal era open unemployment increased, on average, from 6 to 20 per cent of the workforce in Argentina, and from 4 to 10 in Brazil (see Figures 1.5 and 1.6; this excludes underemployment and informal employment, which may reach 70 per cent of the labour force in Argentina, and 50 per cent in Brazil).

Thirdly, *domestic financial liberalization*. It was expected that the deregulation of the financial sector would help to raise savings and the availability of funds for investment. In fact, quite the opposite happened, and both savings and investment rates declined. In Argentina, savings fell from 22 to 17 per cent of GDP in ten years after 1989, while in Brazil they fell from 25 to 20 per cent of GDP in the early years of the neoliberal reforms, and declined further, to only 15 per cent of GDP, towards the end of the *real* plan. In Argentina, investment fell from over 25 per cent to less than 15 per cent of GDP and, in Brazil, it declined from 20–25 per cent of GDP to 15–20 per cent after the reforms (see Figures 1.7 and 1.8).

Fourthly, *fiscal reforms* (especially tax increases and expenditure cuts), in order to address the government budget deficits that plagued both countries and were allegedly the main cause of high inflation. These reforms were largely successful, and led to budget balances or even primary fiscal surpluses.

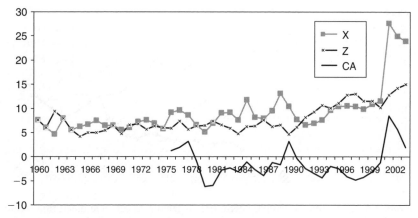

Figure 1.3 Argentina: exports (X) and imports (Z) of goods and services, and current account balance (CA) (% GDP)
Source: World Development Indicators.

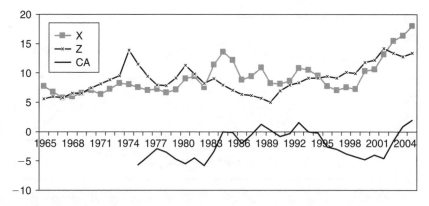

Figure 1.4 Brazil: exports (X) and imports (Z) of goods and services, and current account balance (CA) (% GDP)
Source: World Development Indicators.

However, the cost of servicing the public debt increased sharply because of the high level of the domestic interest rates, which have squeezed non-financial expenditures from the government budget in both countries.

Finally, *liberalization of the capital account of the balance of payments*. This measure was supposedly essential to attract foreign savings and modern technology, but there was much more to it, as was shown above. Capital account liberalization played an essential role in financing the disequilibria created by neoliberalism, and supporting the reorganization of the productive base in both countries.

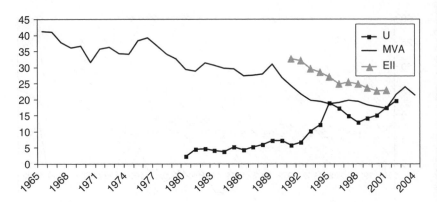

Figure 1.5 Argentina: unemployment (U, % labour force), manufacturing value added (MVA, % GDP), employment in industry (EII, % total employment)
Source: World Development Indicators.

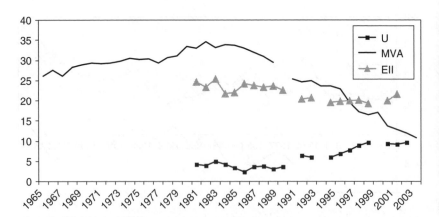

Figure 1.6 Brazil: unemployment (U, % labour force), manufacturing value added (MVA, % GDP), employment in industry (EII, % total employment)
Source: World Development Indicators.

The neoliberal reforms failed to resolve the shortcomings of ISI (explained in section 1.2), and they created new economic problems. They did not relieve the foreign exchange constraint, and increased the dependence of Argentina and Brazil on volatile foreign capital inflows. In both countries, the current account of the balance of payments was initially in equilibrium, but it later shifted to a deficit of 4 per cent of GDP. The financial reforms reduced the availability of savings and did nothing to improve the allocation of investment funds.

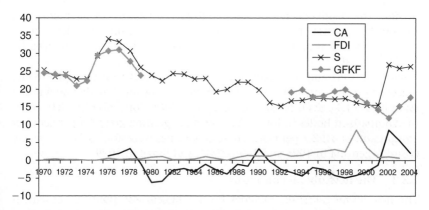

Figure 1.7 Argentina: current account (CA), foreign direct investment (FDI), gross domestic savings (S) and gross domestic fixed capital formation (GFKF) (% GDP)
Source: World Development Indicators.

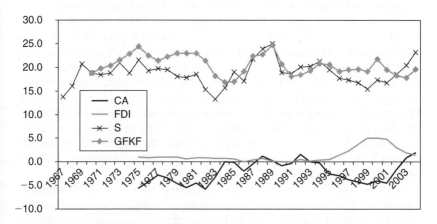

Figure 1.8 Brazil: current account (CA), foreign direct investment (FDI), gross domestic savings (S) and gross domestic fixed capital formation (GFKF) (% GDP)
Source: World Development Indicators.

Fiscal fragility resurfaced almost immediately because of the weight of interest payments on the government budget and the sluggishness of tax revenues due to the economic slowdown. Finally, economic co-ordination suffered from the dismantling of specialist state institutions, the hollowing out of the industrial chains built during ISI and the reduction in the local content of manufacturing production. Wages and profits declined because of competing imports, the rising share of interest in the national income, and the difficulty in developing new competitive industries. Structural unemployment mounted.

In sum, the neoliberal reforms destabilized the balance of payments and the productive system of both countries. Neoliberalism discarded import substitution and promoted, instead, 'production substitution' financed by foreign capital.

Between, 1981 and 2000, Argentina's average annual economic growth rate was only 1.6 per cent, and Brazil's 2.1 per cent (cf. the much higher rates under ISI in Figure 1.1). Even considering only the 1990s, long after the debt crisis, the comparison bodes ill for neoliberalism. Argentina grew 4.5 per cent per annum and Brazil 2.7 per cent. These economies were also rocked by severe crises: Argentina in 1995 and 1998–2002, and Brazil in 1999.

1.5.3   The new liberal consensus

The *new liberal consensus* includes both a hegemonic political settlement (procedural democracy) and a hegemonic set of economic policies and relations (neoliberalism). New liberalism has become the mode of existence of capitalism in Argentina and Brazil – a new system of accumulation – with a specific material basis which corresponds to a particular social structure and given relationships between domestic capital, foreign capital and the state.

It was shown in sections 1.3 and 1.4 that, in the 1980s, the Argentine and Brazilian elites became convinced that economic dynamism could be restored, while securing the existing patterns of social and economic exclusion, only by embracing political democracy, neoliberal economic policies and 'globalization'. Achieving these outcomes required the deployment of state power to impose a new system of accumulation. New liberalism has four defining features: *neoliberal economic policies, the microeconomic integration of domestic capital into transnational circuits* (the denationalization of firms and their restructuring as part of rival international value chains), *the decisive role of financial interests in the formulation of economic policy*, and *political democracy*. These are explained in more detail in what follows.

First, the neoliberal policy reforms, inspired by the (post-)Washington Consensus, dismantled the production structures established during ISI and the social structures and patterns of employment that corresponded to them. The policy reforms led to the privatization of the most productive and financial SOEs, and promoted the alliance between foreign and domestic capital at firm level and the denationalization of industry and infrastructure (see section 1.4).

Secondly, the transnationalization of production and finance ('globalization') which was, to a large extent, a process of international integration at firm level that restructured the 'national' systems of production at a higher level of productivity, and integrated local elites internationally. This was achieved through import liberalization, the denationalization of production and the specialization of Brazilian and (what remains of) Argentine manufacturing industry towards the production of a narrower range of relatively unsophisticated goods. They have eroded the manufacturing base of both countries, and made their economies structurally more dependent on foreign trade, investment and technology.[12] The outcome has been a shift of their productive base away from the long-term requirements of national accumulation, towards the servicing of the short-term imperatives of global accumulation.

Thirdly, the transfer of state capacity to allocate resources intertemporally (the balance between investment and consumption), intersectorally (the distribution of investment, employment and output) and internationally towards an increasingly integrated and US-led financial sector. In doing so, new liberalism facilitated a gigantic transfer of resources to the local rich and, globally, to the United States (Harvey, 2005; Panitch and Gindin, 2005). The restructuring of state capacities has left the Argentine and Brazilian states profoundly depleted in the areas of economic planning, control and policy implementation. In contrast, state capacities in monetary policy implementation, financial sector regulation and security have been extended significantly. Moreover, the financial sector reforms embedded private sector interests in the policy-making process through the decisive role of finance in the pricing of government securities, the determination of interest rates and the financing of the public sector. The reforms also increased the role of the private financial institutions in the foreign exchange market and, therefore, in the country's relations with the rest of the world.

Through these policies and processes, the neoliberal policy reforms have contributed to the disorganization and increased exploitation of workers in both countries, and to a significant shift in power away from the majority *regardless* (and, to some extent, because) of the simultaneous stabilization of democracy. Rather than relying on military force, the new liberal consensus has disciplined the working class through contractionary fiscal and monetary policies, higher unemployment and labour turnover, personal debt, and the permanent threat of inflationary or balance of payments crises should the distributive conflicts get out of hand.

Fourthly, at the political level, democracy has become established as the political form of neoliberalism in Argentina and Brazil. In these countries, the neoliberal transition and the democratic transition were mutually reinforcing and, eventually, became mutually constituting. They were associated with a shift in the mechanisms of social domination towards a combination of democracy and neoliberalism, which contributed to social fragmentation and the dismantling of the resistance movements which had emerged during the dictatorship. The symbiosis between neoliberalism and procedural democracy operates at three levels. First, the neoliberal economic transition was achieved through, and validated by, democratic means (see section 1.4). Secondly, neoliberal policies support the democratic regime because they fragment the working class through unemployment, faster labour turnover, the repression of trade union activity, the curtailment of the social wage and the entitlement systems that benefited the working class, and the rise of economic insecurity. Under neoliberalism, the repression of working-class activity becomes primarily 'economic' rather than 'political' as was the case under the dictatorship. Thirdly, democracy is the optimum political regime for neoliberalism because it offers guarantees of stability and predictability of the 'rules of the game', which makes it more easily controlled by the moneyed interests.

1.6   Summary and conclusions

The new liberal compact is stable in Argentina and Brazil because the economic reforms are self-reinforcing, and they preclude the implementation of alternative economic policies. They also disorganize the working class and other potential sources of opposition to this system of accumulation, including the trade unions, left social movements and political parties. Finally, neoliberalism fosters forms of behaviour that reproduce this system of accumulation at the economic level, and that support the evacuation of democracy at the political level. This reduces drastically the scope for institutional challenges to the new liberal hegemony. In this sense, the disappointing macroeconomic performance in Argentina and Brazil under neoliberalism is a tolerable cost for the economic elites, and it offers no significant internal (economic) incentive for the abandonment of this system of accumulation.

Although the neoliberal reforms have helped to address some of the shortcomings of ISI, especially the propensity to high inflation, they have left unresolved other deficiencies of the previous model, especially the extreme concentration of income and wealth (which undermines the legitimacy of elite rule), the weakness of the domestic financial system, and the insufficiencies of the national system of innovation. Neoliberalism has also failed to create sufficient quality jobs, and contributed decisively to the hollowing out of the manufacturing base in Argentina and Brazil. The democratic reforms, in turn, have established the rule of law and respect for civil rights in several areas of social life (although their implementation remains heavily contingent on circumstances of place and time). However, democracy has been heavily curtailed by the evacuation of meaningful economic debate. The claim that 'There Is No Alternative' to neoliberalism has become entrenched through the institutional structure of the state, and the revealed preference of the electorate for an alternative system of accumulation in both countries has been largely irrelevant.

Neoliberal reforms delivered short-term macroeconomic stability and growth in Argentina and Brazil because they were 'credible' by definition (since they did what was demanded by the moneyed interests), and credibility brings rewards in the form of foreign capital flows and easier refinancing of the domestic public debt. Foreign capital flows financed the growth of investment and consumption, in a virtuous circle that lasted several years. However, the reforms destabilized the productive system and the balance of payments in both countries. Financial liberalization raised interest rates and created financial fragility, and it did not reduce the cost of loans or the availability of credit for domestic firms. High interest rates stimulated the accumulation of foreign debt for investment and speculation, because foreign finance was much cheaper than domestic credit. Consequently, the debt of the private non-financial sector increased rapidly. Debt-financed consumption and cheap imports contributed to euphoria and the impression of the success of neoliberalism, especially in 1991–94 and 1996–98 in Argentina, and between 1994 and 1997 in Brazil. The foreign capital inflows supported the overvaluation of the currency and reduced the competitivity of domestic industry, much of which was wiped out during the 1990s. The currency overvaluation prevented the reduction of the domestic interest rates, because foreign capital flows were needed to finance the trade deficit. However, these high interest rates increased the cost of the domestic debt service, generated fiscal deficits and increased the financial fragility of the private sector. Neoliberal policies also led to wage and industrial profit compression because of competing imports, the rising share of interest in the national income, the loss of industrial competitivity, rising unemployment and the growing fiscal deficit.

In spite of these disappointing outcomes, the new liberal consensus is largely immune to internal challenges. In particular, economic underperformance is insufficient to trigger a shift in the system of accumulation, because unemployment and bankruptcies weaken the capacity of the domestic working class and the urban middle sectors to demand alternatives. Underperformance also compels the domestic producers to shift their capital to more profitable ventures, which are invariably more closely connected with the interests of finance. Only the loss of *political legitimacy* can trigger a successful challenge to new liberalism.

In spite of its basic stability, the neoliberal project suffers from two severe inconsistencies which may offer scope for a political challenge. First, there is a basic tension in new liberalism between the deployment of a politically democratic and inclusive political system to enforce exclusionary economic policies. These policies demand a state hostile to the majority, even though a democratic state is supposedly responsive to majority pressure. This tension has played an important role in the election of several left-wing governments in Latin America and elsewhere, and it continues to exist, even though success in the implementation of alternatives has been limited. Second, the neoliberal reforms have failed to address important shortcomings of ISI, and the combination between the unresolved weaknesses of ISI and the flaws of neoliberalism has entrenched the economic underperformance of Argentina and Brazil.

Transcending neoliberalism in these countries will require both economic and political changes that can be carried out only through the construction of an alternative system of accumulation. This project will require dismantling systematically the material basis of neoliberalism, initially through a set of pro-poor and democratic economic policy initiatives, which will support a shift to a model of development that can generate more equal distributions of income, wealth and power, and higher levels of material welfare. This is a fundamental condition for democracy. These alternative policies should be based on a specific set of controls on capital flows, supported by co-ordinated trade, financial and industrial policies and the expansion of non-revenue-generating social programmes financed through a non-regressive increase in taxation and the reallocation of government spending. These policy measures must be supported by a politically re-articulated working class, as one of the main levers for its own economic recomposition. The difficulty is that this virtuous circle cannot be wished into being. Its elements cannot be addressed purely academically, or through the organization of another political party, or simply through alliances between the existing political forces. The construction of a new economic, social and political model will require mass mobilizations that are sufficiently strong not only to demand change *from* governments, or even changes *of* government, but to embed popular organizations within the state, while preserving their political integrity, mass roots and accountability to the vast majority of the population. The construction of this new wave of popular movements is the most important challenge for the Argentine and Brazilian left during the next decade.

Notes

1 We are grateful to Alison Ayers and Lecio Morais for their helpful and stimulating comments to this chapter. The usual disclaimers apply.
2 Typical examples included Perón's nationalization of transport and infrastructure facilities in the immediate postwar era, and the foundation of Petrobras, the Brazilian state oil monopoly, in 1953.
3 The elite includes the large and medium-sized capitalists, especially financiers, industrial capitalists (based mainly in the Buenos Aires–Rosario region in Argentina, and in the São Paulo–Rio de Janeiro region in Brazil), large exporters and traders, the media, landowners and local political chiefs, their intellectual and political proxies and top civil servants. These fractions of the elite are unrelated to the contrast between domestic and foreign capital, or the conflict between industrial and financial interests.
4 In this chapter, 'consensus' refers to a substantial measure of agreement on strategic political projects among social groups which, by virtue of their institutional power and political influence, can implement these projects through the institutions of the state. This concept is related to the Gramscian notion of hegemony. Neither of them presumes unanimity.
5 The system of accumulation is determined by the economic, political and institutional structures that typify the process of capital accumulation in a specific region, during a particular historical period. This is a relatively concrete concept, with no direct relationship with more abstract concepts such as mode of regulation (in, for example, Aglietta, 1979).
6 Rochon and Mitchell conducted regular surveys on democratic values and desires among Brazilians between 1972 and 1982. During the democratic transition, they note that the '[m]iddle classes were more concerned with the creation of civilian institutions, and less concerned about universal suffrage, whereas [the] working classes and [the] youth were more concerned with universal suffrage and political change, [rather] than with civilian governmental institutions. . . [A]mong the Brazilian public there is a sharp distinction between support for the institutions of

liberal democracy and belief in the empowerment of the public' (Rochon and Mitchell, 1989: 316–17).

7 The political retreat of the Catholic Church has been partly compensated by the growing influence of a myriad of evangelical sects but, on the whole, overtly religious values are less influential than at any time since Brazil's independence in 1822.

8 'The ultimate goal of American foreign policy will be to use power, alone if necessary, to extend free-market democracy around the globe' (Lawrence J. Korb, US assistant secretary of defence, 1981–85, cited in *Canadian Dimension*, Nov–Dec. 2005, 8).

9 Data in this paragraph are derived from the *World Development Indicators*.

10 These fluctuations can be tempered by imports or inventory sales, but these complications will be ignored here.

11 For Cavallo and Cottani (1997, p. 17), the convertibility plan was a 'smashing success. . . it stopped hyperinflation without producing a recession and without causing [a] regressive income redistribution'.

12 For example, the neoliberal reforms led to the 'tertiarization' of Argentina's economy (Basualdo, 2000, p. 217). The profitability of the services sector increased 33 per cent between 1991 and 1998, largely as a result of the privatizations carried out during this period (Schorr, 2002, p. 18; see also Azpiazú, 1998 and Schvarzer, 1998).

References

Acuña, C. and Smith, W. (1994) 'The Political Economy of Structural Adjustment: The Logic of Support and Opposition to Neoliberal Reform', in W. Smith, C. Acuña and E. Gamarra (eds), *Latin America Political Economy in the Age of Neoliberal Reform*. New Brunswick: Transaction.

Aglietta, M. (1979) *The Theory of Capitalist Regulation: The US Experience*. London: Verso.

Altimir, O., Beccaria, L. and Gonzalez Rozada, M. (2002) 'Income Distribution in Argentina 1974–2000', *CEPAL Review* 78, 55–85.

Alves, M.H.M. (1988) 'Dilemmas of the Consolidation of Democracy from the Top in Brazil: A Political Analysis', *Latin American Perspectives* 15(3), 47–63.

Amadeo, E., (1994) *Institutions, Inflation and Unemployment*. Aldershot: Edward Elgar.

Azpiazú, D. (1998) *La Concentración en la Industria Argentina a Mediados de los Anos Noventa*. Buenos Aires: Eudeba.

Basualdo, E. (2000) *Concentración y Centralisation del Capital en la Argentina Durante la Década del Noventa*. Quilmes: Universidad Nacional de Quilmes Ediciones.

Basualdo, E. (2001) *Sistema Político y Modelo de Acumulación*. Quilmes: Universidad Nacional de Quilmes Ediciones.

Bonnet, A.R. (2006) 'Qué se Vayan Todos!: Discussing the Argentine Crisis and Insurrection', *Historical Materialism* 14(1), 157–84.

Borón, A. (2006) 'The Truth about Capitalist Democracy', in L. Panitch and C. Leys (eds), *Socialist Register*. London: Merlin Press.

Bresser-Pereira, L.C. (ed.) (1991) *Populismo Econômico*. São Paulo: Nobel.

Bruton, H.J. (1998) 'A Reconsideration of Import Substitution'. *Journal of Economic Literature*, 36, June, pp. 903–36.

Campbell, A. (2005) 'The Birth of Neoliberalism in the United States: A Reorganisation of Capitalism', in A. Saad-Filho and D. Johnston (eds), *Neoliberalism: A Critical Reader*. London: Pluto Press.

Canitrot, A. and Sigal, S. (1995) 'Economic Reform, Democracy, and the Crisis of the State in Argentina' in J. Nelson (ed.), *Democracy and Economic Reforms in Latin*

America, vol. 2. Washington DC: International Centre for Economic Growth and the Overseas Development Council.

Carranza, M. (1997) 'Transitions to Electoral Regimes and the Future of Civil Military Relations in Argentina and Brazil', *Latin American Perspectives* 24(5), 7–25.

Cavallo D. F. and Cottani J.A. (1997) 'Argentina's Convertibility Plan and the IMF', *American Economic Review* 87(2), 17–27.

Cavarozzi, M. (1994) 'Politics: A Key for the Long Term in South America', in W. Smith, C. Acuña and E. Gamarra (eds), *Latin America Political Economy in the Age of Neoliberal Reform.* New Brunswick: Transaction.

Dahl, R. (1971) *Polyarchy, Participation and Opposition.* New Haven: Yale University Press.

Díaz-Alejandro, C. (1985) 'Good-Bye Financial Repression, Hello Financial Crash', *Journal of Development Economics,* 19, 1–24.

Dornbusch, R. (1993) *Stabilization, Debt and Reform: Policy Analysis for Developing Countries.* London: Harverster Wheatsheaf.

Dornbusch, R. and Edwards, S. (eds), (1991) *The Macroeconomics of Populism in Latin America.* Chicago: University of Chicago Press.

Dornbusch, R. and Simonsen, M. (eds) (1983) *Inflation, Debt and Indexation.* Cambridge, MA: MIT Press.

Dornbusch, R. (1989) 'The Latin American Debt Problem: Anatomy and Solutions', in B. Stallings and R. Kaufman (eds), *Debt and Democracy in Latin America.* Boulder, CO: Westview Press.

Duménil, G. and Lévy, D. (2005) 'The Neoliberal (Counter) Revolution', in A. Saad-Filho and D. Johnson (eds), *Neoliberalism: A Critical Reader.* London: Pluto Press.

Fanelli, J.M. (2003) 'Growth, Instability and the Convertibility Crisis in Argentina', *Cepal Review* 77, 25–43.

Friedman, M. (1962) *Capitalism and Freedom.* Chicago: University of Chicago Press.

Galafassi, G. (2004) 'Argentina: Neoliberismo, Utilitarismo y Crisis del Estado-Nación Capitalista', *Revista Herramienta,* 26, www.herramienta.com.ar/modules.php?op=modload&name=News&file=article&sid=267.

Gramsci, A. (1971) *Selections from the Prison Notebooks.* London: Lawrence & Wishart.

Harvey, D. (2005) *A Brief History of Neoliberalism.* Oxford: Oxford University Press.

Harvey, D. (2006). *Spaces of Global Capitalism: Towards a Theory of Uneven Geographical Development.* London: Verso.

Hirschman, A. (1968) 'The Political Economy of Import Substituting Industrialisation in Latin America', *Quarterly Journal of Economics,* 82(1), 1–32.

Huntington, S.P. (1993) 'Democracy's Third Wave', in L. Diamond and M. Plattner (eds), *The Global Resurgence of Democracy.* Baltimore: The Johns Hopkins University Press.

Mainwairing, S. (1995) 'Democracy in Brazil and the Southern Cone: Achievements and Problems', *Journal of International Studies and World Affairs,* 37(1), 113–179.

Markoff, J. (1997) 'Really Existing Democracy: Learning from Latin America in the Late 1990s', *New Left Review,* 223, 48–68.

Markoff, J. and Baretta, S.R.D (1990) 'Economic Crisis and Regime Change in Brazil: The 1960s and the 1980s', *Comparative Politics* 22(4), 421–44.

Munck, R. (1985) 'The Modern Military Dictatorship in Latin America: The Case of Argentina (1976–1982)', *Latin American Perspectives,* 12(4), 41–76.

Murillo, V. (2000) 'From Populism to Neoliberalism: Labour Unions and Market Reforms in Latin America', *World Politics* 52(2), 135–74.

O'Donnell, G. A. (1982) *1966–1973, El Estado Burocrático Autoritário: Triunfos, Derrotas y Crisis.* Buenos Aires: Belgrano.

Palma, G. (1998) 'Three and a Half Cycles of "Mania, Panic and [Asymmetric] Crash": East Asia and Latin America Compared', *Cambridge Journal of Economics* 22, 789–808.

Panitch, L. and Gindin, S. (2004) 'Global Capitalism and American Empire', in L. Panitch and C. Leys (eds), *Socialist Register*. London: Merlin Press.

Panitch, L. and Gindin, S. (2005) 'Finance and the American Empire', in L. Panitch and C. Leys (eds), *Socialist Register*. London: Merlin Press.

Peralta-Ramos, M. and Waisman, C. H. (1987) *From Military Rule to Liberal Democracy in Argentina*. Boulder, CO: Westview Press.

Rochon, T.R. and Mitchell, M.J. (1989) 'Social Bases of the Transition to Democracy in Brazil', *Comparative Politics* 21(3), 307–22.

Rose, R.S. (2006) *The Unpast: Elite Violence and Social Control in Brazil, 1954–2000*. Athens OH: Ohio University Press.

Saad-Filho, A. and Mollo, M.de Lourdes R. (2002) 'Inflation and Stabilisation in Brazil: a Political Economy Analysis', *Review of Radical Political Economics*, 34(2), 109–35.

Saad-Filho, A and Morais L. (2002) 'Neomonetarist Dreams and Realities: A Review of the Brazilian Experience', in P. Davidson (ed.), *Post Keynesian Perspective on 21st Century Economic Problems*. Altershot: Edward Elgar.

Schorr, M. (2002) 'Mitos y Realidades del Pensamiento Neoliberal: La Evolucion de la Industria Manufacturera Argentina Durante la Década de los Noventa', in *Mas Allá del Pensamiento Único*. Buenos Aires: CLACSO, http://bibliotecavirtual.clacso.org.ar/ar/libros/unesco1/schorr.pdf

Schumpeter, J. (1976) *Capitalism, Socialism and Democracy*. London: Allen and Unwin.

Schvarzer, J. (1981) *El Banco National de Desarrollo y el Desarrollo Tecnológico de la Industria Argentina*. Buenos Aires: CISEA.

Schvarzer, J. (1998) 'Economic Reform in Argentina: Which Social Forces for What Aims?', in P.D. Oxhorn and G. Ducatenzeiler (eds), *What Kind of Democracy? What Kind of Market?* University Park, PA: Pennsylvania State University Press.

Skidmore, T. (1973) 'Politics and Economic Policy Making in Authoritarian Brazil, 1937–71', in A. Stepan (ed.), *Authoritarian Brazil: Origins, Policies and Future* (New Haven: Yale University Press.

Smith, W. C. (1985) 'Reflections on the Political Economy of Authoritarian Rule and Capitalist Reorganisation in Contemporary Argentina', in P. O'Brien and P. Cammack (eds), *Generals in Retreat: The Crisis of Military Rule in Latin America*. Manchester: Manchester University Press.

Smith, W. C. (1989) *Authoritarianism and the Crisis of Argentine Political Economy*. Palo Alto, CA: Stanford University Press.

Smith, W. C. (1991) 'State, Market and Neoliberalism in Post-Transition Argentina: The Menem Experiment', *Journal of Interamerican Studies and World Affairs* 33(4), 45–52.

Tedesco, L. (1999) *Democracy in Argentina: Hope and Disillusion*. London: Frank Cass.

Thorp, R. (1992) 'A Reappraisal of the Origins of Import-Substituting Industrialisation, 1930–1950', *Journal of Latin American Studies*, 24 (quincentenary supplement), 181–95.

Weffort, F. (1989) 'Why Democracy?', in A. Stepan (ed.), *Democratising Brazil*, New York: Oxford University Press.

Weisman, H. (1987) *Reversal of Development in Argentina: Post-war Conterrevolutionary Policies and Their Structural Consequences*. Princeton: Princeton University Press.

Wood, E.M. (1981) 'The Separation of the Economic and the Political in Capitalism', *New Left Review*, I/(127), 66–95.

2

Assessing the Economic Policies of President Lula da Silva in Brazil: Has Fear Defeated Hope?

Philip Arestis
University of Cambridge

Luiz Fernando de Paula
University of the State of Rio de Janeiro and CNPq

Fernando Ferrari-Filho
Federal University of Rio Grande de Sul and CNPq

Abstract

This paper aims to assess President Lula da Silva's economic policies and their impact on the Brazilian economy. We evaluate the president's 'neoliberal' economic policies and the extent to which they have been successful in reaching sustained economic growth. We attempt to gauge the theoretical framework from which the president's economic policies emanate, and also describe the actual policies pursued. The paper also offers an alternative economic policy menu that aims at achieving macroeconomic stability, which would promote sustainable economic growth without the need to introduce policies that are designed to fight inflation through the creation of unemployment.

Keywords: Brazilian economy, economic policy, neoliberalism, Latin America, emerging countries markets.

JEL Classification: E24; E61; E65.

2.1 Introduction*

In his inaugural speech on January 2003, addressed to the Brazilian Congress, President Lula da Silva emphasized that his government would introduce changes

---

* We are grateful to Warren Mosler for helpful comments. The usual disclaimer applies.

that would tackle the social problems of the country and would refuel self-sustained economic growth. In this way, it was hoped, the solution of the problems of unemployment and of distribution of wealth that had plagued Brazilian society for so long would be achieved. In his own words, during his administration 'the hope would defeat fear'. However, the end of President Lula da Silva's four-year term witnessed high and rising unemployment (the monthly average rate is around 10.0 per cent) and unstable economic growth. In addition, ministers and members of the government were involved with corruption, the result of which was that confidence in the administration was considerably shaken.

This chapter seeks to assess President Lula da Silva's economic policies and their impact on the Brazilian economy. These economic policies turned out to be surprisingly different from those that most members and electoral supporters of the Workers' Party – Partido dos Trabalhadores (PT), in Portuguese – might have expected. We attempt to demonstrate that President Lula da Silva's economic policies cannot deliver satisfactory economic outcomes. We suggest alternatives, which we argue are far superior in their ability to deliver and robust and inflation-free economic environment. We, thus, offer an alternative economic policy to aim at macroeconomic stability that would keep inflation under control and promote sustainable economic growth.

We start with Lula da Silva's electoral campaign rhetoric in an attempt to locate the moment and the reasons that led him to adopt a very ambiguous stance in his running for the presidency and the drastic change after his election on those promises (section 2.2).[1] We then proceed to define what we understand as the new consensus in macroeconomics, from which we suggest the 'neoliberal' economic policies of President Lula da Silva emanate (section 2.3). Given the prominence of monetary policy in this theoretical framework, in section 2.4 we briefly look into the operational aspects of the policy as applied in Brazil over the period. In the fifth section, we analyse some main features of the macroeconomic policy regime that has been followed by Brazilian governments since 1999, based on a floating exchange rate regime, an inflation targeting regime, the creation of primary fiscal surplus (the budget surplus excluding interest payments) and liberalisation of the capital account. Section 2.6 focuses on the main macroeconomic policies implemented by the Lula da Silva's government and their results are identified. Section 2.7 outlines some elements for an alternative economic policy strategy. We argue that the suggested alternative economic policies can steer the economy to an economic path that is much more promising than the one offered by President Lula da Silva. Finally, section 2.8 summarizes the argument and concludes.[2]

2.2   Presidential candidate Lula da Silva's campaign rhetoric

Mr Lula da Silva had been the presidential candidate of the leftist PT three times before winning the presidential elections in October 2002. He had lost three previous presidential elections: once to Mr Fernando Collor de Mello in 1989, and twice to Mr Fernando Henrique Cardoso (referred to below as Cardoso) in 1994 and 1998. In the preparations for the 2002 election, a major issue in the strategy debates of the PT, according to the Brazilian press, was that its policies were related to political alliances. In a context under which the PT attempted to make alliances with more centrist parties that could bring Lula da Silva the necessary votes to win a majority vote, the latter, finally, accepted the nomination as presidential candidate for the PT.[3] In fact, an alliance was organized by the PT with the Liberal Party (PL), a small centre-right populist party, which had the privilege of nominating the candidate for vice-president, the entrepreneur Mr José Alencar.

The question of political alliances was important not only because of the immediate effect that a coalition would have in terms of the electoral majority in the presidential election.[4] The main point of the alliance between the PT and the PL (probably too small to make any significant electoral difference) was to gain the confidence of sections of Brazilian society that were traditionally suspicious of the PT. All of the evidence points to the hypothesis that the main lesson extracted by the PT leadership, including Mr Lula da Silva, from past electoral defeats, was the need to attract – or at least to neutralize – those social groups that had been aligned in the past with the more conservative leaders – such as former President Cardoso – and to ensure the confidence of the business sector. During the campaign, Mr Lula da Silva adopted a posture that he himself dubbed 'peace and love', while all other candidates attacked Mr José Serra, the candidate supported by ex-President Cardoso, trying to position themselves as the runner-up in the first round who would face Mr Lula da Silva in the second ballot.

The situation changed in mid-2002, when financial markets finally realized that Lula da Silva's leading position in the presidential run was probably unshakeable. As had been expected, capital flight drove down the exchange rate and a large number of financial investors refrained from purchasing public securities maturing after 1 January 2003, when the new presidential term would begin. In view of the possibility of a Lula da Silva victory, a number of events followed, which may not have been unrelated to that expectation: (i) capital outflows intensified and, as a result, foreign reserves fell from US$42 billion in June 2002 to US$35.6 billion in November 2002; (ii) the *real* weakened from R$2.38 per US dollar in January 2002 to R$3.81 in October 2002 (it ought to be acknowledged, however, that whether weakening of the currency is 'good' or 'bad' could depend on its initial value); (iii) the monthly inflation rate (measured by the IPCA) increased from 0.5 per cent in January 2002 to 1.3 per cent in October 2002, equivalent to around 17 per cent on an annual basis, as a result mainly of the effects of the exchange devaluation on domestic prices;[5] and (iv) the demand for Brazilian securities decreased rapidly and, as a consequence, the 'Brazil risk', measured by J.P. Morgan, increased by almost 600 basis points, at the beginning of the year, to about 2,400 basis points by October 2002.[6]

In this framework, two important related developments took place. A new rescue package from the International Monetary Fund (IMF) was sought and

Mr Lula da Silva was faced by considerable pressure to show his support for this course of action. In fact, the pressure led Lula da Silva's advisors to prepare a 'Letter to the Brazilian People', in which, although in very vague terms, the candidate assured the financial markets of his willingness to abide by the rules set by these markets. Lula da Silva's speeches in the electoral campaign became rich on promises, but short on definitions. His candidature was supported by the voters' memory of what he stood for, rather than by a plan of the prospective government that he in fact never announced.[7]

2.3 New consensus in macroeconomics and policy implications

The theoretical premise of economic policies in Brazil is based on what has come to be known as 'The New Consensus Macroeconomics', NCM for short (see, for example, Meyer, 2001; McCallum, 2001). Here, we rely on an interpretation of the NCM when extended to an open economy as in Arestis (2007) – see also Agénor (2002). We may summarize the main features of the NCM, and highlight its policy implications. They are the following.

(i) The primary feature is that the focus of the policy objective is on price stability. This is monetary policy's primary long-term objective, along with the further assumption that inflation is a monetary phenomenon. Inflation targeting is a monetary policy framework whereby public announcement of the official inflation target is undertaken. In doing so, the central bank pursues the principle of 'constrained discretion', which is the middle ground between 'rules' and 'discretion'. Monetary policy is, thus, taken as the main instrument of macroeconomic policy, but it should not be operated by politicians but by experts: 'independent' central banks.

(ii) The level of economic activity fluctuates around a supply-side equilibrium, which corresponds to a zero output gap or to NAIRU (non-accelerating inflation rate of unemployment), a supply-side phenomenon closely related to the workings of the labour market. The source of domestic inflation (relative to the expected rate of inflation) is seen to arise from unemployment falling below the NAIRU, and inflation is postulated to accelerate if unemployment is held below the NAIRU. However, in the long run there is no trade-off between inflation and unemployment, and the economy has to operate (on average) at the NAIRU if accelerating inflation is to be avoided. Say's Law holds, namely the level of effective demand does not play an independent role in the long-run level of economic activity, and adjusts to underpin the supply-side determined level of economic activity (which itself corresponds to the NAIRU). The adjustment of demand to the supply-side equilibrium is effected by interest rate decisions whereby the 'equilibrium interest rate' is the rate at which demand and supply are equalized. However, it should be noted that the adjustment process is an administrative one operated by the central bank in the setting of interest rates. Shocks to the level of demand can be met by variations in the rate of interest to ensure that inflation does not develop (if unemployment falls below the NAIRU). The implication of this analysis is that monetary policy cannot have permanent effects on the level of economic activity. It can only have temporary effects, which persist for a number of periods in the short run before they completely dissipate in price adjustments.

(iii) Inflation targeting is a monetary policy framework in which the public announcement of official inflation targets, or target ranges, is undertaken alongside an explicit acknowledgement that price stability, meaning low and stable inflation, is the primary long-term objective of monetary policy. The price stability goal may be accompanied by output stabilization so long as price stability is not violated. Explicit numerical targets for inflation are published, either as a point or a range, along with a time horizon for reaching the targets. Such a monetary policy framework improves communication between the public, business and markets on the one hand, and policy makers on the other, and provides discipline, accountability, transparency and flexibility in monetary policy. The focus is on price stability, along with three other objectives: credibility (the framework should command trust); flexibility (the framework should allow monetary policy to react optimally to unanticipated shocks); and legitimacy (the framework should attract public and parliamentary support). In fact, credibility is recognised as paramount in the conduct of monetary policy to avoid problems associated with time-inconsistency (Barro and Gordon, 1983). It is argued that a policy, which lacks credibility because of time-inconsistency, is neither optimal nor feasible (Kydland and Prescott, 1977; Calvo, 1978; Barro and Gordon, 1983).

(iv) A further role of inflation targeting is to 'lock in' the gains from 'taming' inflation. Bernanke *et al.* (1999) are explicit on this issue, when they argue that 'one of the main benefits of inflation targets is that they may help to "lock in" earlier disinflationary gains particularly in the face of one-time inflationary shocks' (p. 288). In an important contribution, however, Johnson (2003) finds rather mixed results for this contention. Johnson compares actual forecasts with predicted forecasts undertaken by professional forecasters for five consecutive 12-month periods after the announcement of inflation targets. The study isolates the additional effect of the announcement of inflation targets on the level of expected inflation in the cases of Australia, Canada, New Zealand, Sweden and the UK. Immediate reduction in expected inflation is registered in New Zealand and Sweden with a smaller effect and slower impact in Australia and Canada; inflation targets do not appear to have a significant impact in the UK.

(v) In this framework, monetary policy is taken to be the main instrument of macroeconomic policy. Fiscal policy is no longer viewed as a powerful macroeconomic instrument (in any case it is hostage to the slow and uncertain legislative process); in this way, 'monetary policy moves first and dominates, forcing fiscal policy to align with monetary policy' (Mishkin, 2000, p. 4). Monetary policy is a flexible instrument for achieving medium-term stabilization objectives, in that it can be adjusted quickly in response to macroeconomic developments. Indeed, monetary policy is viewed as the most direct determinant of inflation, so much so that in the long run the inflation rate is the only macroeconomic variable that monetary policy can affect. Monetary policy cannot affect economic activity, for example output and employment, in the long run.

(vi) Monetary policy should be operated by experts rather than by politicians (whether banks, economists or others) in the form of an 'independent' central bank. Politicians would be tempted to use monetary policy for short-term gain (lower unemployment) at the expense of long-term loss (higher inflation), the time-inconsistency problem (Kydland and Prescott, 1977). An 'independent' central bank would also have greater credibility in the financial markets and be seen to have a stronger commitment to low inflation than politicians do. There is also the question of instrument independence, when the monetary policy instrument is under the control of the independent central bank, and goal independence, when the independent central bank sets the goal of monetary policy (Debelle and Fischer, 1994; Fischer, 1994). It is argued that instrument independence is preferable to insulate the independent central bank from time-inconsistent policies. However, in terms of the goals of monetary policy, it is thought that an independent central bank should be goal dependent so that its long-run preferences coincide with society's preferences, i.e. that of the elected government (Bernanke *et al.*, 1999).

(vii) A mechanism for openness, transparency and accountability should be in place with respect to monetary policy formulation. Openness and transparency in the conduct of monetary policy improve credibility. In the context of inflation targeting, central banks publish inflation reports that might include not only an outlook for inflation, but also output and other macroeconomic variables, along with an assessment of economic conditions. There is also some accountability mechanism: if the inflation target is not met, there should be specific steps in place for the central bank to follow; this may include publishing an explanation, or submitting a letter to the government explaining the reasons for missing the target and how to return to it. Furthermore, transparency reduces uncertainty about the central bank's preferences, which is expected to lead to lower expected rate of inflation.

(viii) In the case of inflation targeting in an open economy, exchange rate considerations are of crucial importance, and we highlight this aspect in the case of emerging countries, and Brazil in particular in what follows in this chapter. They transmit both certain effects of changes in the policy instrument, interest rates, and various foreign shocks. Given this critical role of the exchange rate in the transmission process of monetary policy, excessive fluctuations in interest rates can produce excessive fluctuations in output by inducing significant changes in exchange rates. This may suggest exchange rate targeting. However, the experience of a number of developing countries, which pursued exchange rate targeting but experienced financial crises because their policies were not perceived as credible, is relevant to the argument. The adoption of inflation targeting, by contrast, may lead to a more stable currency since it signals a clear commitment to price stability in a freely floating exchange rate system. This, of course, does not mean that monitoring exchange rate developments should not be undertaken. Indeed, weighting them into decisions on setting monetary policy instruments is thought desirable. Such an approach is thought to make undesirable exchange rate fluctuations less likely, thereby promoting the objective of financial and price stability (Bernanke and Gertler, 1999).

2.4 Operational aspects of monetary policy

In terms of the operational framework of monetary policy in Brazil, that is, the inflation targeting type of policy, a number of issues suggest themselves. To begin with, there is the establishment of inflation targets. This is the setting of a point target or a band and choosing the time period over which the target is expected to be achieved. It is important to note that the target horizon (over which the central bank is expected to achieve its inflation target) cannot be shorter than the control horizon (over which the policy is expected to affect the target variable). Clearly, choosing a range as opposed to a point for the inflation target involves a degree of flexibility, not only for output stabilization but also for accommodating large movements in the nominal exchange rate; this is a particularly thorny issue in the case of emerging countries, and Brazil in particular, as shown below. In those cases where a range is chosen, there is the question of symmetrical/asymmetrical response with respect to the central target. Symmetrical behaviour purports to show equal concern for both inflation and deflation. Such an approach reduces the likelihood of output declines and deflation, and indicates that the central bank cares about output fluctuations; this helps to maintain support for its independence. An asymmetric approach to inflation targeting may be advantageous when high inflation rates threaten credibility. This is often the case for developing and emerging countries adopting inflation targeting. A greater weight on overshoots than undershoots in the loss function is suggested under these circumstances.

Inflation targeting also requires the setting up of a model or methodology that can provide information on future inflation, an issue that relates to the necessity of forecasting inflation. There is also the key issue of how to measure inflation. A relevant question in this context is whether the chosen price index should reflect the prices of goods and services for current consumption only, or for both current and future consumption. In the latter case constructing such a price index is, of course, not feasible. Then there is the problem of noisy or erratic short-run movements in prices, which suggests that an adjusted or core (long-term) price index should be used. Such an index might exclude from the general or headline price index items such as food and energy prices, shocks to the exchange rate, indirect tax or regulated prices on the assumption that such changes are the result of temporary and self-correcting short-term shocks that contain very little information on long-term price movements. Another important excluded category of items relates to changes directly associated with the policy change. Items which vary directly with the policy instrument, such as mortgage payments, may be excluded from the definition of the targeted price index. Such effects, however, may contain significant and protracted second-round effects. For example, a rise in indirect taxes that lowers inflation temporarily, can affect aggregate demand, which may lower prices in the long run, thereby implying important loss of information on future price developments.

There is still the question of the trade-off between reducing deviations of inflation from the target, and preventing a high degree of output variability. This is particularly pertinent in the case of supply shocks that cause inflation to exceed the target and are associated simultaneously with lower output. Monetary authorities have a serious dilemma in these circumstances: the quicker the disinflation, the shorter the period of actual inflation being above its target. But then the quicker disinflation is, the greater the potential output variability. Policy preferences are an important determinant of this trade-off in addition to the magnitude of the supply shock. Flexibility is required in this context, which, however, may conflict with credibility if agents interpret it as reluctance by the central bank to deflate. There is, thus, another trade-off in this case between credibility and flexibility (Garfinkel and Oh, 1993).

This discussion highlights another important operational aspect. This relates to the question of monetary rules. Central banks on the whole are assumed to follow one form or another of Taylor rules (Taylor, 1993); in its original formulation this monetary rule took the *ad hoc* formulation as shown in equation (2.1):

$$R_t = RR^* + p^T + d_1 Y^g{}_t + d_2(p_{t-1} - p^T) \tag{2.1}$$

where the symbols are as above, with the exception of p^T which in the original Taylor (*op. cit.*) formulation is desired inflation (clearly, in current parlance it is the inflation target set by the central bank as explained in section 2.3).

Equations of the type depicted in (2.1) are what is called Taylor rules, since Taylor (1993) who showed that a simple equation of this form, with $d_1 = 0.5$ and $d_2 = 1.5$, can be employed to capture the behaviour of the US federal-funds rate and the Federal Reserve System (Fed) monetary policy. The nominal rate is increased more than one-to-one with respect to any increase in inflation. This policy reaction ensures that the real rate of interest will act to lower inflation. Given inflation, the real rate of interest is also increased as a result of output-gap positive changes. Taylor rules, therefore, require monetary policy to act automatically to inflation and output. These Taylor-type rules have been criticized (for example, Svensson, 2004) in terms of the possibility of real indeterminacy: if the rise in the nominal rate of interest in response to a rise in expected inflation is not high enough, then the real rate of interest falls, raising demand which fails to check inflation. *Mutatis mutandis*, an excessive rise in the nominal rate of interest in response to a rise in expected inflation would also cause indeterminacy. However, indeterminacy can be avoided if monetary authorities respond rather aggressively, that is with a coefficient above unity to expected inflation, but not overly higher than unity. This result has been demonstrated in the closed-economy case (Clarida, Galí and Gertler, 2000) as well as in the small open-economy case (De Fiore and Liu, 2002).

The Brazilian inflation-targeting monetary policy regime is modelled on the basis of the British inflation-targeting model. The National Monetary Council (CMN) sets the inflation target, which is proposed by the Minister of Finance. The Brazilian Central Bank (BCB) Monetary Policy Committee (COPOM) has to achieve the inflation target through the manipulation of the short-term interest rate. In fact the BCB makes use of the Taylor rule as its reaction function. It is actually a slightly modified form of equation (2.1), as this is apparent from (2.2), which is adapted from Minella *et al.* (2003, p. 11). The relevant relationship is:

$$R_t = \alpha_1 \, p_{t-1} + (1 - \alpha_1) \, [\alpha_0 + \alpha_2 \, (E_t P_{t+j} - P^*_{t+j})] + \alpha_3 Y^g_{t-1} + \alpha_4 \, \Delta e_{t-1},$$
(2.2)

where R_t is the 'Sistema Especial de Liquidação e Custodia' (Selic), that is, the rate of interest set by the COPOM, $E_t P_{t+j}$ is inflation expectations and P^*_{t+j} is the inflation target, both referring to some period in the future,[8] Y^g is the output gap (obtained by the difference between the actual and the Hodrick-Prescott – HP – filtered series), and Δe_{t-1} is the nominal exchange rate variation. Therefore, the Brazilian Taylor rule relates the interest rate to deviations of expected inflation from the target, allowing also for some interest rate smoothing (R_{t-1}) and reaction to the output gap as well as movements in the exchange rate. The Brazilian inflation targeting regime sets year-end inflation targets for the current and the following two years. Inflation targets are based on the headline inflation index – that is, extensive national consumer price index (IPCA).[9] A certain degree of flexibility is introduced through defining inflation targeting within a range, which has varied between 2.0 or 2.5 percentage points above and below the central point target. The other main reason for the introduction of this flexibility is that it helps the BCB to achieve its inflation target in view of the serious supply shocks to which the Brazilian economy is exposed.

Brazil is the only country in the world where the central bank determines directly the interest rate that remunerates public debt and also uses the same rate as the operational target for the reserves of the banking sector. This anomalous situation is a heritage of the high inflation era that still remains intact nowadays. Indeed, as more than 40 per cent of federal securities are indexed to the overnight rate (Selic[10]) and they are used by the banks to back up fixed income funds (short-term funds that are very popular in Brazil), any increase in the interest rate results in an immediate increase in the total stock of public debt.[11] It follows that under such circumstances, a rise in the interest rate (Selic) by BCB, is followed, *ceteris paribus*, by an increase in the liquidity conditions of the economy as measured by broad monetary aggregates. It can also cause a higher level of consumption expenditures by firms and households, as the increase in the remuneration of the fixed income funds results in a positive wealth effect in consumption. This increase in expenditure outweighs the negative impact on consumption as a result of the higher rate of interest (Nakano, 2005). There are two consequences of this *modus operandi* of monetary policy in Brazil. First, in order to have some effect over demand, BCB needs to increase the rate of interest sufficiently high so that banks are forced to ration credit due to the increased default risk. Secondly, the increase in the rate of interest, due to the arbitrage between domestic and foreign interest rates, can arguably cause an appreciation of the exchange rate. This works as a positive shock on the supply side of the economy, since it reduces the cost of imported raw materials and the price of the tradable goods in the domestic market; it works negatively, of course, on the demand side. Under these conditions it would mainly be through the exchange rate channel that monetary policy is most effective in countries like Brazil. However, it is very well known that the evidence on this issue is very sparse.

Still it should be emphasized that the inflation-targeting regime in Brazil can only account for demand-type shocks, not supply-side shocks. It is also pertinent to note that if inflation is a function of indexation policies, as is the case to some extent in Brazil (see below), then attempting to control and fight inflation with policies such as interest rate manipulation and tight fiscal policy could potentially create a great deal of slack and unemployment in the system.

2.5 Main features of the macroeconomic policy regime in Brazil

We argued earlier in this contribution that the theoretical focus of President Lula da Silva's economic policies is based on the NCM. While this is true, it is also the case that prior to President Lula da Silva's election, indeed since the beginning of the 1990s, Brazil had followed a pattern of economic development, which in broader terms was inspired by another consensus, which has been proposed to encapsulate what appeared to be at the time relevant debates. Those debates, which were taking place in the late 1980s, evolved extensively on the reforms that were taking place in Latin America. The consensus in question was the result of proposals of what appeared 'to be the central areas of policy reform that most people in Washington thought were needed in most Latin American countries at that time' (Arestis, 2004–05, p. 195; see also Williamson, 1990). Arestis (2004–05) provides a comprehensive critique of this consensus in relation to another important discussion, which had been going on for a while, that of financial liberalization). This is what has come to be as the 'Washington Consensus'.[12] This framework is not really different from NCM. It includes a set of liberalizing and market-friendly policies such as privatization, trade liberalization, stimulus to foreign direct investment (FDI), financial liberalization (including both foreign banks entry and capital account opening up), fiscal discipline, tax reform, labour and social security reforms, price stabilization, secure property rights, independence of the central bank and so on. The new pattern of development had two basic dimensions: economic integration commanded by the market and a new role for the state, which should include the promotion of price stability, and the improvement of market performance. While it is true that the former Cardoso's government followed the 'Washington Consensus', indeed 'neoliberal', type of policies extensively,[13] the Lula da Silva government although did not depart from them then, it did, nonetheless, pursue the NCM principles more closely as we argue below.

As is well known, at the beginning of 1994, Brazil implemented a stabilization programme, more specifically the Real Plan. The Brazilian Real Plan differed from Argentina's Convertibility Plan in that it adopted a more flexible exchange rate anchor. At the launch of the Brazilian programme in July 1994, the government's commitment was to maintain an exchange rate ceiling of one-to-one parity with the dollar. Moreover, the relationship between changes in the monetary base and foreign reserve movements was not explicitly stated, allowing some discretionary leeway. After the Mexican crisis, the exchange rate policy was reviewed and, in the context of a crawling exchange rate range, the nominal rate began to undergo gradual devaluation.

The Real Plan was successful in bringing inflation down rapidly, due to the combination of exchange rate appreciation, high interest rates and a huge reduction in import taxes.[14] However, the expansion of demand, which had come from the fiscal side, and the overvalued exchange rate created immediate difficulties for Brazil's external sector. For while in 1994 the trade balance was around US$10.4 billion in surplus and the current account was in balance, from 1995 to 1998 the trade balance accumulated a deficit of around US$22.3 billion and the current account registered a deficit of around US$105.6 billion.

Under the pressure of the speculative attack on the domestic currency, the main tool available for the Central Bank to defend the *real* (Brazilian currency) was to increase the rate of interest. As a result of this external imbalance, the Brazilian economy suffered many speculative attacks on the *real*, 'a mix of a "contagious crisis" arising out of the effects on Brazil of the [Mexican crisis], East Asian and Russian crises and an outbreak of speculative activity triggered by market operators who perceived evident macroeconomic imbalances in Brazil' (Ferrari Filho and Paula, 2003, p. 77).

Despite the fact that, on several occasions during this period, the IMF 'offered' financial support to Brazil, the crisis in Russia affected Brazil's external capital account and, as a result, the capital started flowing out of the country and foreign reserves fell rapidly. Under the circumstances of macroeconomic imbalances and uncertainties about the Real Plan's future, Brazil was unable to defend its currency and, in January 1999, Cardoso's government changed the exchange rate regime. The 'fixed' exchange rate regime was replaced by a floating exchange rate regime.

The 1999 switch from an exchange anchor to a floating exchange rate regime plus an inflation-targeting regime brought no significant improvement in the macroeconomic variables (such as GDP growth, inflation rate and unemployment rate), although in terms of the balance of payments the accounts did improve in 2003–04, mainly due to the increase in the trade balance surplus. One might have expected that adopting a floating exchange regime might have allowed interest rates to be lowered more quickly in Brazil. Although the rate of interest did decline, it rose again during 2001, in view of the turbulence on international markets (the Argentina crisis and the effects of 11 September 2001, among others), and again in 2003 due to the market turbulence in the beginning of Lula da Silva's government (see Figures 2.1 and 2.2). Those 1999 developments inaugurated a period, spanning to this day, over which the NCM is more appropriate as a theoretical framework able to explain the President Lula da Silva economic policies than the 'Washington Consensus'. Indeed, under the NCM framework, interest rates increase because the central bank raises them. Under such circumstances, and under a floating exchange rate system, direct market forces on interest rates are limited.

The *modus operandi* of inflation-targeting regime plus the adoption of a floating exchange rate regime, under the conditions of full opening of the capital account, has resulted in sharp instability of the nominal exchange rate. Indeed, since the end of the 1980s and the beginning of the 1990s, Brazil and other Latin American countries, began gradually, but continually, to liberalize their capital account.[16] Capital outflows can induce a sharp exchange rate devaluation that affects domestic prices ('pass-through effect'), which can jeopardize the BCB's inflation target. Under these conditions, BCB is compelled to increase the interest rate in order to seek to avoid both capital outflow and pass-through effect.[17] The BCB's reaction to exchange rate movements causes a decline in output and employment, at the same time increasing the volume

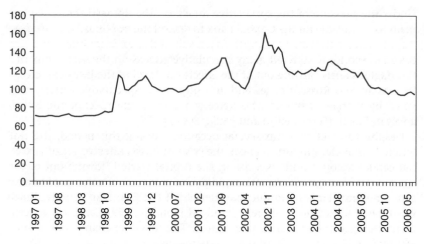

Figure 2.1   Brazil: effective real exchange rate[15]
Source: IPEADATA.
Note: 2000 = 100.

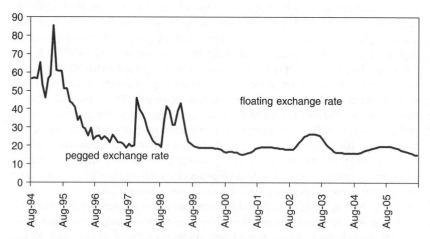

Figure 2.2   Brazil: nominal interest rate (% p.y.)
Source: BCB.

of public debt, although it should be readily acknowledged that such a decline in output is likely also to emanate from other sources. It should also be acknowledged that in terms of domestic currency the deficit can be sustained at any level necessary for full employment in conjunction with a policy of very low interest rates. This is particularly relevant in the case of Brazil, where a low interest rate policy would be a major contractionary force to the extent that the full budget deficit would vanish and perhaps go into surplus in tandem with the low interest rate policy. This implies, of course, that a low interest rate policy would need to be matched by a tax cut or spending increase to be fiscally neutral. However, during 'tranquil times', in which the country has abundant capital inflows, the interest rate is used in order to attract capital flows that results in the exchange rate appreciation that serves for the purpose of the inflation targets. Since 1999, there has, therefore, been a connection between exchange rate oscillations and interest rate movements in Brazil (see Figures 2.1 and 2.2), although it should be noted that the 'inflows' are not normally associated with interest rates under a floating exchange rate policy.

The rate of interest (real as well as nominal) has been high in Brazil because it serves multiple functions. First and foremost, it is designed to influence and achieve the inflation targets, in view of the inflation-targeting regime in the context of various macroeconomic constraints; also to limit exchange devaluation, to attract foreign capital, to roll over public debt, and to reduce trade deficits by curbing domestic demand (Bresser-Pereira and Nakano, 2002). High interest rates in Brazil have had two effects: (i) constrained economic growth, through the price of credit (loan rates) and entrepreneurs' negative expectations; and (ii) increased public deficit through interest payments, which is formed mainly by indexed bonds to overnight rate or short-term pre-fixed bonds. Despite the significant improvement in the current account of the balance of payments figures since 2003, essentially as a result of the increasing trade balance surplus, Brazil's recent experience shows that countries with a high level of external debt and a fully-liberalized capital account, external capital flows can cause periods of intense exchange rate instability. This situation has also caused low economic growth, because monetary authorities tend to increase interest rates during periods of external turbulence in order to meet inflation targets, and also stabilize exchange rates. A rising interest rate punishes firms, that need credit to operate, and workers, who lose their jobs when firms face difficulties, but rewards *rentiers* richly. Moreover, high interest rates also increase fiscal expenditures, deepening any fiscal imbalance that could already be present.

Another factor that weakens the efficacy of monetary policy in Brazil is the weight of administered prices in the extensive national consumer price index (IPCA). Monitored or administered prices are defined as those that are relatively insensitive to domestic demand and supply conditions or that are in some way regulated by a public agency. The group includes oil by-products, telephone fees, residential electricity, and public transportation. Its dynamics differ from those of market prices in three ways: '(i) dependence on international prices in the case of oil by-products; (ii) greater pass-through from the exchange rate; and (iii) stronger backward-looking behaviour' (Minella *et al.*, 2003, p. 7).[18] This is since electricity and telephones rates are generally adjusted annually by the General Price Index (IGP).[19] Our estimation of the percentage of monitored prices to IPCA is around 28 per cent on average from April 2003 to December

2005 (see Figure 2.3). Furthermore, administered prices have increased more than market prices. Indeed, while the accumulated inflation rate related to market prices was 57.0 per cent from 1999 to 2005, the administered price rate was 137.0 per cent – that is, it increased by more than 50.0 per cent in relation to the former.[20] Administered prices in Brazil are set by contracts based on past variations in the price index. It is for this reason that some degree of persistence is evident in the formation of this particular price index. Consequently, in view of the importance of administered prices in the determination of the Brazilian inflation rate, inflation pressures result in the BCB having to increase interest rates higher than might be necessary to restrain inflation that derives from market prices. This is so since the BCB has to account for the secondary effects that emanate from the shocks of monitored prices. Given also that wages in Brazil are centrally administered, it follows that under such conditions it becomes illogical and contradictory to attempt to fight inflation through the normal means of manipulating the rate of interest.

Under the current conditions of the operation of macroeconomic policy in Brazil, the government has to generate primary fiscal surplus in order to maintain some fiscal balance due to the effects of movements in the rate of interest and the exchange rate on the public debt. However, orthodox economists (for example, Pastore and Pinotti, 2005) argue that fiscal imbalance is the main problem of the Brazilian economy. However, they do not explain the origins of such an unbalanced situation. Indeed, the reasons are both important and pertinent. The international financial integration of the Brazilian economy

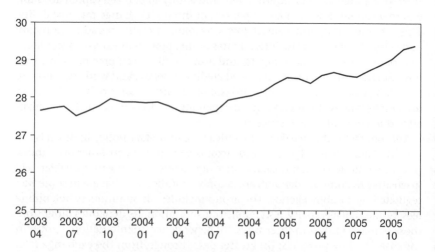

Figure 2.3   Brazil: percentage of administered prices over IPCA
Source: Authors' calculations based on data from IBGE (www.ibge.gov.br).
Note: Administered prices include utilities services, oil by-products, private health plans, that are, prices that are or determined (or authorized) directly by government (oil, private health plans) or are governmental permission that include some sort of price indexation.

has resulted in the instability of both the exchange rate and the rate of interest. It has also restricted the government's degrees of freedom over fiscal policy. Primary fiscal surplus has been more than 3 per cent of GDP since 1999 and reached almost 5 per cent in 2005 (Table 2.1). The amount of primary surplus necessary to stabilize the public debt ratio over GDP is determined partly by movements in the rate of interest and the exchange rate. As public expenditures are very sticky due to the existence of some mandatory public expenditures (education, health, Fund against Poverty etc.),[21] the only option to generate fiscal primary surplus is to combine increasing public revenues, as they arise through taxation, with the decrease in public expenditures due mostly to lower public investment.[22] As a result, the tax burden[23] (see Table 2.1) increased from 30 per cent of GDP in 1998 to around 35 per cent in 2004, which generated a great many complaints from the business sector in Brazil. Under such circumstances, there is no role for contra-cyclical fiscal policy. In the next section, we will see that Lula da Silva's economic policies are a relevant example of this sort of constraint.

2.6   Lula da Silva government's orthodox economic policies

The showdown of mid-2002 was decisive to show wealth-owners in Brazil the extension of their power over the new government. After some specialists in economic matters of the PT were vetoed by the financial markets, President Lula da Silva nominated Antonio Palocci, an unknown politician from the right wing of the PT, for the Ministry of Finance. The president also appointed Henrique Meirelles, a former chair of BankBoston in Latin America, and elected congressman by Cardoso's political party (the Brazilian Social Democratic Party – PSDB), as chairman of the BCB. Antonio Palocci's team and BCB's direction were constituted mostly by neoliberal economists and/or economists that were working in some big banks in Brazil. As a result, the economic policies

Table 2.1   Public sector accounts, 1998–2005 (percentage of GDP)

Year	Primary fiscal surplus	Interest rate expenditures (nominal)	Nominal public deficit	Tax burden
1998	0.02	7.49	7.47	29.6
1999	3.23	9.05	5.82	31.7
2000	3.46	7.08	3.61	33.4
2001	3.64	7.20	3.57	35.1
2002	3.89	8.47	4.58	36.6
2003	4.25	9.33	5.08	35.9
2004	4.59	7.26	2.67	37.0
2005	4.83	8.13	3.29	38.9

Source: BCB and also Afonso and Meirelles (2006) for the tax burden data.

have been marked by the continuation, and in some aspects radicalization, of Cardoso's economic policies, during his second term, 1999–2002. In broader terms, there are some slight differences between Cardoso's economic policies and those of Lula da Silva. First, the latter deepened the process of financial liberalization with the adoption of a set of new regulations, that included both facilitation to outward transactions (elimination of the limits that residents can convert real in foreign currencies, with the end of the CC5 accounts) and inward transactions (fiscal incentives to foreign investors to buy domestic public securities).[24] Secondly, primary fiscal surplus were increased from around 3.5 per cent to more than 4.25 per cent of GDP during Lula da Silva's government, in order to assure the conditions of fiscal solvency. So fiscal policy has been definitely set as the main anchor of the regime of macroeconomic policies in Brazil, following the neoliberal view, according to which the effects of fiscal policy are explained by the role of current policy in shaping expectations of future policy changes. This is seen as essential to improving the credibility of the economic authorities (Bertola and Drazen, 1993). It is also clear that this is consistent with NCM, whereby fiscal policy has been downgraded as a short-term stabilization instrument. Thirdly, Lula da Silva's government has been helped by much better international conditions than Cardoso's; the latter had to face the contagious of a lot of external crises, such as Asian crises, Russian crisis, and Argentinean crisis.

Indeed, the favourable international conditions have included both greater economic growth (and as a result an increase in international trade) and increasing liquidity in the international financial markets, which resulted in the retaking of the voluntary capital flows to emerging countries. The recovery of the global economy since 2001, due to American economic growth and mainly to Chinese economic growth, has had as a consequence an increase in both demand and prices of commodities in the international trade. As the main item of the Brazilian exports are commodities, such as soy, steel and iron, the increase in the price of most of the commodities exported by Brazil explains why trade balance arose from US$24.9 billion in 2003 to US$44.8 billion in 2005, although the real exchange rate was continuously appreciating since 2003 (see Figure 2.1; also Prates, 2006, for more details). Net exports were the main source of growth for the Brazilian economy from 2002 to 2005 and allowed the BCB to increase exchange reserves from US$37.8 billion in 2002 to US$53.8 billion in 2005 (Table 2.2). In fact, the commodity boom is the entire explanation for the Brazilian 'success' and how it avoided default on its external debt obligations. It is the case, actually, that a lot of questionable policy was overshadowed by the commodity boom. When that ends Brazil may very well suffer from a situation where success has been attributed to success of the wrong factors.

In spite of the improved international conditions, GDP has taken a 'stop and go' pattern during Lula da Silva's government. GDP growth was 0.5 per cent in 2003, 4.9 per cent in 2004, 2.3 per cent in 2005 and it is estimated to

Table 2.2 Some macroeconomic indicators of the Brazilian economy

Macroeconomic indicators/year	1999	2000	2001	2002	2003	2004	2005	2006[2]
IPCA (%)	8.94	5.97	7.67	12.53	9.30	7.6	5.69	3.8
GDP growth (%)	0.8	4.4	1.3	1.9	0.5	4.9	2.3	3.5
Unemployment rate (%)[1]	8.3	7.9	6.8	7.9	12.3	11.5	9.8	10.2[3]
Interest rate (Selic), average (%)	25.5	17.4	17.3	19.2	23.0	16.4	19.2	15.3
Exchange rate, average R$/US$)	1.815	1.829	2.350	2.926	3.077	2.922	2.43	2.19
Exports (US$ billion)	48	55.1	58.2	60.4	73.1	96.5	118.3	n.a.
Imports (US$ billion)	49.2	55.8	55.6	47.2	48.3	63.0	73.5	n.a.
Trade balance (US$ billion)	−1.2	−0.7	2.6	13.1	24.8	33.5	44.8	41.2
Current account (US$ billion)	−25.3	−24.2	−23.2	−7.6	4	11.6	14.2	9.0
Foreign debt (US$ billion)	241.5	236.2	209.9	210.7	214.9	201.4	168.8	n.a.
Foreign reserves (US$ billion)	36.3	33.0	35.9	37.8	49.3	52.9	53.8	n.a.
Country risk/ EMBI, average	1,030	730	890	1,380	830	542	313.8	n.a.
Fiscal surplus/ GDP (%)	3.2	3.5	3.6	3.9	4.3	4.6	4.8	4.25
Net Public debt/GDP (%)	46.9	49.9	53.3	56.5	58.7	51.8	51.0	50.5
Investment rate (% of GDP, 1980 prices)	14.8	14.8	14.8	13.9	13.1	13.8	13.8	n.a.

Notes: (1) Unemployment rate according to the IBGE methodology. (2) BCB expectations based on weekly report of August 21, 2006. (3) Average unemployment rate from January to July.
Source: IBGE, IPEADATA and BCB.

be around 3.5 per cent in 2006. The growth rates are very low for Brazilian needs, and also very low when compared with those of other big emerging countries over the same period.[25] It is the purpose of the rest of this section to attempt to provide an explanation of this performance.

The increase in the primary surplus was from 3.75 per cent in 2002 to 4.25 per cent of GDP in 2003, and the institutional improvements to ensure financial discipline at all levels of government and a high average basic interest rate (Selic) (around 23.0 per cent) allowed Brazil to reach policy credibility with domestic and international financial investors. Accordingly, there was a significant improvement in the risk premium charged on Brazilian bonds. In 2002 the average EMBI for Brazil was 1,380 basis points, while in 2003 it was reduced to 830 basis points; an increase in the value of Brazilian bonds in the international secondary market also took place.[26] In addition to this, two important points that strengthened the market's 'confidence' concerning Lula da Silva's economic policy were the fact that the inflation rate, despite having reached 9.3 per cent in 2003 (0.8 per cent above the 'adjusted target' adopted by BCB), was kept under control and the trade surplus increased from US$13.1 billion in 2002, to US$24.8 billion in 2003. To sum up, according to international and domestic financial markets, the Lula da Silva administration has done a 'good job' in restoring confidence. But it appears that the 'good job' has been performed in the main by international commodity prices, denominated in dollars, rather than by policy.

Nevertheless, the results were far from bright with regard to real economic activity, perhaps as a consequence of the very high interest rate (as it was shown above, the annual average basic interest in 2003 was 23 per cent). The economic policy mix led to poor economic growth in 2003, the GDP increased only by a poor 0.5 per cent, with the productive capacity declining in several strategic sectors because of the continuing lack of investment. The average rate of unemployment was 12.3 per cent and the distribution of income deteriorated according to the Brazilian Institute of Geography and Statistics (IBGE). In general, workers' average real income decreased by almost 15.0 per cent in 2003.

In 2004, following a few years of poor growth, GDP increased by 4.9 per cent, the fastest expansion in five years. Domestic demand picked up, consumers and business also increased and private investment actually recovered. The inflation rate was 7.6 per cent, only 0.4 per cent below the maximum limit of inflation target proposed by BCB. Moreover, the average unemployment rate decreased (from 12.3 per cent in 2003 to 11.5 per cent in 2004) and the workers' average real income dropped only by 0.75 per cent. At least two reasons can explain the Brazilian economic performance in 2004. On the one hand, the average basic interest rate dropped from 23.0 per cent in 2003 to 16.4 per cent; on the other, the record trade and current account surpluses (the trade balance was around US$33.5 billion, built basically by robust export growth rather than by a fall in imports; and the current account balance was US$11.6 billion) contributed to an increase of output and national income, and also made the Brazilian economy less vulnerable to external shocks. Thus, the main indicator of vulnerability – that is to say, the ratio of external indebtedness to exports – improved markedly. Fiscal conditions also improved in 2004, as is clear from the reduction of public indebtedness from 58.7 per cent of GDP in 2003 to 51.8 per cent in 2004, due to a combination of output growth with low basic interest rate and exchange rate appreciation. The reduction in the interest-rate-sensitive expenditures contributed to a better performance of the nominal public deficit, which declined to just 2.67 per cent of GDP (see Table 2.1). As a result, the average country risk dropped to 542 basis points. At that time, President Lula da Silva stated that, at last, 'recovery was to last and the "amazing growth" had started'.

However, 2005 showed that sustained recovery of the Brazilian economy was not really under way in view of the fact that productive activity slowed sharply in 2005. According to the IBGE, GDP increased only 2.3 per cent in 2005.[27] It is possible to identify at least four reasons for this poor performance of GDP growth. First, to aim at keeping the inflation on target (5.1 per cent), when the actual inflation rate was 5.69 per cent in 2005, the BCB pursued an overly restrictive monetary policy, and, as a result, the basic interest rate was very high (the annual average overnight Selic interest rate in 2005 was 19.2 per cent); secondly, fiscal adjustment, predominantly by raising taxes and cutting back public investments, was too tight (the ratio of primary fiscal surplus over GDP reached 4.8 per cent); thirdly, the exchange rate dramatically appreciated – in 2003 the annual average exchange rate was a R$3.01 per US dollar, while in 2005 the annual average exchange rate had dropped to R$2.43 per US dollar; and, finally, the performance of domestic demand, especially the agricultural sector, was very weak. It is important to emphasize that the economic growth rate did not decline even more only due to the fact that the international scenario was so favourable to the Brazilian economy.[28] In this context, the trade balance and the surplus of current account reached US$44.8 billion and US$14.2 billion, respectively. As a result of this external performance, the average country risk was 313.8 basis points.

For 2006, there are signs of a pick-up in activity and some reasons why growth is expected to strengthen a little. The most important sign is the fact that, since the third quarter of 2005, a gradual reduction of interest rates has been observed; furthermore, primary fiscal surplus is expected to decline from 4.8 per cent of GDP in 2005 to 4.25 per cent in 2006. As a result, domestic demand has been more robust, with private consumption and industrial production increasing and the level of investment recovering. Moreover, at least two further reasons could suggest some better perspective for the Brazilian economy in 2006. First, as a result of corruption problems, the finance minister, Antonio Palocci, was replaced by Guido Mantega, the former president of the Brazilian Development Bank (BNDES). In contrast to Antonio Palocci, Guido Mantega is an economist who, since 2003, has been criticizing the core of Lula da Silva's economic policies. In this respect, there is a distinct possibility that in 2006 some flexibility in fiscal and monetary policies may be introduced, implying that economic policy in Brazil may be moving away from the inflation-targeting principles.[29] Secondly, due to the presidential election in October, Lula da Silva is running for his possible second term. It means that monetary and, specially, fiscal policies may be more relaxed. In this context, according to the weekly report of BCB (21 August 2006), the expectations for the main indicators of the Brazilian economy for 2006 are: GDP will increase by 3.5 per cent, the average interest rate and the average exchange rate will be around 15.2 per cent and 2.19 per US dollar, respectively, the inflation rate will be 3.8 per cent, slightly lower than the centre of the target inflation rate (4.5 per cent), and net exports are expected to reach around US$41.2 billion (see Table 2.2).

Assuming that, at the end of 2006, the main indicators of the Brazilian economy are similar to the BCB expectations, it means that Lula da Silva's economic performance, from 2003 to 2006, could show the following characteristics: (i) despite the fact that inflation rate would be kept under control, its average rate would be relatively high at 6.6 per cent per year on average since the introduction of the inflation strategy. This is high, especially when it is noted that Brazil has adopted an inflation-targeting regime which is supposed not only to tame inflation but also to 'lock-in' inflation rates to low levels; (ii) the annual nominal interest rate would be around 18.4 per cent, while the average real interest rate would reach 11.1 per cent; and (iii) the average annual growth rate of GDP would be only 2.8 per cent.[30] Finally, it is important to emphasize that the course and results of Lula da Silva's economic policies, based on inflation targeting, a primary fiscal surplus and a flexible exchange rate regime, are not performing as well as they might be expected to by conventional wisdom, although some indicators have improved recently.

We can actually summarize the results of Cardoso's (during his second term) and Lula da Silva's economic policies, based on the inflation-targeting regime, flexible exchange rate and fiscal surplus regime, as follows:

- It is notable that over the period 1999–2005 actual inflation rates in Brazil were only within the targeted range in four of the seven years of the operation of this monetary policy strategy (it is important to state that in 2003 and 2004 the inflation target was changed halfway through the period). The targets were missed in 2001, 2002 and 2003 by a substantial margin, especially in 2002 (see Table 2.3). On another occasion (2004), the inflation target was met (it was 0.4 per cent below the inflation target proposed by BCB) only after the target itself had been raised. It may, thus, be concluded that inflation targeting in Brazil was not completely successful over the first eight years of its implementation. It should also be noted that its average rate is relatively high at 6.6 per cent per year on average since the introduction of the inflation targeting strategy.
- Despite the fact that the ratio of the primary fiscal surplus over GDP has increased since 1999, in 2006, due to the presidential election, the primary fiscal surplus/GDP probably might be reduced to 4.25 per cent, the net public debt over GDP, after a reduction in 2004, has been more or less stable and over 50 per cent. As a result, the primary fiscal surplus is not enough to reduce the ratio of net public debt over GDP, which has been one of the main constraints for the management of economic policies in Brazil. There is, thus, some evidence of excluding fiscal policy from the panoply of stabilization instruments, under a regime of macroeconomic policies in which exchange rate and interest rate movements are prominent as the main tools

Table 2.3   Brazil – inflation targets and headline consumer price index (IPCA)

Year	Inflation target (%)	Tolerance intervals +/−(%)	IPCA (%)
1999	8.0	2.0	8.94
2000	6.0	2.0	5.97
2001	4.0	2.0	7.67
2002	3.5	2.0	12.53
2003	4.0*	2.5	9.30
2004	5.5*	2.5	7.60
2005	5.1	2.5	5.69
2006	4.5	2.0	3.8**

Source: BCB (data obtained in August 2006).
Notes: *The original inflation target was 3.25 per cent (tolerance interval of 2.0 per cent) in 2003 and 3.75 per cent (tolerance interval of 2.5 per cent) in 2004. Later BCB decided to change again the inflation target in 2003 to the maximum limit of 8.5 per cent, that was known as 'adjusted target'. **As expected by the BCB based on the weekly report of 21 August 2006.

of stabilization policy. There is also some concern about the quality of the fiscal adjustment due to the income distributive effects of interest payments to *rentiers*, the very high level of the tax burden and the fact that reduction in the public expenditures has been done at the expense of mainly investment expenditures.

• Due to the good performance of the trade position and also to the reduction of the external debt (both public and private) and the increase in the amount of foreign reserves, external vulnerability indicators in general improved over the period 2003–05. The ratio of net external debt over exports (external solvency indicator) has declined sharply since 2002, although the broader indicator, the ratio of foreign liability over exports, has not improved so well, due to the increase in FDI and portfolio investment over the period (Figure 2.4). However, there is a great deal of concern about the future of the trade balance performance. This is due essentially to two reasons: (i) continuous real exchange rate appreciation has reduced the growth rate of exports in 2006; and (ii) the possible reduction in the volume of international trade, mainly commodities, if a decline in the economic growth of USA and China were to materialize. Brazilian exports are still very much concentrated on agricultural and industrial commodities, natural resources, and technological low-intensive industrial products, while there is an important presence in its import contents of products that rely extensively on technology.[31]

2.7   Possible alternative economic policies

In this section we seek to advance a set of policies, which do not sit comfortably with the policies implemented in Brazil by the two most recent regimes.

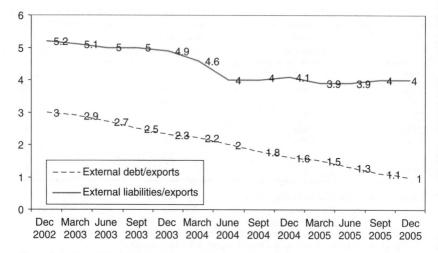

Figure 2.4   Brazil: indicators of external solvency
Note: External liabilities include foreign debt, FDI stock and portfolio investments stock.
Source: Prates (2006, p. 149).

Many critics of the neoliberal economic policies implemented in Brazil have advanced proposals to change the course of economic policies. Many of these proposals are designed to reach results that may be more or less radically different from those achieved so far. A sample of these proposals may be summarized succinctly. Most of the debate around Lula da Silva's economic policies has taken place, understandably, in the newspapers. Among the relatively few debates already published as books, one could mention, Sicsú, Oreiro and Paula (2003) and Sicsú, Michel and Paula (2005). Oreiro and Paula (2007) present a Keynesian strategy of economic policy that aims to achieve higher, stable and sustained economic growth in Brazil. The basic features of this strategy are: (i) adoption of a *crawling-peg exchange rate regime* in which the devaluation rate of domestic currency was set by the BCB at a rate equal to the difference between a *target inflation rate* and *average inflation rate* of Brazil's most important trade partners; (ii) adoption of *market-based capital controls* in order to increase the autonomy of the BCB to set nominal interest rates according to domestic objectives (mainly to promote a robust growth); (iii) reduction of nominal interest rate to a level compatible with a real interest rate of 6.0 per cent per year; and (iv) reduction of primary surplus from the current 4.5 per cent of GDP to 3.0 per cent of GDP. According to the authors' calculations these elements are fundamental for the required increase in the investment rate of Brazilian economy from the current 20 per cent of GDP to 27 per cent of GDP, a rate that is needed for a sustained growth of 5 per cent per year.

It is clear from this short summary that, most frequently, it is monetary policy that is singled out. In general, the basic idea is that monetary policy is too rigid and insensitive to the need to grow, and that some flexibility could be introduced in the inflation-targeting regime (such as the use of a core inflation index instead of the headline consumer index). In this context, many economists argue that interest rates could be reduced more extensively in the short term with virtuous impacts on the economy. They also argue for: (i) reduction of public debt and consequent decline of interest payments with beneficial effects on the fiscal balance; (ii) increase in the supply of credit; and (iii) mechanisms to stimulate productive investment decisions with beneficial effects on economic growth.

A second line of criticism, even if agreeing with the argument stressed above about the need to reduce interest rates more boldly, insists that it may not be enough. Some economists defend the view that capital controls should also be adopted to protect the Brazilian economy against external shocks, to increase the degrees of freedom in the conduct of monetary policy and also to avoid excessive exchange rate appreciation due to the capital flows movements. Moreover, they are in favour of implementing a sort of 'managing floating exchange regime', which would aim at the same time to preserve some flexibility in the short-term nominal exchange rate (although avoiding high volatility in the exchange rate), in order to discourage short-term speculative capital flows. It would also aim to reach a stable and competitive real exchange rate (RER) in order to stimulate the expansion of tradable sectors. The strategic need for a strong growth of exports, at the same time preserving the feasibility of implementing active development policies, means that trade negotiations, including the Free Trade Area of the Americas (FTAA) and at the World Trade Organization (WTO), all these dimensions are of dramatic importance to Brazil.[32]

We actually share the views summarized above in this section. A minimal programme would be one that focuses on the attainment of full employment and the creation of conditions for a recovery of private and public investment. In fact, the conditions favourable to the promotion of full employment and the recovery of investment largely overlap. On the macroeconomic side, it is necessary to wake up and stimulate the *animal spirits* of the entrepreneurs, by signalling that policies supporting aggregate demand, rather than the opposite, would be pursued. Not only does this mean that monetary policies should explicitly consider the goal of maintaining employment stability along with price stability, but also that fiscal policy should be reoriented to enable expansion in public investment, rather than debt service or even current expenditure. Monetary policies should be refocused and the BCB should be assigned employment *and* inflation targets. In other words, the BCB should be given a broader mandate than the current monolithic concentration on price stability. There is nothing particularly revolutionary about this suggestion. It is in fact very closely to the policy framework of the US Federal Reserve in the United States, which arguably has been practised in this country with considerable success for a number of years now. It is not without its problems. But it avoids the monolithic concentration on price stability, which does not appear to have been applied in the history of mankind with any particular success. Fiscal policy, on the other hand, should not sacrifice all other objectives simply in order to guarantee the service of public debt at any price. Some reduction in the primary fiscal surplus and some control over current expenditure in the long run should be necessary in order to increase public investment in economic and social infrastructure in Brazil. We propose that the entire reduction in primary surplus is used to increase public investment. Note that the reduction of the ratio of public debt over GDP could be obtained, even with some reduction in the primary fiscal surplus if combined with a reduction in the real interest rate and an increase in the GDP growth.[33] Reduction of the ratio of public debt to GDP could contribute to reaching the long-run objective of fiscal balance, so that fiscal policies could operate again as an important contra-cyclical tool.[34]

Monetary policy has to be formulated jointly with other macroeconomic policies and their implementation often coordinated. Since in developing countries like Brazil, exchange rate is the main transmission mechanism that affects inflation, a more stable exchange rate can contribute to avoid inflation acceleration. The new mix of fiscal, monetary and exchange rate policies should strengthen *animal spirits* through influencing expectations that earned profits would further encourage increases in aggregate demand. Macroeconomic policies are closely interconnected and should be coherently designed and implemented. The new mix of policies, however, would not stand a chance if the current degree of capital account liberalization was maintained, thereby allowing residents to promote capital flight as easily as is presently the case. For this reason, the regulation of capital flows through the adoption of market-based capital controls that could create market incentives for the reduction of short-term capital flows would be necessary in order to preserve some autonomy of domestic economic policies.[35]

Under the scenario discussed, reaching full employment can go hand-in-hand with stimulating growth and investment in order to provide the capital equipment upon which the workers can be employed. But to achieve this objective, interventionist policies are vitally necessary – not merely to expand economic activity, but also to produce significant distribution-type effects, so desperately needed in Brazil to alleviate, if not fight poverty entirely. Active economic policies are clearly necessary. In addition, healthy industrial policies would also be necessary to coordinate private and public efforts at accumulating capital at the necessary rate. This is a neglected area in economic policy, but one that recently has received a great deal of attention in the case of the EU countries. This work shows that unless capital stock is increased it may be difficult to fight unemployment successfully (see, for example, Arestis and Biefang-Frisancho Mariscal, 2000). This is also an important issue, we suggest, in the case of other countries, including Brazil. This may be a pertinent issue mainly in the more dynamic manufacturing sectors that could contribute towards stimulating exports in goods with greater income elasticity.[36] It would certainly be more plausible to assume that growth policies would have a higher probability of success in situations where aggregate demand was not maintained at low levels by macroeconomic policies, as is the current practice in Brazil. In such a case, maintaining and expanding trade surplus is a strategic element for economic growth. On the one hand, the implementation of a 'managing floating exchange regime', as discussed above, to promote the profitability of tradable activities and to provide incentives to firms to invest and expand production and employment through a stable and competitive real exchange rate should be desirable.[37] On the other hand, resisting the demands of industrial countries to liberalize non-traditional sectors, such as government procurement, is essential to establishing the feasibility of any efficient industrial policy. We recognize that the work of the Ministry of Foreign Affairs of Lula da Silva's government would be helped by giving priority to trade and financial partnerships with Mercosur block countries and other emerging countries. This is important in the attempt to increase the bargaining power of Brazil and other block countries in trade talks, such as the FTAA.

To sum up, to address the objective of expanding effective demand and stabilizing the inflation process, the government should (i) operate fiscal policy to implement social programmes and to promote investments, in particular to rebuild public utilities in energy production and road construction, among others; (ii) ensure that monetary policy has a positive impact on the level of economic activity; this, however, can only be done by very low interest rates; (iii) implement a 'managing floating exchange regime' that aims at maintaining a stable and competitive real exchange rate. To be sure, this is only a short-term measure for 'market-making' purposes, but certainly not as a policy that accumulates foreign exchange. All that the latter achieves is either to export real savings or reduce and/or defer domestic standards of living with a very high risk of never getting real compensation; (iv) operate an industrial policy that should aim at integrating the Brazilian economy in the international scene. This would create the context in which Brazil can incorporate the technological innovations occurring in the world in her relevant sectors, and enable her to attract FDI that would add aggregate value to exports. In other words, industrial policy should be used both to increase and change the composition of Brazil's exports, in order to incorporate other products with high levels of aggregate value. Alternatively, and perhaps more promisingly, the exporters could be organized to maximize export profits nationally and utilize any international market power that could be gained by organizing export strategies. Domestic industries need not be forced to compete individually in world markets if they can collude for export purposes in the national interest; at the end of the day it is true that it is full domestic employment policy that attracts FDI – a good example here is the USA that gets so much inflow of FDI in healthy economic circumstances; (vi) implement trade and financial agreements with other developing countries, such as Mercosur countries, Latin America countries and emerging countries in Asia; drop all import restrictions unilaterally may not be a bad idea – either can help greatly in this respect; (vii) create efficient anti-speculation mechanisms to regulate movements of capital in order to prevent exchange rate crises and augment the autonomy of domestic economic policies; this may become unnecessary if banks were to be well regulated; (viii) adopt incomes policies to regulate wages and prices, in which case the private sector would necessarily follow and not lead; and (ix) introduce fiscal initiatives, such as really progressive income tax schedules and capital levies, guaranteed minimum income and social expenditure, with the objective to improve the standard of living of poor people. Such policies are paramount and urgently required to promote personal income redistribution. We might add at this point that transactions taxes are necessarily counterproductive and that other progressive taxation would accomplish the same ends more efficiently. In terms of guaranteeing minimum income and social expenditure, offering a job with benefits to anyone willing and able to work automatically can do the job very well (Mosler, 1997).

Full employment policy is so important that the last observation becomes paramount. The policy description under what has come to be known as 'employer of last resort' (ELR) is a significant contribution in this regard.[38] This can be done, as Mosler (1997) argues, by the government proceeding directly to zero unemployment by offering a public service job to anyone who wants one as a supplement to the current budget. Furthermore, by fixing the wage paid under this ELR programme at a level that does not disrupt existing labour markets, i.e. a wage level close to the existing minimum wage, substantive price stability can be expected (p. 2). Indeed, 'Lower real interest rates will tend to keep more individuals in need of employment. Combined with a well-run ELR policy, low rates should increase output dramatically with much of the increased output being investment. It may be possible, for example, to repair, rebuild, enhance and maintain the public infrastructure without a decrease in private consumption from current levels' (p. 26). The counter argument to this proposal is that it may require substantial government deficits to implement it, in which case it becomes politically unacceptable. The response to this is that the growth in the economy that would emanate from the policy could very well produce the necessary receipts to the Brazilian treasury so that the deficit does not become excessive, if any at all. It could also be the case that such policies are implemented when deficits do not threaten to be become a burden to the economy.

2.8   Summary and conclusions

We have attempted in this contribution to examine the economic policies of President Lula da Silva. We have demonstrated the theoretical premise of the president's economic policies, and have discussed their performance over the life of President Lula da Silva's government. In conclusion, we may ask the legitimate question: what is macroeconomic stability in the context of these policies? The monetary authorities appointed by President Lula da Silva, as those appointed by former President Cardoso, seem to believe inflation stabilization is the only goal of macroeconomic policy. From the fiscal side, all that matters is building credibility with financial agents. As John Maynard Keynes once suggested, macroeconomic stability should mean a combination of full employment and stable prices. For developing countries, we should add, macroeconomic stability also means long-term economic growth and social development. In this context, economic stabilization cannot neglect fiscal, monetary, exchange rate, trade and income policies as instruments for stabilizing prices and expanding effective demand.

It is very unfortunate that President Lula da Silva has not advanced a more progressive vision and project for Brazil. His electoral slogan, 'hope has defeated fear', has been so deflated that not even the president himself mentions it anymore in his speeches. There is very little to show for hope, but a lot for fear. Unemployment is still high, and rising, the GDP performance is below par and it is led almost by the export sector only helped by the healthy international economic conditions. No long-term vision of Brazil's future has been offered. Inflation targeting was implemented in 1999, when the balance of payments crisis led to the change in the exchange regime as a new nominal anchor for price stabilization purposes. Eight years later, the regime has become a straight-jacket holding back real activity. Instead of an inflation-targeting regime, what Brazil really needs is an *economic growth regime*. President Lula da Silva was elected on the promise that he would move the country away from the many years of stagnation promoted by President Cardoso. Regrettably, the opposite is true. In other words, it seems that fear has defeated hope!

Notes

1 Brazil is a democratic state by right, with a presidential system of government. The President of the Republic performs two functions: those of the Head of State and Head of the Federal Government. The Presidency of the Republic and the Vice-presidency are in the foremost position of federal public administration, assisted by ministers. There is subordination of the government bureau, public companies and other directly or indirectly controlled entities to the Presidency. With the country's return to democracy during the 1980s – from 1964 to 1985, Brazil was under military dictatorship – presidential elections have been carried out by means of a direct and secret voting system. The first Brazilian presidential election, after the return of democracy, was in 1989.

2 It should be noted that when the paper was written, just before the 2006 presidential election, we utilised data as available in August 2006.

3 In the Brazilian electoral system, a candidate to executive posts has to reach 50.0 per cent plus one of the votes in two ballots to be declared a winner.

4 After the election, Lula da Silva's government enlarged its political alliance with other non-ideological parties, such as the Brazilian Labour Party (PTB), the Popular Party (PP) and parts of the Brazilian Democratic Movement Party (PMDB). Later a National Congress' inquiry found out a corruption scandal related to the purchase of votes in the Congress that involved a lot of deputies of the government's alliance, including some of the PT.

5 Extensive national consumer index (IPCA) covers a sample of families with a multiple of up to 40 times the minimum wage, which is determined every year by the Brazilian federal government. The sample covered by IPCA has a broad geographical basis that includes families in the biggest cities of Brazil (Belém, Belo Horizonte, Fortaleza, Goiânia, Porto Alegre, Recife, Rio de Janeiro, Salvador, São Paulo and Distrito Federal). IPCA is calculated by IBGE (Brazilian Institute of Geography and Statistics).

6 It should be noted that the increased 'Brazil risk' applied only for external, foreign-denominated debt. Brazil does not need this. Domestic currency debt is not affected by it. Brazil was and is heavily involved in indexed domestic currency debt, which is a mistake, very much like external debt.

7 The PT prepared a detailed programme to be implemented in case of victory. The candidate himself, however, never showed any special attachment to what had been proposed by PT.

8 In order to have a single measurement of the deviation of inflation from the target, BCB has used a weighted average of current year and following year expected deviation of inflation from the target, where the weights are inversely proportional to the number of months remaining in the year.

9 See footnote 5 for a precise definition of IPCA.

10 The interest rate target set by the BCB is the target for the Selic interest rate, the interest rate for overnight interbank loans, collateralized by those government bonds that are registered with and traded on the Selic. This is the interest rate equivalent to the *Federal Funds* rate in the United States.

11 According to data from IPEADATA, the ratio of net public debt-over-GDP increased from 34.4 per cent in 1997 to 52.6 per cent in 2001, and since then it has been more than 50.0 per cent. Lula da Silva's government has succeeded in reducing the part of domestic public debt that is indexed to the exchange rate, but this policy has been followed by a reduction of the average maturity of public securities.

12 'Washington Consensus' (WC) is a set of liberalizing propositions that intended to create conditions for economic growth in Latin American countries, and was first suggested by Williamson (1990; see, also 2004–05). The set of reforms could be summarized in ten propositions: fiscal discipline, redirection of public expenditure priorities towards fields offering both high economic returns and the potential to improve income distribution, tax reform, interest rate liberalization, a competitive exchange rate, trade liberalization, liberalization of inflows of foreign direct investment, privatization, deregulation and secure property rights. It ought to be noted that, as stressed later by Williamson (2000), the ten propositions did not include capital account liberalization in the original version of WC, although IMF included it in its own WC.

13 Saad-Filho and Morais (2002) show that Cardoso's economic policies were neoliberal style policies.

14 In August 1994, the Brazilian government reduced tariffs on imports of more than 4,000 products, to a maximum of 20 per cent.

15 Real effective exchange rate (REER) is defined as a nominal effective rate index (this is the ratio of the index of the period's average exchange rate of the currency

in question divided by the weighted average of the exchange rates of the currencies of selected countries) adjusted for the relative movements in the national price of the home country and selected countries. It should be stressed that REER in Brazil and other Latin American countries is calculated differently from the conventional way, that is REER is calculated by multiplying the nominal exchange rate by the inflation rate of the home country and dividing it by that of a partner country. The most frequently utilized REER is calculated by multiplying the nominal exchange rate by the inflation rate of a partner country and dividing it that of the home country. As a result, in the case of Brazil when REER increases this means depreciation and when it declines it means appreciation.

16 In 1991 the Brazilian government permitted the acquisition by institutional investors of equities of Brazilian firms. In 1992 BCB allowed a broad liberalization of exchange rate markets as it permitted that a special banking account called CC5 could be operated more freely by foreign financial institutions as a result of acquisition or sale of foreign currencies. This norm in practice created a privileged way to short-term capital flight that was used during periods of contagious of currency crises, as any agent (resident and non-resident) with access to a foreign bank could send dollars abroad. In 1994 BCB implemented a tax on capital inflows in order to lengthen maturities of capital flows and to give some degree of freedom for monetary policy as Brazil had adopted a semi-fixed exchange rate. After the 1999 Brazilian currency crisis and the adoption of a floating exchange regime, economic authorities implemented a lot of norms that resulted in greater flexibility in exchange rate markets, including the unification of the exchange rate markets (floating and free ones), simplification of the procedures related to the capital remittance to other countries and extension of maturities for exchange rate coverage related to exports operations, among others.

17 While exchange rate volatility had been reduced by the end of 1998, when Brazil adopted a crawling-peg exchange rate regime, after the adoption of the flexible exchange rate regime, nominal exchange rate volatility increased a great deal.

18 According to Minella *et al.* (2003), '[t]here are three basic links: (i) the price of oil by-products for consumption depends on international oil prices denominated in domestic currency; (ii) part of the resetting of electricity rates is linked to changes in the exchange rate; and (iii) the contracts for price adjustments for electricity and telephone rates link these adjustments, at least partially, to the General Price Index (IGP), which is more affected by the exchange rate than the consumer price indexes' (p. 7).

19 IGP is prepared by the Getúlio Vargas Foundation, a private foundation, and it is calculated through a weighted index that includes the wholesale price index (60.0 per cent), consumer price index (30.0 per cent) and the national index of building costs (10.0 per cent). The reason for the use of this index to adjust electricity and telephones rates (instead of IPCA) is that when these services were privatized in the second half of the 1990s, the Brazilian government was interested to attract foreign firms, and for these firms IGP is better than IPCA, as it is much more sensitive to exchange rate variations (due to the high weight of the wholesale price on it).

20 The synthetic IPCA, which includes both market and monitored prices, from 1999 to 2005, was 73.9 per cent, according to the authors' own calculations.

21 The ratio of mandatory public expenditures over total public expenditures was 90.1 per cent in 2004, according to data from the Planning Ministry. For a comprehensive analysis of fiscal policy in Brazil see Lopreato (2006).

22 Public investments in infrastructure (percentage of GDP) declined from 2.8 per cent in 1998 to 1.7 per cent in 2003 (Afonso, 2006, table 5, p. 11).

23 Tax burden is defined as the ratio of a country's total taxes over GDP.

24   See footnote 16 above for some information relating to external financial liberalization in Brazil.

25   Ferrari Filho and Paula (2006) report that GDP growth in China, India and Russia was in 2000–2004, on average, 6.8 per cent, 5.7 per cent and 8.5 per cent, respectively.

26   Once again, it is important to say that, during the presidential election, in October 2002, the risk premium had reached the 2,400-point mark.

27   Despite this poor GDP performance, the average unemployment rate decreased a little (from 11.5 per cent in 2004 to 9.8 per cent in 2005) and the workers' average income increased by 5.8 per cent.

28   The international prices and the global demand for Brazilian commodities was still high, the growth rate of the main trade partners (United States, Argentina and China) were higher than the world average growth, and foreign investment, direct and portfolio, were 'flying' into Brazil.

29   In fact in the election of 29 October 2006, Lula da Silva was re-elected in the second round for a new term, 2007–2010. Despite some allegations of corruption and his orthodox economic policies, Lula da Silva managed 60.8 per cent of the votes while his opponent, Geraldo Alckimin of the Social Democratic Party (PSDB) had 39.2 per cent of the votes. The success of Lula da Silva's re-election was his welfare project, Bolsa Família (family grant), in reducing poverty. According to this welfare project, around 11 million families reached between R$15.00 and R$95.00 per month (US$7.00 and US$45.00, respectively – as per the relevant exchange rate on 30 October 2006). As reported in the *Guardian* (30 October 2006), cabinet members promised a post-election departure from the orthodox economic policies of the first Lula da Silva government.

30   A recent Bulletin of the National Confederation of Industry – CNI ('Informe Conjuntural CNI', July 2006; and reported in the *Financial Times*, 25 September 2006), revised the GDP growth for 2006 to be around 2.9 per cent, far below the government's 4–4.5 per cent and rather close to the 2003–06 average. According to CNI the main factor that contributes to the downgrade of the GDP growth in 2006 is the performance of the trade balance. This is due to the reduction in both income and quantum of exports, which is the result mainly of the exchange rate appreciation.

31   An interesting recent study by Ferreira (2007) on Brazil, Argentina and Mexico deals with the trade and financial liberalizations carried out in the 1980 and 1990s in these countries to conclude that these type of policies never helped income growth.

32   The suggestions discussed in the text have been proposed by a number of contributors, and a good example is Frenkel (2004). Note that the operation of this sort of exchange rate regime would require both a comfortable level of foreign reserves and some restrictions on capital flows in order to increase central bank's ability to intervene in the exchange markets.

33   The required level of primary surplus is determined by government intertemporal solvency condition, as follows:

$$s = \left[\frac{r - g}{1 + g}\right] b$$

where s is the primary surplus as a ratio to GDP, r is the level of real interest rate, g is the growth rate of real GDP, and b is the ratio of public debt to GDP.

34   On this particular matter, and following Keynesian lines, Kregel (1994–95) suggests that a budgetary policy that aims at reaching a full employment growth should include: (i) the government budget should be divided into a current and a capital account; (ii) the current account should be in balance or run a surplus that

is transferred to the capital budget, which serves to offset exogenous cyclical changes in investment spending; (iii) although the capital budget may be in deficit, it should be balanced over the long run; (iv) investment spending financed by the capital budget should be countercyclical relative to private spending on plant and equipment; (v) the capital and current account budgets should balance at a long-run target rate of unemployment between 3 and 5 per cent.

35 This could include Chilean-style capital controls (reserve requirements on capital inflows), in order to avoid short-term capital inflows, and also some restrictions on capital outflows, that have been the main culprit during periods of speculation against Brazilian domestic currency (*real*).

36 Developing countries, particularly, can face a structural problem in their balance of payments, due to the effect known as Thirlwall's law (Thirlwall, 2002). This law states a link between the rate of economic growth and the income-elasticity of imports and exports of an economy. According to this law, in the long run, demand-side variables play a key role in economic growth through the 'balance of trade constraint'; a country cannot grow at a rate higher than what is consistent with its balance of trade equilibrium. The low income-elasticity of products of smaller aggregate value exported by developing countries *vis-à-vis* the greater income-elasticity of products imported from developed countries can generate structural deficits in the balance of payments of the former countries. These increasing deficits can result in a significant constraint for economic growth in developing countries, as the maintenance of a non-exploding deficit requires that the domestic growth rate is maintained below the world growth rate so that imports and exports grow in line with one another. Holland and Canuto (2001) estimated in the case of the ten most important Latin American economies (including of course Brazil), for the period 1950–2000, that for each 1 per cent of GDP growth, total imports increased between 2 per cent to 4.5 per cent. This means that there is some evidence of balance of payments constraint to economic growth in these economies.

37 Hausmann, Pritchett and Rodrik (2004), analysing experiences of growth accelerations (economic growth that is sustained for at least eight years), found that growth accelerations tend to be correlated with increases in investment and trade, *and with real exchange rate depreciations*.

38 This policy could sit very comfortably with additional programmes that aim to redistribute income and wealth more fairly in Brazil.

References

Afonso, J.R. (2006) 'Gestão de choque: um ajuste que está desajustando'. Paper presented in the III Forum of Economy of Getúlio Vargas Foundation, August.

Afonso, J.R. and Meirelles, B.B. (2006) 'Carga tributária global no Brasil, 2000–2005: cálculos revisitados'. Cadernos NEPP/UNICAMP, no. 61, March.

Agénor, P. (2002) 'Monetary Policy under Flexible Exchange Rates: An Introduction to Inflation Targeting', in N. Loayza and N. Soto (eds), *Inflation Targeting: Design, Performance, Challenges*. Santiago, Chile: Central Bank of Chile.

Arestis, P. (2004–05) 'Washington Consensus and Financial Liberalization', *Journal of Post Keynesian Economiucs*, 27(2), 251–71.

Arestis, P. (2007) 'What is the New Consensus in Macroeconomics?', in P. Arestis (ed.), *Is There a New Consensus in Macroeconomics?* Basingstoke: Palgrave Macmillan.

Arestis, P. and Biefang-Frisancho Mariscal, I. (2000) 'Capital Shortages, Unemployment and Wages in the UK and Germany', *Scottish Journal of Political Economy*, 47(5), 487–503.

Banco Central do Brasil. www.bcb.gov.br. Accessed August 2006.

Barro, R.J. and Gordon, D.B. (1983) 'A Positive Theory of Monetary Policy in a Natural Rate Model', *Journal of Political Economy*, 91(3), 589–619.

Bernanke, B.S. and Gertler, M. (1999) 'Monetary Policy and Asset Price Volatility', in *New Challenges for Monetary Policy*, Proceedings of the Symposium Sponsored by the Federal Reserve Bank of Kansas City, Jackson Hole, Wyoming, August 26–28.

Bernanke, B.S., Gertler, M. and Gilchrist, S. (1999) 'The Financial Accelerator in a Quantitative business cycle framework', in J. Taylor and M. Woodford, (eds), *Handbook of Macroeconomics*, volume 1. Amsterdam: North-Holland.

Bernanke, B.S. and Mishkin, F.S. (1997) 'Inflation Targeting: A New Framework for Monetary Policy?', *Journal of Economic Perspectives*, 11(2), 97–116.

Bertola, G. and Drazen, A. (1990) 'Trigger Point and Budget Cuts: Explaining the Effects of Fiscal austerity', *American Economic Review*, 83(1), 11–26.

Bresser Pereira, L.C. and Nakano, Y. (2002) 'Uma estratégia de desenvolvimento com estabilidade', *Brazilian Journal of Political Economy*, 22(3), 146–77.

Calvo, G. (1978) 'On the Time Consistency of Optimal Policy in the Monetary Economy', *Econometrica*, 46(4), 1411–28.

Clarida, R., Galí, J. and Gertler, M. (2000) 'Monetary Policy Rules and Macroeconomic Stability: Evidence and Some Theory', *Quarterly Journal of Economics*, 115(1), 147–80.

Debelle, G. and Fischer, S. (1994) 'How Independent Should a Central Bank Be?', in J.C. Fuhrer (ed.), *Goals, Guidelines, and Constraints Facing Monetary Policymakers*. Boston: Federal Reserve Bank of Boston, pp. 195–221.

De Fiore, F. and Liu, Z. (2002) 'Openness and Equilibrium Determinacy under Interest Rate Rules', *European Central Bank Working Paper No. 173*. Frankfurt: European Central Bank.

Ferrari Filho, F. and Paula, L.F. (2003) 'The Legacy of the *Real* Plan and an Alternative Agenda for the Brazilian Economy', *Investigación Económica*, 244, 57–92.

Ferrari Filho, F. and Paula, L.F. (2003) 'Regime cambial, conversibilidade da conta de capital e performance econômica: a experiência recente de Brasil, Rússia, Índia e China', in J. Sicsú and F. Ferrari Filho, *Câmbio e Controles de Capitais: Avaliando a Eficiência de Modelos Macroeconômicos*. Rio de Janeiro: Editora Campus.

Ferreira, A.L. (2007) 'On the Transmission Mechanism of Monetary Constraints to the Real side of the Economy', *International Review of Applied Economics*, 21(1).

Fischer, S. (1994) 'Modern Central Banking', in F. Capie, C. Goodhart, S. Fischer and N. Schnadt (eds), *The Future of Central Banking*. Cambridge: Cambridge University Press, pp. 262–308.

Frenkel, R. (2004) 'Real Exchange Rate and Employment: Argentina, Brazil, Chile and México'. Paper prepared for the G24.

Garfinkel, M.R. and S. Oh (1993) 'Strategic Discipline in Monetary Policy with Private Information: Optimal Targeting Horizons', *American Economic Review*, 83(1), 99–117.

Hausmann, R., Pritchett, L. and Rodrik, D. (2004) 'Growth Accelerations', *NBER Working Paper Series* no. 10566, June.

Holland, M. and Canuto, O. (2001) 'Macroeconomic Interdependence and Exchange Rates in Latin America'. Paper presented in the International Conference on International Financial Architecture. Rio de Janeiro, 25–6 July.

Instituto Brasileiro De Geografia e Estatística. www.ibge.gov.br. Accessed in August 2006.

Instituto De Pesquisa Econômica Aplicada – IPEADATA. www.ipeadata.gov.br. Accessed in August 2006.

Johnson, D.R. (2003) 'The Effect of Inflation Targets on the Level of Expected Inflation in Five Countries', *Review of Economics and Statistics*, 85(4), 1076–81.

Kregel, J. (1994–95) 'The Viability of Economic Policy and the Priorities of Economic policy', *Journal of Post Keynesian Economics*, 17(2), 261–77.

Kydland, F. and Prescott, E.C. (1977) 'Rules Rather than Discretion: The Inconsistency of Optimal Plans', *Journal of Political Economy*, 85(3), 473–92.

Lopreato, F.L. (2006) 'Política fiscal: mudanças e perspectivas', in *Política Econômica em Foco*. Campinas: IE/UNICAMP.

Meyer, L.H. (2001) 'Does Money Matter?', *Federal Reserve Bank of St. Louis Review*, 83(5), 1–15.

McCallum, B.T. (2001) 'Monetary Policy Analysis in Models without Money', *Federal Reserve Bank of St. Louis Review*, 83(4), 145–60.

Minella, A., Freitas, P., Goldfajn, I. and Muinhos, M. (2003), 'Inflation Targeting in Brazil: Constructing Credibility Under Exchange Rate Volatility', *Working Papers Series, 77, Banco Central do Brasil*, November, 1–32.

Mishkin, F.S. (2000) 'What Should Central Banks Do?', *Federal Reserve Bank of St. Louis Review*, 82(6), 1–13.

Mosler, W. (1997) 'Full Employment and Price Stability'. Available at http://www.epicoalition.org/docs/essay1.htm.

Nakano, Y. (2005) 'O regime monetário e de dívida pública brasileira e a alta taxa de juros', *Revista de Conjuntura Econômica*, 59(11), 10–12.

Oreiro, J.L. and Paula, L.F. (2007) 'Strategy for Economic Growth in Brazil: A Post Keynesian Approach', in P. Arestis, M. Baddeley and J. McCombie (eds), *Economic Growth: New Directions in Theory and Policy*. Cheltenham: Edward Elgar.

Pastore, A.C. and Pinotti, M.C. (2005) 'As condições macroeconômicas: política fiscal e balanço de pagamentos', in J.P.R. Velloso (ed.), *O Desafio da China e Índia: A Resposta do Brasil*. Rio de Janeiro: José Olympio.

Prates, D. (2006) 'A inserção externa da economia brasileira no governo Lula', in *Política Econômica em Foco*. Campinas: IE/UNICAMP.

Saad-Filho, A. and Morais, L. (2002) 'Neomonetarist Dreams and Realities: A Review of the Brazilian Experience', in P. Davidson (ed.), *A Post Keynesian Perspective on 21st Century Economic Problems*. Cheltenham: Edward Elgar, pp. 29–55.

Sicsú, J., Oreiro, J.L. and Paula, L.F. (eds) (2003) *Agenda Brasil. Políticas Econômicas para o Crescimento com Estabilidade de Preços*. Barueri: Manole/Fundação Konrad Adenauer.

Sicsú, J., Michel, R. and Paula, L.F. (eds) (2005) *Novo Desenvolvimentismo: um Projeto Nacional de Crescimento com Eqüidade Social*. Barueri: Manole/ Fundação Konrad Adenauer.

Svensson, L.E.O. (2004) 'Commentary on Meyer: Practical Problems and Obstacles to Inflation Targeting', *Federal Reserve Bank of St. Louis Review*, 86(4), 161–4.

Taylor, J.B. (1993) 'Discretion versus Policy Rules in Practice', *Carnegie-Rochester Conference Series on Public Policy*, December, 195–214.

Thirlwall, A. (2002) *The Nature of Economic Growth*. Cheltenham, UK: Edward Elgar.

Williamson, J. (1990) 'What Washington Means by Policy Reform', in J. Williamson (ed.), *Latin American Adjustment: How Much Has Happened?* Washington: Institute for International Economics.

Williamson, J. (2000) 'What Should the World Bank Think about the Washington Consensus?', *The World Bank Research Observer*, 15(2): 251–64.

Williamson, J. (2004–05) 'The Strange History of the Washington Consensus', *Journal of Post Keynesian Economics*, 27(2), 195–206.

3
Chile Between Neo-liberalism and Equitable Growth

Ricardo Ffrench-Davis
University of Chile

Abstract

This paper revises the last three decades of reforms and economic policies in Chile. The neo-liberal experiment implemented in the 1970s and 1980s and the return to democracy since 1990 are evaluated, determining the main economic and social differences in design and in outcomes in both periods of 16 years. It is stressed that there has been significant diversity between the three decades, moving from 'pure neo-liberalism' in the 1970s, to a more pragmatic policy with some heterodox ingredients during the 1980s that we classify as 'regressive pragmatism', and reforms to the neo-liberal reforms in the search of growth with equity since the return to democracy in 1990. Additionally, we study the counter-cyclical management of the capital account developed in the first half of the1990s, introducing the concept of Macroeconomics for Development. Finally, follows a brief discussion on the evolution of poverty and income distribution in the full period covered.

Keywords: Chilean economy, economic policy, macroeconomics, neo-liberalism, Latin America.

JEL Classification: E3, E6, F4, N26, O1, O54

3.1 Introduction*

The Chilean experience is a valuable source of lessons for Latin America and other developing nations, with respect to the implementation of a free market

---

* Detailed analysis of economic reforms and policies in Chile since the 1970s can be found in Ffrench-Davis (2002). Economic reforms and policies in Latin America, under the Washington Consensus, are examined in Ffrench Davis (2005). I have made partial use of chapter 1 of the former and chapter IX of the latter books.

economic model. The main reason why this particular case is so important resides in the depth of transformations and the long period since the Chilean economy started this process. The first intense reforms were launched in 1973, under the harsh dictatorial regime of Pinochet. Usually, it has been generalized the idea that there is 'one' successful Chilean model. The fact is that this one-third of a century includes several subperiods, characterized by different emphases and diverse economic and social outcomes. This diversity is of great significance, since Chile not only teaches of good successes but also of deep mistakes that must be avoided.

The first stage of the reform process (1973–81) was characterized by the implementation of a neo-liberal model in its purest form. Deep trade and financial liberalizations, and the elimination of 'selectivity' in economic policies, were accompanied by massive privatizations. In general, by 1981, success was achieved in reducing inflation rate and eliminating the fiscal deficit, but at the expense of the external balance. The consequence was an economic and social debacle in 1982, with a GDP fall of 14 per cent, high unemployment that exceeded 30 per cent of the labour force, and a significant increase in poverty together with a worsening of income distribution.

The second stage (1982–89) involved moves towards more pragmatic policies to overcome the effects of the crisis. It implied a series of foreign debt renegotiations, several policies aimed to balance the external deficit – as tariff increases and 'selective' export incentives – and the direct takeover of the collapsed financial system and then privatizing it again when their balance sheets were in order thanks to heavy public subsidies to banks and also to debtors. At the end of this period, which started with a severe recession, the economy had recovered. During this recovery, actual GDP grew vigorously, but after due consideration of the 1982 recession, it emerges that average growth was under 3 per cent in both the 1980s and the whole period covered by the Pinochet regime. By the early 1990s, the Chilean economy faced the challenges of achieving a sustained high average GDP growth and of serving the great social debt accumulated in the years of dictatorship, both in the 1970s and in the 1980s.

Thus, a third variant of the Chilean model begins in 1990, under democracy. We have named this stage the *reforms to the reforms*, since there were significant improvements of the market model, strengthening the social component and correcting severe failures of the economic policies. It included labour reforms (that restored labour rights) and a tax reform (that raised public revenue in order to improve social expenditure). In addition, substantive changes in fiscal, monetary, capital markets, exchange rate and regulative policies were implemented, with the aim of obtaining a stable and sustainable macroeconomic environment, functional for economic development. It was in this context in which Chile expanded its productive capacity, in a sustainable manner in the 1990s, growing at annual rates around 7 per cent, improving at the same time the social indicators; that is, it has partly achieved the elusive economic growth with equity. Nevertheless, Chile was not capable of isolating its economy from the turbulence created by the Asian crisis, exhibiting a stagnating actual output and a drop in the growth of potential GDP in 1999–2003. After significant recovery in 2004–05, today it seeks reforms to the model that would allow a resumption of growth after the mediocre economic performance of the 1999–2003 period. We analyze all these situations across the text.

In this chapter we present a brief summary of the most outstanding features of the Chilean economy since the military coup of 1973. Section 3.2 focuses on the Pinochet regime. Section 3.3 summarizes the three democratic governments of presidents Aylwin, Frei Ruiz-Tagle and Lagos. Section 3.4 examines the macroeconomic and capital account reforms of the early 1990s, particularly the active regulation of capital inflows. Section 3.5 discusses the evolution of poverty and income distribution in the past three decades. Section 3.6 concludes.

3.2 The neo-liberal strategy, 1973–89[1]

The long period of Pinochet's government can be divided into two halves.[2] The first one, between 1973 and 1981, is a case of orthodoxy or neo-liberalism in its purest – or extreme – form. The second one, from 1982 until March 1990, within the same general approach, introduced numerous heterodox interventions, which gave it a more pragmatic tinge. They were stimulated by the severe crisis resulting from the most ideological policies of the first half. This second period can be identified as a pragmatism (what is positive because it tries to adapt to the real economy); nevertheless, many of the interventions had a regressive bias (evidently negative), favouring sectors with high incomes and at the expense of medium- and low-income sectors.

3.2.1 Pure neo-liberalism, 1973–81

The initial concerns of Pinochet's dictatorial government were with controlling the macroeconomic disequilibria and especially the high inflation rate that prevailed in 1973.[3] Soon the focus shifted to facing the inefficiencies of the prevailing economic system in accordance with neo-liberal beliefs, which became increasingly fashionable abroad in the following years. As an extreme neo-liberal group extended its power until it dominated public policy making, the range and depth of the structural changes increased.

The main reforms during this period were the abolition of price controls; across-the-board import liberalization; sharp deregulation of the domestic financial market, followed at the end of the decade by a broad deregulation of capital flows; reduction of the public sector and restrictions on the activities of public enterprises; privatization of the pension system (see Uthoff, 2001) and part of the national health service (see Titelman, 2001); the return of expropriated businesses and lands to their former owners; privatization of many traditional public enterprises; suppression of most current labour union rights; and a tax reform, which, along with eliminating some distortions (for example, the cumulative effects of sales taxes corrected by implementing a value added tax), sharply reduced the share of direct and progressive taxes.

The traditional role of the state, as entrepreneur and promoter of investment and industrialization, was to be curtailed as quickly as possible so that those functions were to be fulfilled exclusively on the basis of decisions taken by private agents in liberalized open markets, under the 'neutral' rules of a free market economy.

Economic activity recovered in the first 12 months following the military coup of September 1973. Labour discipline (imposed through the repression of unions and persecution of leaders), the liberalization of prices, exchange rate devaluation, increased public works investment, and high copper prices, removed bottlenecks and favoured higher use of installed capacity and potential GDP. Rising copper prices in 1973–74 more than offset increased spending on oil imports, with a net improvement in the terms of trade equivalent to almost 5 per cent of GDP in 1974 compared with 1972.

These developments helped to lower inflation to 370 per cent in 1974. Nevertheless, the price of copper dropped sharply in the second half of 1974, while the oil shock persisted, with a net negative overall effect amounting to 6.4 per cent of GDP in 1975 as compared to 1972.[4] This negative shock, coupled with persistent inflation, prompted the government to introduce a sharp adjustment programme, based on a reduction of aggregate demand, led by fiscal and monetary contraction and significant exchange rate devaluation.

Soon economic activity began to slow, with a sharp decline in imports and an increase in non-traditional exports. Once again, the intense and rapid response of the trade balance to large shocks of aggregate demand was portrayed. The novel element for Chile was the strength of the increase in export volume (see Table 3.1). There were four causes of this increase: (i) a very sharp real devaluation, (ii) export capacity installed in earlier years, (iii) removal of bottlenecks in the sector, and (iv) a sharp reduction in domestic demand (see Ffrench-Davis, 1979). Inflation, on the other hand, was slow to respond. Existing indexation and inertial expectations concentrated the impact of the restriction of aggregate demand mainly on the level of economic activity. For three years, the inflation rate hovered around 300 per cent, diminishing only after mid-1976 when the government introduced other stabilization mechanisms besides money supply control (Foxley, 1983; Ramos, 1986). One of the mechanisms was rather peculiar, consisting of an implicit deindexation through the manipulation of the consumer price index, which was underestimated month after month from 1976 to 1978. Another mechanism consisted of a series of profusely publicized exchange rate revaluations in order to influence expectations.

A sharp 17 per cent drop in GDP in 1975 and the slow pace of the subsequent recovery generated a high average underutilization of capacity between 1975

Table 3.1   Macroeconomic variables during the military regime, 1974–89[a] (annual averages)

	1974–81	1982–89	1974–89
GDP growth (%)	3.0	2.9	2.9
Exports growth (%)	13.6	7.8	10.7
Inflation rate (%)[b]	138.9	20.8	79.9
Total unemployment rate (%)[c]	16.9	19.2	18.0
Official unemployment rate (%)	13.0	13.6	13.3
Real wages (1970 = 100)	75.7	88.0	81.8
Fixed investment (% of GDP)			
In 1977 pesos	15.9	16.0	15.9
In 1996 pesos	15.4	15.5	15.4
Fiscal balance (% of GDP)	1.6	−1.1	0.3

Sources: Central Bank and the Budget Office (DIPRES).
[a] Annual growth rates of GDP and exports; average of annual rates of inflation and unemployment.
[b] From December to December.
[c] With emergency employment included.

and 1979 (see Figure 3.1).[5] The predominance of sharp demand-reducing policies over a weak set of switching policies explains the significant under-utilization of productive capacity or output gap. This manifested itself in terms of high unemployment, depressed wages, numerous bankruptcies, and low levels of capital formation. Given the deep recession, subsequently Chile could sustain a vigorous recovery for several years, with significant actual GDP growth, while potential GDP rose slowly (with the investment ratio averaging low levels). The noticeable recovery generated an image of economic and financial success, which was advantageous in light of the plebiscite of 1980, which institutionalized the authoritarian regime. Something similar occurred in the 1980s, when the crisis of 1982–83 was followed by recovery and a period of economic expansion, reaching the productive frontier or capacity in 1989. It is paradoxical that a technical failure, which implies deepening a recessive situation, becomes a source of political success.

In 1979 a new stage of passive macroeconomic adjustments was introduced when the government fully accepted the monetary approach to the balance of payments. It pegged the nominal exchange rate to the dollar, and allowed the supply of money to be determined exclusively by changes in inter-national reserves, with no intervention by the Central Bank on interest rates. This policy is similar to the 'Convertibility Law' adopted by Argentina in 1991. The aim was to anchor the Chilean economy to the current world inflation rate, which, although it was then at a two-digit level, was only one-third of Chile's 36 per cent. Heavy foreign lending supported this policy, which more than covered, until 1981, an expanding external deficit.

Economic policy was successful in curbing inflation, which at the beginning of 1982 stood at the international level, even below zero in some months.[6] But once again the severity of other macroeconomic imbalances was underestimated. The concentration on bringing down inflation had meant that external equilibrium and investment in human and physical capital were overlooked. Since 1979, the real exchange rate had lost one-third of its purchasing power, the external debt doubled, the export boom faltered in 1981–82, and the current account deficit had climbed to 21 per cent of GDP in 1981.[7]

Those disequilibria had been induced by excessive domestic spending on the part of the private sector, spurred by financial liberalization, huge capital inflows and the so-called monetary approach to the balance of payments. Underlying these disequilibria there was a serious diagnostic error. The government assumed that, since it had achieved a fiscal surplus and private agents were opting for external borrowing, a foreign exchange crisis would never occur. The explicit and strong support of the International Monetary Fund (see Robichek, 1981) reassured the government in that wrong assumption. It failed to realize that an unsustainable medium-term deficit could be generated in the private sector (Marfán, 2005).

In 1982, the high rate of external borrowing, followed by a sudden stop of inflows, led the country into a new recessionary crisis that was every bit as severe as the preceding one. For the second time in a decade, the Chilean economy underwent a recession of considerable magnitude, the worst in Latin America in 1982, with GDP declining by 14 per cent, followed by a widespread bank crisis and massive unemployment in 1983.

With the crisis, the productive sectors – including agriculture, manufacturing, and construction – faced massive bankruptcies. Political discontent against the ironfisted dictatorship spread, while demonstrations of opposition proliferated even amongst many of the regime's former supporters.

3.2.2 Introduction of regressive pragmatism, 1982–89

As the government's power weakened, it was compelled to revise its strategies in several respects. The debt crisis demonstrated the extreme vulnerability to external shocks created by neo-liberal policies and the passivity of the state. The apparent economic success of the late 1970s was based on a shaky policy of external and domestic borrowing with minimal regulations. The monetarist model led to a deep recession, and the climate of discontent and protest made possible the reconstitution of some social movements that had been dismantled – especially labour unions and the political parties of the Centre and Left. In the economic arena, several attempts at adjustment were made, including successive devaluations, the reintroduction of some protective tariffs, band prices for the main agricultural imports, subsidies to non-traditional exports, stringent regulation of the financial system, implicit nationalization of private debt, renegotiations of foreign debt with creditor banks, and massive financial aid to the private sector. This was associated with a substantial change in fiscal policy, which after exhibiting a strong surplus until 1981 went on to a deficit averaging 3.4 per cent of GDP in 1983–85.

The government yielded to business pressures to adopt a more pragmatic strategy, with several forms of intervention on markets by the authorities, in stark contrast to the neutral and passive approach adopted in the first half of the dictatorship. However, this greater pragmatism was biased in favour of upper-income sectors, including generous subsidies, while a tough position was maintained towards labour and grassroots organizations. The consequence was a further deterioration in income distribution; indeed, the year 1987 registered the worst income distribution since statistics are available (see Ffrench-Davis, 2002, chap. 9).

A strong and sustained recovery of economic activity and domestic production began in 1986. In 1986–87, the recovery proceeded gradually in a sustainable macroeconomic framework, though with limited external financing. In the next two years, the situation changed, with the disappearance of the restriction of external financing, due to a spectacular rise of the copper price. Then, the expansion of demand and economic activity accelerated, culminating in the overheating of the economy in 1989, when GDP increased by 10 per cent. The difference between that figure and the forecast of about 5 per cent per year in 1988–89 was associated with the increase in aggregate demand resulting from expansion of the money supply, tax reduction, import liberalization and some exchange rate appreciation, which made imports cheaper. The installed capacity still available by 1987 and a sharp improvement in the terms of trade (copper prices) in 1988–89 made a sharp jump in economic activity feasible.

The 1980s ended with the Chilean economy enjoying a high rate of capacity utilization. The economy, however, did show substantial disequilibria. During 1988–89, a number of macroeconomic variables exhibited inconsistent trends over the medium term. Aggregate demand had grown swiftly – 22 per cent – in the biennium, and GDP had risen by 18 per cent. Exports grew vigorously during the two-year period, but imports rose even faster. The gap between changes in spending and production was compensated by an improvement in the terms of trade equivalent to 5 per cent of GDP in 1989 as compared to 1987. Output, in turn, rose sharply due to idle capacity. However, productive capacity was expanding by less than a total 8 per cent in the biennium. The contrast with the 18 per cent increase in actual GDP led to the full utilization of installed capacity and the overheating of the economy. This manifested itself in accelerating inflation and a deteriorating external sector. At the beginning of 1990, the annual rate of inflation in 12 months reached 23 per cent, twice the 1988 rate.[8]

3.2.3   Learning from the reforms of this period

It is interesting that economic growth recorded similar annual averages in both halves of Pinochet's government: 3 per cent and 2.9 per cent, respectively (see Table 3.1). How can similar results be explained when some key policies were significantly different? The low average of both periods was associated with the severe crises of 1975 and 1982–83, and with the gradualism of recovery processes, which in both cases involved high rates of underutilization of productive capacity for several years. This gap between actual and potential GDP, in turn, was the main factor discouraging capital formation (Servén and Solimano, 1993), which was under 16 per cent of GDP in each period; that is, around five points lower than in the1960s.

The reforms had significantly different effects on productive structure in both subperiods. Trade liberalization applied simultaneously with a tough monetary stabilization policy induced a depression, illustrated by a 26 per cent drop in industrial output in 1975. Despite numerous bankruptcies, the sector achieved a recovery based on a rise in productivity among those companies that survived and also dynamic export expansion. While between 1969–70 and 1978 the industrial sector grew by only 0.2 per cent per annum, exports rose by an average of 15 per cent, with great heterogeneity in the sector. Some branches showed notable gross productivity per worker and export dynamism, while many others either did not survive or stagnated.

The high rate of business bankruptcies cannot necessarily be attributed to inefficiency resulting from protection under the earlier development strategy. In fact, after 1973, the long recession, real annual interest rates at an average of 38 per cent, and the accelerated import liberalization, together with exchange rate revaluation, can be identified as the decisive factors leading to business mortality. Manufacturing lost a significant share of GDP. Exports, on the other hand, achieved great dynamism, particularly non-traditional goods. Between 1974 and 1980, the share of non-traditional exports (including industrial products) in total sales abroad rose from 9 per cent to 19 per cent. These exports exhibited a falling share in 1981–85 (averaging 16 per cent) and then resumed an upward trend to 22 per cent of exports of goods in 1989. In all, in the period 1974–89, the volume of non-copper exports averaged an annual growth of 15 per cent, undoubtedly a significant figure.

The rejuvenated business sector witnessed a surge of new groups exhibiting vigorous innovative competitiveness. Furthermore, many classical conditions for development arose, among them, 'correction' of some prices (especially exchange rate depreciation in the 1980s and reduced cost of imported inputs), market deregulation and guaranteed property rights. But it also contributed the substantial fall of real wages and of taxes on capital, and the elimination of many labour rights. At the end, there was a notable progress of some people, with exclusion of many others.

Until 1982 the 'price corrections' were very contradictory. In fact, the neoliberal orthodoxy did not consider that financial liberalization could lead to extremely high interest rates or that trade liberalization could be accompanied by continuous exchange rate appreciation, as was the case between 1979 and 1982. Neither was it foreseen that the private sector would be 'promoted' amidst a sharp restriction of aggregate demand, as in 1975–76 and 1982–83.

In turn, the debt crisis dismantled the financial system and the government resultingly felt obliged to allocate the equivalent of 35 per cent of an annual GDP to the rescue of some affected sectors, diverting these resources from the generation of economic and social development. This combination of reasons helps to explain why modernization was associated with a mediocre average economic growth rate of 2.9 per cent between 1974 and 1989 and why the average investment ratio was notoriously below the sixties level.

As on many other occasions in Chilean history, economic policy was strongly influenced by temporary improvements in copper prices. During the last two years of the regime, copper enjoyed a notably high price. It is undeniable that 1988–89 would have been very different had there been a 'normal' copper market in those years. Based on that abnormal price of copper, in 1988–89 the Pinochet regime could finally boast an economy with impressive export and GDP growth figures and a modernized portion of the productive sector. But modernization had still eluded the large majority of firms, and evident macro-economic imbalances had to be corrected in 1990. In fact, as was evidently to be expected, copper prices did decline from late 1989. This explains the strong adjustment carried out in January 1990 – in full transition from dictatorship to democracy – in order to stop an overheating led by aggregate demand.

In turn, income inequality was notably greater than two decades earlier; for instance, in 1989, average and minimum real wages were still below those in 1970. In political terms, the salient development was the effective organization of social movements and political parties, which were able to compel the democratization of the system – even under the rules unilaterally imposed by the dictatorial regime. Following the triumph of the opposition in the October 1988 plebiscite and the December 1989 presidential election, a democratic president, Patricio Aylwin, took office in March 1990.

3.3   Democracy, reforming the reforms, and development, 1990–2005[9]

After 1990 the political arena was dominated by the administration of the *Concertación de Partidos por la Democracia* (Democratic Concertation), which assumed power with the successive elections of Patricio Aylwin (1990–94), Eduardo Frei Ruiz-Tagle (1994–2000) and Ricardo Lagos (2000–06). The first two administrations gave rise to a period of the greatest prosperity in Chilean economic history, with a sustained average annual GDP growth rate of 7 per cent between 1990 and 1998, which marked a clear break with the historical trend (see Table 3.2 and Figure 3.1), with high capital formation and a generalized atmosphere of stability until 1998, when the so-called Asian crisis hit Latin American countries.

The vigorous growth was led by an annual expansion of exports of around 10 per cent, a figure similar to the average registered in the 1970s and 1980s. Nevertheless, GDP growth was radically different: 6.3 per cent in the 1990s

Table 3.2 Chile: macroeconomic indicators, 1974–2005[a]

	1974–89	1990–2005	1974–81	1982–89	1990–98	1999–2003	2004–05
Actual GDP growth (%)	2.9	5.6	3.0	2.9	7.1	2.6	6.3
Potential GDP growth (%)[b]	2.5	6.0	1.9	3.0	7.4	4.2	4.1
Average output gap (% of potential GDP)	10.3	3.4	8.8	11.9	– 0.1	8.5	6.7
Fixed investment (% of GDP)	15.4	24.0	15.4	15.5	23.8	23.1	27.0
Exports growth (%)	10.7	8.4	13.6	7.8	9.9	5.5	8.9
Non-exported GDP growth (%)	1.6	4.8	1.5	1.7	6.5	1.7	5.2
Inflation rate (%)[c]	79.9	7.8	138.9	20.8	11.7	2.7	3.1
Unemployment rate (% of labour force)[d]	18.0	8.5	16.9	19.2	7.0	10.5	10.0
Real wage index (1970 = 100)	82	124	76	88	112	137	145
Fiscal actual balance (% of GDP)	0.3	1.2	1.6	– 1.1	1.9	– 1.0	3.5
Fiscal structural balance (% of GDP)	n.a	0.7	n.a	n.a	0.8	0.4	1.0

Source: Central Bank and the Budget Office.
[a] Annual growth rates of actual, potential and non-exported GDP, and exports; average of annual inflation rates.
[b] Growth of potential GDP that could be 'generated' in each period; methodology is discussed in Ffrench-Davis (2002, chap. 1).
[c] From December to December.
[d] With emergency employment included.

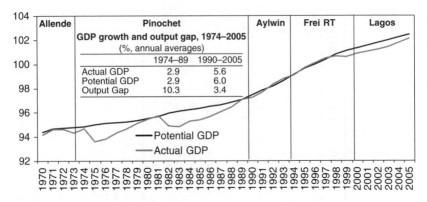

Figure 3.1   Actual and potential GDP, 1970–2005 (log scale, 1996 = 100)
Source: Based on Ffrench-Davis (2002, chap. 1) and updated official figures.

and 2.9 per cent in the two previous decades. Given the good export performance, however, the main factor explaining the success in the 1990s was the strong expansion of the rest of GDP (non-tradables and import substitutes) which expanded by 6.5 per cent annually in 1990–98. As in the three decades (1965–95) of intensive development of Korea and Taiwan, a key of success were the links between the export sector with the rest of the economy and the persistence of a comprehensive real macroeconomic balance.

The end of the Frei administration (1999) and the first two-thirds of President Lagos (2000–03) period were characterized by a depressed economic environment that frustrated the expectations of a rapid recovery. The sharp and sustained fall in economic activity was located in the non-exported GDP, which represents around 70 per cent of the whole economy. A drop in exports dynamism – undoubtedly, very significant – only explains 1.0 out of 4.6 points of the lower growth achieved in 1999–2003 with respect to 1990–98.

In all, the rate of growth of actual GDP averaged 5.6 per cent in the 16 years between 1990 and 2005. In turn, per capita GDP expanded 4.1 per cent annually in the same period, in contrast with 1.3 per cent in the period 1974–89. This notable difference that is associated with improvements in the quality of macroeconomic policies since 1990s, explains the substantive economic and social progress achieved in the 1990s. As well, the sharp stop of the vigorous trend in 1998 is partly associated with setbacks in the quality of macroeconomic management.

3.3.1   From the reform of the reforms to the Asian contagion, 1990–98

The new administration of Patricio Aylwin concentrated its efforts on stabilizing the economy after the 1988–89 boom generated by the Pinochet regime and achieving stronger, more stable, and more sustainable and equitable GDP growth. This required, among other things, an increasing investment ratio, the implementation of macroeconomic policies achieving sustained equilibria in financial markets and in the real economy, diminishing the economy's vulnerability to external shocks, and progress in the solution of the most urgent social demands by enabling larger segments of population to benefit from the modernization of the economy. The aim was to reconcile macroeconomic and macrosocial equilibria,[10] and to implement a style of economic policy that would become legitimate within the new democratic framework.

The government decided to avoid a radical change in existing economic policy, seeking 'a change in continuity' and thus breaking with the rehashing tradition of several previous governments. In order to accomplish this goal, the government of President Aylwin had to obtain support of the trade unions and incorporate workers into the macrosocial decision-making process. This was intended to benefit groups that had suffered most from the effects of the long adjustment period of the 1980s.

The new administration had to cope with the potential conflict between macroeconomic stability and demands for more resources to be allocated to lower-income groups. On the one hand, it changed the composition of public expenditure, increasing the share of social spending in the budget, and, on the other, it rapidly presented to the Parliament a tax reform to increase fiscal income.[11] Tax reform included a reintroduction of profit taxes abolished in 1988, and an increase of 2 percentage points of the value-added tax.[12]

Likewise, in 1990 the government proposed a reform of the labour code to Congress. It was aimed at balancing the bargaining powers of employers and workers and sought to endow current labour legislation with greater legitimacy. In order to secure the passage of this law, an agreement was reached between the government, labour and employer organizations, and most political parties. However, the reforms agreed (including the tax reform) were always less comprehensive than those originally proposed by the government (Cortázar, 1996; Marfán, 1998). A determining factor was the group of senators that had been appointed under the Constitution designed by Pinochet, which more than compensated for the majority achieved by candidates of the new government in 1989 and 1993.

In 1990, a tripartite agreement was also reached between the government and the representatives of unionized workers and employers; this agreement provided for an increase of 28 per cent in the real minimum wage between 1989 and 1993. In April 1991, it was agreed that after this recovery stage any future real increase in the minimum wage would be linked to labour productivity gains and that criteria for nominal adjustments would be forward looking, not past inflation.[13]

In the early 1990s, significant progress in income distribution and poverty reduction was achieved in this constructive climate. After 1993, progress in equality seemed to grind to a halt (to that issue we return in section 3.4);

nevertheless, poverty continued to decline. While 45 per cent of the population lived in poverty in 1987, by 2003 this share had been reduced to 19 per cent.

It should be pointed out that greater social effort was attained with notable fiscal responsibility. As a result of the 1990 tax reform, the expansion of economic activity and imports, a higher than expected copper price (captured by Chile thanks to the nationalization of large copper mines, now grouped under Corporación Nacional del Cobre, CODELCO), and a decline in tax evasion, fiscal income rose significantly – by 3 per cent of GDP. This allowed the government to increase public spending, in particular social expenditure, and at the same time to expand non-financial public sector savings from 2 per cent in the 1980s to nearly 5 per cent of GDP in the 1990s.[14] Higher savings not only financed public investment but also generated an average fiscal surplus of 1.8 per cent of GDP in 1990–97; the surplus was used to reduce the high stock of public debt accumulated during the dramatic financial crisis of 1982–83.

A new political agreement in 1993 enabled the approval of several previously transitory modifications on a more definite basis. Subsequent evidence rejected the prediction of critics of the reform, who said that it would have a negative impact on investment. After a decline in 1991 – associated with the lagged effect of the 1990 adjustment – capital formation increased in 1992 and again in 1993, reaching record levels in the next five years never achieved in any of the previous three decades (see Table 3.1). This high productive investment was the main explanation behind the outstanding annual GDP growth, which rose from below 3 per cent in 1974–89 to 7 per cent in 1990–98. As empirical studies show robustly, private investment, given its irreversibility, is positively correlated with macroeconomic equilibria whenever they appear to be sustainable and fulfil two key conditions. First, effective demand has to be consistent with productive capacity being generated, and, second, macroeconomic key prices (interest and exchange rates) must be *right* (see Agosin, 1998; Coeymans, 1999; Ffrench-Davis, 2005, chap. II; Servén and Solimano, 1993). This is what we call real macroeconomic balance.

Given the macroeconomic disequilibria generated in 1988–89, a severe adjustment through the increase in interest rates was carried out in order to control the expansion of aggregate demand and a new outbreak of inflation. This adjustment was considerably complicated soon after by large capital inflows, which, like other economies in the region, Chile had been receiving since the early 1990s (see section 3.3). The gap between domestic and international interest rates had increased significantly. In the meantime, risk-rating agencies had upgraded the Chilean economy, inducing a strong inflow of short-term 'hot money' and an appreciation in the exchange rate in the second half of 1990 (with a drop from the depreciated ceiling to the appreciated floor of its 10 per cent crawling band of the price in pesos of the US dollar). The Central Bank was forced to buy large amounts of foreign currency to defend the band's floor.

The strong external supply of both short-term and portfolio capital threatened to diminish considerably the capacity of the authorities to conduct monetary policy independently of external events, since they intended to avoid excessive fluctuations in the real exchange rate and aggregate demand.

In particular, economic authorities faced the need to differentiate between permanent appreciation pressures, resulting from Chile's net improvement in productivity and from having surmounted the debt crisis, and transitory pressures. Having identified the former, an attempt was made to avoid the latter in order to maintain the competitiveness of tradables.

Faced with a massive capital inflow, Chilean authorities sought to reconcile these two objectives – an interest rate suited to keeping domestic balances and an exchange rate consistent with external balances – by applying several policy measures. Among these were active exchange rate policy and monetary sterilization; selective liberalization of capital outflows; a reserve requirement (*encaje*) increasing the cost of foreign loans and liquid inflows; and the extension of a tax, which had previously applied only to domestic currency loans, to include foreign currency loans.

These policies were successful in reducing short-term and volatile inflows. But foreign direct investment (FDI) – both risk capital exempted from the reserve requirement and associated credits subject to it – became increasingly large. FDI was stimulated by the attractive features of the Chilean economy: rich natural resources and the almost tax-free transfer of the economic rent abroad (a loophole inherited from the dictatorship that required correction), high quality macroeconomic policies, and the positive perception of the democratization process. Therefore, a large surplus in the capital account, much higher than the deficit in the current account, was generated. The Central Bank responded with active purchases of foreign currency and open market monetary sterilization.

The set of policies, especially those affecting short-term capital inflows, contributed to keeping the current account deficit within sustainable levels (2.3 per cent of GDP in 1990–95) and preventing an excessive increase in more volatile external liabilities. In so doing, Chilean economic authorities contributed significantly to macroeconomic stability, to the export strategy, and to overall growth. This became evident when Chile showed nearly complete immunity to the effects of the Mexican crisis of 1994–95.

In 1990–95, GDP growth peaked at an annual rate of 7.8 per cent. If one compares the growth achieved in this period with that of other years of good performance in the past three decades (1966, 1971, 1981, and 1989), it can be seen that, in contrast to previous occasions, this time: (i) GDP growth, both actual and potential, was sustained for several rather than one or two years; (ii) growth occurred in a context of real macroeconomic equilibrium, with high productive investment; (iii) growth occurred without significant inflationary or external account pressures; and (iv) an orderly fiscal balance was maintained. Both in 1966 and in the 1990s, considerable GDP growth was achieved without placing significant pressure on the rate of inflation, but in 1966 growth was based on an increase in public spending, while in the 1990s it was induced by exports and productive investment. In the other three episodes of considerable GDP rise (1971, 1981 and 1988–89), significant imbalances occurred. In 1971 and 1989, domestic productive capacity became exhausted, generating an inflationary surge, while in 1981 an external imbalance equivalent to 21 per cent of GDP occurred.

After each of these episodes of unsustainable macroeconomic performance in the past four decades, an adjustment programme with significant welfare costs had to be implemented. These sizeable changes in the macroeconomic environment reflect, on the external front, the instability of the terms of trade and financing. On the domestic front, they reflect the high sensitivity of external balances to aggregate demand, especially when the economy is operating close to its productive frontier.

The impact of the adjustment programme in 1990 on other economic variables was less severe and quickly reversed. As mentioned earlier, investment ratios recovered in 1992 and reached record levels after 1993. The main merit of policies in 1990–95 is that they resisted successfully the temptation of achieving a faster disinflation with an increased domestic absorption of capital inflows and at the expense of appreciating the exchange rate and a larger external deficit. Up to 1995, authorities implemented an effective monitoring of the regulation on capital inflows. The strength of regulations (the cost and extent of the *encaje*) was adjusted continuously to the strength of the external supply of funding.

In the six-year period 1990–1995, actual and potential GDP rose at similar rates, with the economy working close to the production frontier (that is, with a minor output gap). However, policies lost their strength after 1995, and could not prevent real appreciation of the peso and imbalances in the external accounts in 1996–97. Consequently, Chile entered the 'vulnerability zone', where it was caught by the Asian crisis. What was the cause of the change? Various factors can be mentioned. First of all, the strength shown by the Chilean economy in face of the Mexican crisis in 1995 created a misleading sense of invulnerability. The immunity had been the result of a policy approach that prevented excessive exchange rate appreciation, avoiding a high current account deficit, and a significant stock of liquid external liabilities. Secondly, after 1995 a change in Central Bank priorities could be observed, with the prevalence of anti-inflationary targeting. Thirdly, the belief that financial crises would not occur in the future prevailed in international circles, and this implicitly or explicitly supported proposals for full financial opening; understandably, such overoptimism was absorbed domestically by private leaders and some public authorities. Fourthly, the outstanding performance of Chile transformed it into a preferred destination for foreign investors in a context in which huge amounts of capital were being supplied to emerging economies. Chile, despite this larger capital surge, kept most of its regulations unchanged.

The outcome was a net inflow equivalent to 8 per cent of GDP in 1997. Therefore, when the Asian contagion reached Chile in 1998, with a strong negative terms of trade shock, the economy had accumulated significant imbalances: the real exchange rate had appreciated 16 per cent between 1995 and October 1997, and the current account deficit had jumped to 4.5 per cent of GDP in 1996–97, as compared to 2.3 per cent in 1990–95, which worsened further in 1998 under a negative terms of trade shock, the main contagion from the Asian crisis.

3.3.2   Recessive adjustment, 1999–2003

The Asian 1997 crisis contagion arrived in Chile through two channels. On the one hand, there was an intense deterioration in the terms of trade (around 3 per cent of GDP). On the other hand, a widespread reduction of capital flows towards emerging economies took place. Thus, since late 1997 there arose strong expectations of a depreciation of the currency, which the Central Bank resisted during 1998, due to the fear of an inflationary overheating and the explicit concern of allowing domestic economic groups to reduce their debt denominated in dollars. First, massive sales of foreign currency were carried out with an artificially low market price. Then, by mid-1998, the Bank reduced drastically the crawling band spread to give a signal of nominal exchange rate stability, in combination with a rise in the real interest rate, which reached 14.5 per cent. In this critical context, not only was there a reduction of foreign credits, but a residents' capital flight also took place. In fact, from January 1998, there were voluminous capital outflows, principally from the private pension funds – speculating against the domestic currency – totalling almost 5 per cent of GDP in 18 months (see Ffrench-Davis and Tapia, 2001; Zahler, 2006). Naturally, it had a strong impact on domestic liquidity and aggregate demand.

Again, adjustment, after macroeconomic disequilibria led by excessive capital inflows in 1996–97, was costly for both economic growth and equity. Beginning in mid-1998, aggregate demand fell sharply (with a 6 per cent drop in 1999, while GDP decreased by 0.8 per cent). Since productive capacity kept rising, resting on the still high investment ratio of 1998, a large gap emerged between actual and potential GDP.

It is useful to examine in some detail the size and evolution of the output gap; that is, the gap between actual and potential GDP. Potential GDP is economically productive capacity that was in use in 1997, to which we discount an estimate of non-sustainable output in that year; and we add new capacity that was being created at a rate of about 7 per cent per year which continued in 1998 and 1999, determined by the high investment ratios up to and including 1998. The downward adjustment started by mid-1998, with actual GDP rising by only 3.2 per cent in 1998 and falling by 0.8 per cent in 1999. Altogether a gap of about 8 per cent of potential GDP was generated in 1999. That was the key determinant of the sharp drop in the investment ratio in 1999–2003. A high output gap was still persisting in 2003, having increased gradually instead of decreasing.

In fact, in the four-year period 2000–03, the potential annual GDP grew around 4 per cent per year, while actual annual GDP growth averaged 3.3 per cent.

Assertions that fiscal policy was responsible for disequilibria are not supported empirically: 90 per cent of excess demand in 1996–97 was located in the private sector and was financed with net capital inflows. The fiscal expenditure was over-financed with new tax revenue, as attested by a rising surplus and the fact that public savings reached its higher level during the period (see Table 3.3). Indeed, a stronger counter-cyclical approach would have implied a moderation of fiscal expenditure or an increase of taxes during that biennium, but this would not have been enough to compensate the great private sector imbalance; as said, 90 per cent of over-expenditure (and more than 100 per cent of indebtedness used). The source of disequilibria – that is, capital inflows – should have been tackled directly.

As we have shown repeatedly, a significant gap between actual GDP and the production frontier is followed, usually (or perhaps always), by a drop in productive investment. As in Mexico 1995, Argentina 1995 and 1999–2001, and Korea 1998, in Chile the investment ratio diminished substantially (by 18 per cent in 1999) and remained low until 2003; the output gap plus the drop in investment had a deepening impact on employment, too. Both reduced the speed at which the production frontier was moving in the 1990s: from 7 per cent per year to 4 per cent.

The presidential campaign of 1999 was marked by the premise of a fast return to 6–7 per cent growth rates. Both government and opposition constructed their programmes on the basis of expectations that ex-post turned out to be over optimistic.

This mismatch between official expectations of an imminent reactivation and a depressed economy, with a stagnated aggregate demand, determined an imbalance between the necessary resources to fulfil the government programme and the depressed tax revenues. To face this context, the government

Table 3.3   Public and private budget balances, 1990–2005 (% of GDP at current prices)[a]

	Total	Private sector	Public sector
1990–95	−2.3	−4.4	2.1
1996–97	−4.5	−6.6	2.1
1998	−5.1	−5.5	0.4
1999–2003	−1.0	0.0	−1.0
2004–05	1.1	−2.3	3.4

Source: Author's calculations based on data from the Central Bank and the Budget Office.
[a] Total balance is the current account deficit or net use of external savings. Public sector corresponds to the Central Government (does not include public enterprises). Private sector is constructed by difference.

implemented a new fiscal rule that operates with the concept of fiscal structural balance (see Marcel *et al.*, 2001; Tapia, 2003). The rule consists of supporting a level of expenses consistent with structural fiscal income; that is, for each budget year it is estimated the fiscal income as if the economy were fully using the 'potential' GDP and were facing the expected medium-term copper price. Consequently, when the economy is overheated it accumulates funds; and when it is under a recession it uses those funds to cover the foregone fiscal revenue associated with an economic activity below potential GDP. This new fiscal policy seems to us a great conceptual advance in fiscal and macroeconomic management, given the volatility of international trade and financial markets. In order to cope with international volatility, there is need for effective counter-cyclical policies to stabilize economic activity. As we have repeated through this text, that one is an essential ingredient of real macroeconomic balances.

This positive fiscal rule was accompanied by two features that are not intrinsic of the rule, but they constitute options of how applying it. One is to define as a goal a structural surplus of 1 per cent; the other one is to define as potential GDP what has been the trend GDP of the Chilean economy, which evidently includes the intense recessions that it has suffered. Obviously, trend GDP moves well below potential GDP or the full employment productive frontier.

The features of the Chilean rule allowed to support an expenditure level consistent with the estimated medium-term trends of GDP and copper price during the recessive years of this period. It implied a neutral fiscal policy with respect to the economic cycle, which implies a progress with respect to the procyclical traditional norm of balancing actual fiscal budget period after period.[15]

The Central Bank foreign exchange policy was evolving from the mid-1990s, when the monetary authorities began to lose confidence in the available instruments. In September 1999, the exchange rate was fully liberalized, leaving behind the crawling band. During 2000–01, in what it was considered to be a policy consistent with the new floating exchange rate, it eliminated the majority of the remaining controls to financial transactions with the rest of the world. One of the effects has been the intense financial activism, with voluminous inflows and outflows. Associated with the recessive environment, helping to keep it like that, in 2002–03 a net outflow of portfolio investments equivalent to about 3 per cent of GDP took place. Thus, national investors joined international markets in their pro-cyclical attitude.

Notwithstanding the persistent output gap, the government continued to develop social reforms. In October 2002, an unemployment insurance system was created by the government that was licensed to a society formed by all private pension funds. In September 2001 there was a second reform enhancing labour rights. In addition, temporary public employment programmes were intensified, covering nearly 2 per cent of jobs in 2002–03. It continued with the educational reforms, the complete day school, infrastructure improvements and modernization of educational programmes. The 'Chile Solidario' and 'Chile Barrio' programmes were begun, in order to incorporate indigents into the social network supported by the state and to eradicate shanty towns.

All of these advances, very novel and promissory, have been limited in their financing because of the output gap. But as significant is the impact the gap has on the labour market in the present and in the future.

In the period between mid-1998 and 2003, the number of occupied workers (including personnel in special programmes financed by the government) grew by only 3.3 per cent, while the 15-year-old or over population increased 8.7 per cent. The rate of participation, which had been rising during the 1990s but was still low by 1998, diminished 3 per cent (from 1998 to 2002) and open unemployment rose four percentage points. The main determining factor of this labour market deterioration was the macroeconomic imbalance, as we define it here: the high gap between actual and potential GDP, that implied under-utilization of labour and capital, discouraged productive investment. In fact, the investment ratio in 1999–2003 was four points below the average recorded in 1995–98.

3.3.3   Recovery led by a positive external shock, 2004–06

During 2003 the world economy observed a sharp improvement of commodity prices in international markets, which implied a strong positive shock. In fact, terms of trade improved for Chile the equivalent of 10 per cent of GDP between the recessionary 1998–2003 period and 2004–05. That was an exogenous shock contributing to a significant jump in GDP growth from 2.7 per cent to 6.3 per cent in the same subperiods. Given that potential output was rising only about 4 per cent, this implied a noticeable reduction of the output gap (by over four points of GDP).

Naturally, the merits accumulated by the Chilean economy were one factor supporting the sharp recovery. But the leading force was the positive external shock.[16] This reveals a macroeconomic weakness, since the merits of the Chilean economy were present in the recessionary period, including large international reserves, and low external liabilities of the public sector. Thus, the conditions for a domestic reactivating shock were at hand since the very moment the excessive external deficit and the appreciated exchange rate had been corrected in 1999.[17] With recovery, with a usual lag, productive investment started to rise. As a consequence, by 2006 both actual and potential GDP were rising by about 5.5 per cent and employment was also expanding.

The fiscal rule continued in force. The structural surplus of 1 per cent of GDP that implied an actual deficit of 0.7 per cent in 2001–03, moved to a huge 4.8 per cent surplus in 2005, rising further in 2006. The responsible variable was a spectacular rise in the price of copper, the corresponding profits of CODELCO (the public copper firm) and taxes paid by private producers. Naturally, generalized improved terms of trade enhanced the spending capacity of the private sector directly, and expectations became optimistic. In the meantime, authorities (the autonomous Central Bank) allowed the real exchange rate to appreciate 13 per cent between 2003 and the first half of 2006. This fact reinforced an increase in aggregate demand. Given a large output gap by the start of the external shock, domestic supply was able to respond with a rising GDP and low inflation pressures (within a target band of 2–4 per cent set by the Central Bank).

3.3.4   Lessons from the period examined

Notwithstanding the gap in 1998–2003, actual GDP rose 5.6 per cent in 1990–2005 – that is, nearly twice as fast as in the 1970s and 1980s. The leading force behind that outstanding performance was the vigorous investment ratio achieved in the 1990s. The average ratio (24 per cent in 1990–2005) was almost ten points larger than during the neo-liberal experiment (15 per cent in 1974–89; all in 1996 prices). It is important to stress that though foreign direct investment (FDI) had a very significant recovery, 82 per cent of the generation of productive capacity in the 1990s was realized by domestic agents. After the recessionary adjustment of 1999, FDI also contracted, but the major reduction focused on private national investment, demonstrating the strong sensitivity of domestic investment ratio under a context of a persistent output gap. In all, capital formation in 1999–2005 was significantly above those of the 1970s and 1980s and sustains a potential GDP growth rate of 4 per cent.

On the other hand, during the 1990s the national savings ratio averaged 22 per cent, the highest in recent decades, and one-third higher than the 16.4 per cent achieved in the period 1985–89. That ratio provided financing for 86 per cent of total investment. The higher savings ratio since 1990 was associated with the stimulating macroeconomic environment faced by firms, leading to greater use of installed capacity, higher profit margins, and larger reinvestment of profits (Agosin, 1998).[18]

The savings capacity is strongly affected by the terms of trade. They continue to be extremely unstable for Chile. For instance, in 1989 the high price of copper implied additional inflows into the copper buffer fund (CBF) equivalent to 3.7 per cent of GDP, which is a source of public and domestic savings. On the contrary, in 1999 the fund lost 0.6 per cent of GDP. This represents a net difference of 4.3 percentage points, which ought to be used to adjust the gross figures of public and national savings, in order to improve the quality of data on actual savings effort in each year. However, that is only part of the story. The CBF covers just a fraction of the change in the proceeds of copper exports due to price fluctuations. First, copper price changes have a residual effect on the net profits of the large copper public firm (CODELCO) and all of these profits are transferred to the Treasury. Second, the price of copper effects tax proceeds from the private copper enterprises. Thus, fluctuations of that price have an impact on national savings beyond those on the CBF. On the other hand, the savings of the private sector are also affected by the terms of trade, particularly when they impact on exports of domestic firms.

In 1990–2005, the volume of exports of goods and services grew at a rate of 8.4 per cent per annum, while potential GDP expanded by 6 per cent. Thus, exports and investment (which rose 7.8 per cent annually in this period) were the driving forces behind economic growth, increasing the external links of the Chilean economy and its potential for sustainable growth.[19] It is interesting to note that the rate of export growth was relatively similar in the last three decades. In this context, it is remarkable that GDP growth in the 1990s performed notably better because non-exports also grew dynamically, reflecting broader systemic competitiveness and the positive impact of sustainable macroeconomic equilibria.

Income distribution in Chile continues to be very regressive. Nevertheless, it must be recognized, considering the diverse available precedents, that in 1990–98 an improvement on income distribution was registered. In spite of the recent deterioration of the distribution, it is not as regressive as in any of the years 1982–89. Nevertheless, it is much worse than in the 1960s.

In summary, the *Concertación* administration compares favourably with all regimes since the 1950s in terms of GDP growth, inflation, real wages, and fiscal surplus (see Table 3.2). The performance of investment and savings and the generation of new productive capacity were also considerably improved. However, the unemployment rate, though lower than one-half the average rate under the Pinochet regime, did not recover to the level of the 1960s in a sustainable pattern. Moreover, by 2005, after a long recessive gap in 1999–2003, unemployment was posing one of the greatest challenges for recovering growth with equity. Another big challenge was to find the way back to sustainable macroeconomic equilibria and the recovery of productive investment after some confusing swings between the neo-liberal and growth-with-equity approaches.

3.4   A macroeconomics for development: the experience in 1990–95

Chile's recent history includes three interesting episodes of capital surges since the 1970s. The first episode ended with the 1982 debt crisis; the second started in the early 1990s and continued until the Tequila crisis; and the third took place for a couple of years preceding the Asian crisis. All three originated in (i) a capital surge that flew into the private sector of emerging economies (EEs); (ii) each of these financial booms was followed by an international financial crisis; (iii) host EEs held an outstanding image as 'successful' economies; and (iv) in the 1990s several EEs exhibited balanced or surplus fiscal budgets, particularly Chile and the East Asian economies. However, Chile experienced different outcomes in each of the three surges. A severe financial and currency crisis in 1982; a continued vigorous and sustainable economic growth in 1995, while Argentina, Mexico and Uruguay suffered deep crises; a soft, but long-lasting recession (with recession defined as a significant actual/potential GDP gap) in 1998–2003, while most LACs experienced a deeper recession with drops in per capita GDP during this six-year period. Here we focus on the second episode.

The return to democracy in 1990 coincided with the beginning of a new episode of abundant capital flows into emerging economies. Conscious of the risks involved, Chilean policy makers adopted a set of active macroeconomic policies to regulate the capital surge in order to achieve real macroeconomic balances. As a result, during this period, potential GDP expanded vigorously and the economy was running close to full capacity. This was a determining factor in creating a virtuous circle of rapid capital formation.

3.4.1 Capital surges in 1990–95

In the 1990s Chile was one of the LACs earlier to attract renewed inflows of private capital, and was among the countries facing the largest supply in relation to its economic size.

Chilean policy in the first half of the 1990s represented a significant step towards a pragmatic approach to macroeconomic management. In brief, policy makers responded to the massive availability of foreign capital by moderating short-term inflows while keeping the door open to long-term flows. Specifically, an unremunerated reserve requirement (URR) was established to raise the cost of bringing in short-term capital; this is a market-based instrument affecting relative costs. Authorities also intervened in the foreign currency market to hold down the appreciation of the real exchange rate in face of those flows that surpassed the reserve barrier, and sterilization of the monetary effects of foreign exchange operations. These tools were used in support of a development strategy that encouraged export growth and its diversification.

The policy was highly successful, in the sense that in the period 1990–95 the current account deficit was moderate, the currency appreciated less than in most LACs, and the total short-term external debt was held at a fairly low level. When the Mexican currency crisis exploded in late 1994, the Chilean economy proved to have significantly reduced its vulnerability.

For a country to be the target of interest rate arbitrage, domestic interest rates must exceed international rates by a margin that more than offsets the currency's expected depreciation and the country risk. Such conditions obtained in Chile from the early 1990s. On the one hand, in 1992 and 1993, international rates on dollar loans were at their lowest level for thirty years, and though they later rose, they remained far below their levels in the 1980s. On the other hand, Chile is a capital-scarce country with a stock consistent with a GDP per capita, at present, of about one-quarter that of developed economies. Because scarcity entails a higher price, the interest rate as well as profit rates in EEs tend to be higher than in developed countries.

Other conditions for interest rate arbitrage also encouraged inflows. After a cumulative real depreciation of 130 per cent in the 1980s, the exchange rate began to appreciate gradually in the 1990s. As in the case of other countries in the region, Chile's country risk premium fell. An atmosphere of emerging markets mania (*à la* Kindleberger) on the part of international investors generated a spectacular drop in perceived country risk. Private short-term capital inflows were substantial well into 1992, after which they began to fall as a result of the policy measures taken to regulate them.

Portfolio inflows took two forms: investment through large international mutual funds and the issuing of American depositary receipts (ADRs) by major Chilean firms. Primary issues of ADRs represent an opportunity for a firm to expand its capital at a relatively low cost, given that costs of capital in international markets naturally tend to be below that in the Chilean financial market. Secondary issues of ADRs occur when foreigners purchase securities available on the Chilean stock market and subsequently convert them into ADRs. This operation constitutes a change of ownership from nationals to foreigners, without a direct financial effect on the firm. These changes of ownership exposed the economy to an additional degree of uncertainty and volatility, since foreign investors can easily withdraw their investments.[20] Such flows actually played a destabilizing role in the economy. They contributed to the bubbles in the securities market in 1994 and 1997 and depressed the market in 1995 and 1998, operating pro-cyclically.

3.4.2 The response of macroeconomic policies and their effects

Monetary authorities in Chile deployed a wide range of measures to regulate the surge in financial capital in the period 1990–95. The Central Bank took steps to discourage inflows of short-term, liquid capital by means of the URR. It moderated the impact of those waves of capital by: (i) intervening in the foreign exchange market to prevent an overabundance of foreign currency from appreciating the real exchange rate too much (seeking a deficit on current account not larger than 3 per cent of GDP); (ii) sterilizing the monetary effects of the accumulation of international reserves that crossed the barriers of the reserve requirements; and (iii) active regulation of the domestic interest rate.

Four other policies contributed to the success in managing capital inflows. First, fiscal policy was extremely responsible. Increases in social spending were financed with new taxes. Consequently, Chile had a significant public sector surplus of 1 or 2 per cent of GDP. This prudential approach, which included observing the regulations of a stabilization fund for public copper revenues, facilitated the monetary authorities' task of regulating capital inflows. Of course, running a fiscal surplus does not guarantee, by itself, financial stability. The great 1982 crisis occurred despite Chile having had several years of budget surpluses; the soft recession of 1999 was preceded by three years of a 2 per cent GDP surplus. A similar fiscal behaviour happened in Mexico before the Tequila crisis and in Korea before the Asian crisis. In all these cases, the external deficit was led by the private sector, misinformed by a two-pillar rather than three-pillar macroeconomic balances (see Ffrench-Davis, 2005, chap. II).

Secondly, there was an active exchange rate policy, with a crawling band, directed to keep the real exchange rate at a level consistent with the external balance in the mid-term. Allowing a significant appreciation evidently makes notably difficult the regulation of capital flows.

Thirdly, prudential banking regulations had been introduced in response to the banking crisis of 1982–83, and the regulatory system had then been improved over the years. Authorities effectively resisted pressures to weaken supervision when lobbying, financial and academic sectors argued that the system was mature enough for self-regulation; in fact, prudential supervision was strongly intensified by democratic economic authorities. This made it difficult for capital inflows to trigger another unsustainable credit boom in the commercial banks, which in turn helped keep the current account deficit and exchange rate within sustainable limits until 1995. It is important to note that, usually, a significant share of financial flows is not channelled through local banks. This phenomenon became decidedly more pronounced in the 1990s, with the development of portfolio investment funds and derivatives markets.

Fourthly, authorities continually monitored aggregate demand and its consistency with productive capacity; and they actually conducted several *mini-adjustments* in monetary policy. Consequently, macroeconomic disequilibria were not allowed to accumulate. When the Tequila crisis exploded, Chile had a moderate external deficit, large international reserves, and space for increasing economic activity. Those conditions would not have been feasible without regulating capital inflows, managing the exchange rate, and pursuing an active monetary policy.[21]

3.4.2.1 *Managing capital inflows*

Strategic features of the policies used went against the fashion of capital account liberalization. The two main targets of exchange rate and inflows management policies were, first, achieving sustained macroeconomic stability in an economy prone to huge cycles (recall that Chile experienced the sharpest recessions in the whole of Latin America in 1975 and 1982) and, secondly, supporting the growth model adopted by the authorities, which gave the expansion and diversification of exports a crucial role.

In the face of a plentiful supply of foreign funds, Chilean authorities opted to regulate the foreign currency market in order to prevent large misalignments in the real exchange rate relative to its medium-term trend. The natural short-term horizon of financial markets can lead to exchange rate values that are inconsistent with medium- and long-run trends, which negatively affects decisions in the productive sector. The authorities sought to preserve the predominance of medium-term fundamentals over short-term factors influencing the exchange rate.

In June 1991, the financial environment was leading to an accelerated GDP growth based on rising capital inflows and a high copper price – factors considered to have a significant transitory component. The authorities reacted by establishing an Unremunerated Reserve Requirement (URR) of 20 per cent on foreign credit (covering the entire spectrum of foreign financial inflows, including loans associated with FDI to trade credit). The reserve was to be on deposit at the Central Bank for a minimum of 90 days and a maximum of one year, according to the time frame of the operation. It was heavily onerous for very short-term inflows. At the same time, an up to 1.2 per cent tax on domestic loans was extended to foreign loans.

Since capital inflows persisted, the reserve requirement was tightened and its coverage expanded. In January 1992 it was extended to cover time deposits in foreign currency; in May the rate was raised to 30 per cent, and in July 1995 the coverage enclosed the purchase of Chilean stocks (secondary ADRs) by foreigners.[22] The term of the deposit was raised to one year, independent of the maturity of the loan.[23] With some lag, authorities took measures to eliminate a loophole that made it possible to circumvent the reserve requirement by means of FDI (since risk capital was exempt, though had to be held in Chile at least for a full year). This was accomplished by scrutinizing FDI applications. Permission for exemptions from reserve requirements granted to productive FDI was denied when it was determined that the inflow was disguised financial capital.

Beginning in 1991, measures were put in place to facilitate capital outflows as a way of lightening pressure on the exchange rate. The most relevant one, with strong pro-cyclical effects several years later, was a change allowing Chilean pension funds to invest a given percentage of their total assets abroad.[24] The greater profitability of financial assets in Chile compared to financial investments abroad, along with expectations of an appreciating exchange rate, discouraged, until 1998, investments abroad by pension funds and by the mutual funds created at that time.

The immediate effect of deregulating outflows was probably to encourage new inflows thanks to the greater certainty that it gave potential investors coming into Chile. This scenario may actually produce the opposite of the desired effect, because the market takes advantage of the opportunity to move foreign currency abroad principally when expectations of appreciation are replaced by expectations of depreciation, which is precisely when the economy is most vulnerable and likely to suffer from speculative attacks (see Williamson, 1993). The progressive deregulation of outflows can thus imply a risk of capital flight not only from the sudden exit of capital that previously came in, but also from domestic funds seeking to speculate against the peso. This pro-cyclical feature weakens the effect of measures such as the reserve requirement on inflows, as was sharply proved in 1998–99.

3.4.2.2　Exchange rate policy

In the late 1980s Chile was emerging from the depths of a debt crisis, that had been faced with exchange rate depreciation. The real exchange rate had reached historic highs, such that there was room for some appreciation.

However, the economy was moving from a shortage to a very abundant supply of foreign savings, and authorities wanted to avoid an excessive and overly rapid adjustment in the exchange rate (see Zahler, 1998). One particularly problematic aspect of the situation involved foreign expectations: as pessimism turns to optimism, foreign investors tend to rapidly define a new stock of desired investments in the emerging market; this generates excessive inflows of capital, whose high levels are naturally transitory, rather than permanent.

In response to the capital surge, the crawling band was broadened in January 1992. This produced a wave of expectations of currency revaluation fed by capital inflows, stimulated by the understanding that the Central Bank would not intervene within the set band. For many months, the Central Bank had been analyzing a proposal to initiate a dirty floating within the crawling band. The sudden revaluation of almost 10 per cent in the observed rate between January and February 1992 contributed to the Bank's initiation of the dirty float in March. The observed rate then fluctuated generally off the bottom of the band, with frequent active purchases by the Bank, though also with some sales from time to time.

By establishing the intra-band intervention, the Central Bank regained a greater macroeconomic role over short-term and speculative participants, which allowed the Bank to strengthen the long-term variables that determine the exchange rate faced by producers of exportables and importables.

In subsequent months, US interest rates continued to be reduced by the Fed, putting pressure on the Central Bank of Chile to also ease its monetary stance. Nevertheless, since the domestic economy was experiencing a notable boom, the Bank wanted to raise rather than lower interest rates for the sake of domestic macroeconomic balances. So it increased the policy interest rate and, in order to deter arbitrage, it increased the rate of the URR. The effectiveness of the reserve requirement and its flexible application at that juncture facilitated monetary policy and avoided the accumulation of macroeconomic imbalances.

The actual market performance indicates strongly that the exchange rate appreciation during this period represented equilibrating movements. This is consistent both with reverting the adjustments brought by the 1980s crisis – thus allowing the elimination of the over-devaluation – and with the net improvements of productivity for Chilean tradables in the 1990s. A revealed proof is the fact that the current account deficit was quite moderate in 1990–95: 2.3 per cent of GDP.

3.4.2.3 *Stronger banking regulation and supervision*

Among the elements of prudential regulation and supervision adopted after the Chilean banking crises of 1981–86 are: the continuous monitoring of the quality of bank assets; strict limits on banks' lending to related agents; automatic mechanisms to adjust banks' capital when its market value falls beneath thresholds set by regulators; and the authority to freeze bank operations, prevent troubled banks from transferring funds to third parties, and restrict dividend payments by institutions not complying with capital requirements.

Despite the quality of prudential supervision, however, macroeconomic imbalances that lead to sudden massive devaluations and very high interest rates can unexpectedly affect the quality of banks' portfolios, as can exploding bubbles in asset markets. Sustainable macroeconomic balances are an essential partner of sustainable prudential regulation and supervision of financial markets.

3.4.3   Effectiveness of policies for stabilizing macroeconomic variables

The Chilean mechanism for prudential macroeconomic regulation attracted considerable international attention, and many studies attempt to measure its effectiveness.[25] Various tests seek to determine how the URR affects the composition and volume of flows, as well as their impact on the exchange rate and the authorities' ability to make monetary policy and regulate aggregate demand. There is robust evidence and broad agreement that Chile's regulations on foreign capital changed the maturity structure of inflows, reducing the short-term component. This evidence points to a very positive feature of the instrument, since the liquidity of foreign liabilities is a major factor in the probability and severity of crises (see Rodrik and Velasco, 2000).

Disagreement arises, however, on the effect on the overall volume of flows, since some econometric studies fail to find an impact on the total volume or on exchange rates, notwithstanding the effect on the composition of flows. The implication of critics is that there is a high substitution between short- and long-term flows. Three counter-points are relevant here. First, part of this compensatory phenomenon between flows of different maturities should be expected, if long-term investors (greenfield FDI) are attracted by a more stable economy (as emerged in Chile from the implementation of the URR); that actually is a point in support of the URR. Secondly, FDI flows normally encompass a different investor with a different behaviour, closely connected to productive investment. Thirdly, it has been tested robustly that FDI in Chile has behaved as a permanent variable, while other flows have acted as transitory disturbances (Ffrench-Davis, 2002, chap. 10). One outstanding implication is that FDI creates new capacity, which contributes to capital formation (higher GDP) and increased imports of capital goods (higher demand for foreign currency). Given a volume of FDI inflows, therefore, the foreign currency market experiences a smaller excess supply than in the case of identical volume of financial inflows.

Some observers have stated that the effectiveness of measures to discourage capital inflows is only temporary, since private sector agents generally find ways around such measures. In principle, a number of loopholes facilitate such evasion. But they usually imply costs, and some may have undesirable repercussions on the tax liabilities of those circumventing reserve requirements. Anyway, the effective answer of Chilean authorities was the permanent monitoring of the market to identify and close loopholes that did appear from time to time during the first half of the 1990s when the regulation of capital inflows remained active. Though a certain level of evasion is inevitable, there is no evidence suggesting large-scale evasion of measures to discourage short-term capital, as shown by the URR deposits actually made and the collection of the equivalent fee by the Central Bank (Le Fort and Lehmann, 2003).

The most recent studies tend to confirm that the reserve requirement also reduced total inflows and moderated exchange rate appreciation. Qualitative analysis reinforces the conclusion: Chile confronted a supply of foreign funds that was proportionally greater (in relation to its GDP) than other LACs, owing to its more attractive economic performance and its greater political stability in the early 1990s. Nevertheless, exchange rate appreciation and the current account deficit (as a fraction of GDP or exports) were smaller, on average, than in the other LACs that received large amounts of foreign capital (see Ffrench-Davis, 2005, chap. VII, tables VII.2 and VII.3).

All of these studies coincide in their assessment that the reserve requirement, by maintaining an adequate spread between domestic and international interest rates, provided room for effective counter-cyclical monetary policy during a capital surge. This factor was important in the process of sustained growth seen throughout the decade, since frequent *mini-adjustments* by the Central Bank prevented the need for *maxi-adjustments* and allowed the economy to remain persistently close to its production frontier. Actual output thus coincided with potential output. The resulting perception of real sustainable stability stimulated a sharp increase in capital formation, and the growth of productive capacity and employment.

Based on the Chilean case, some authors have highlighted the microeconomic costs of capital controls (see Forbes, 2003). The crucial point is what is the net effect of capital controls on overall welfare, after contrasting both their eventual microeconomic costs and their macroeconomic benefits. From the point of view of investment and growth, the impressive growth performance experienced during the 1990s indicates that the positive effect of the whole macroeconomic Chilean approach, including the capital controls and their management, was much stronger than any associated microeconomic costs. Actually, the investment ratio of Chile in the 1990s was the highest recorded in its history. In this sense, 'financial constraints' as defined and reported by Forbes (2003) were far from being an impediment for expanding the productive capacity. Moreover, the microeconomic switch from debt to retained earnings in the financial structure, as well as the shift towards longer-term liabilities of 'small' firms, can be considered as a positive by-product of Chilean capital controls. Indeed, the main source of private savings in EEs, as has been well documented for Chile, tends to be non-distributed profits and depreciation reserves of firms.

The combination of policies used involved social costs for the economy since the accumulation of large volumes of foreign currency implies a significant opportunity cost. This also generates a financial cost for the public sector, since the profitability of these assets abroad is naturally less than the interest payments on the Central Bank liabilities issued to sterilize the domestic monetary effects of accumulating reserves. However, evidence shows that disincentives to short-term, liquid capital inflows tended to reduce the magnitude of the financial costs of sterilization and generated substantial macroeconomic benefits. Even more timely management of the intensity and coverage of the reserve requirement and additional mechanisms by the monetary authority would undoubtedly have kept the financial costs lower.[26] Furthermore, the existence of high levels of reserves has frequently been a very significant stabilizing factor in EEs facing crisis situations, as was proved in Chile in the episode of the contagion of the Asian crisis.[27]

3.4.4   The price of success

In 1996–97 Chile recorded vigorous growth that could be judged sustainable thanks to high domestic investment rates, but during this period the economy was becoming vulnerable to changes in the international environment. Crises are usually the consequence of badly managed booms (Ffrench-Davis, 2005, chap. VI).

Paradoxically, satisfactory performance was one of the causes of the disequilibria built in 1996–97. In the first place, foreign investors' confidence in the strength of the Chilean economy encouraged them to invest massively, which created additional pressure on the exchange rate and tested the economy's capacity for efficient absorption. Secondly, a generalized optimism characterized the world financial environment, based on the notion that the international community had learned how to handle international crises and that those virulent crises were gone forever. Lobbying pressure and a strong fashion towards financial liberalization were well received by many actors in Chile, a country which had resulted immune from the effects of the Tequila crisis of 1995. Thirdly, some officials, particularly from the Central Bank, understandably let themselves be swayed by this euphoric atmosphere, accepting as sustainable a rising external deficit and a sharp appreciation of the real exchange rate. Chile thus gave in, partially, to the pressures of the dominant international and domestic environment at the time (the *financieristic* forces). It indeed managed to reduce inflation quickly, but it paid a price in the form of the imbalances being gradually generated in 1996–97. The general policy was kept in place, against the fashion, but the authorities failed to strengthen measures in the face of the very abundant supply of capital during that biennium. The combination of policies and the intensity with which they were applied remained constant, while monitoring for loopholes lost force. The capital surge clearly weakened the fundamentals of the Chilean economy: the current account deficit rose, the exchange rate appreciated, and the stock of liquid foreign liabilities grew somewhat. The deterioration certainly could have been checked during the boom by means of higher reserve requirements and other measures. Nevertheless, a notorious complacency reigned while the new boom made the country increasingly vulnerable to external shocks. Imbalances were externally generated and overwhelmingly private. The government's responsibility in this case lay in its failure to enforce coordination between the Central Bank and the Ministry of Finance.[28] This shortcoming was related to the Central Bank's specific form of autonomy and its imbalanced priority for the inflation target (there is not a single form of autonomy in the world, but rather several alternative ones).

As a result of the lack of timely and sufficiently strong measures, the Asian crisis found Chile with a significantly appreciated exchange rate, an overstimulated aggregate demand, and a high current account deficit that in 1996–97 doubled the 1990–95 average (4.5 per cent and 2.3 per cent, respectively).

Financial capital began to flow out in late 1997 and this trend accelerated in 1998–99. The outlier nominal exchange rate depreciated to correct for misalignment. This time the impact of the capital outflow was aggravated by the outflows associated with pension funds, which intensified the devaluating pressures on the exchange rate. The channels that had been progressively opened up over the course of the decade, under the argument that they would moderate the abundance of foreign currency in boom periods and diversify risk, were effectively used only during the bust. Actually, the mechanism caused a significant loss of international reserves during the crisis, a monetary contraction, and a sharpening of the recessionary adjustment in 1998–99.

The cumulative current account deficit was moderate during the whole decade thanks to the active management of inflows in the first half of the 1990s and the persistence of regulations in the following years with only gradual liberalization. The stock of foreign liabilities was relatively low, and volatile funds played only a minor role, creating external imbalances only in 1996 and 1997. These conditions, together with the country's considerable international reserves, put Chile on a better footing than in the previous crises for confronting the hardships of trade and financial shocks caused by the Asian recession. The domestic financial system did not suffer radically, as a result of the strictness of the Chilean banking commission. Non-performing loans as a percentage of total loans rose from 0.97 per cent in December 1997 to 1.8 per cent at its worst moment in April 1999 – a level comparable to 1992, a crisis-free year. This is remarkable given that aggregate demand fell 6 per cent in 1999.

In September 1999, the Central Bank allowed the exchange rate adjustment by adopting a free-floating exchange rate regime. From 2000 onwards, the government and the Central Bank moved together to a new macroeconomic framework featured by the removal of most of the remaining regulations on the capital account. Thus, in May 2000 the minimum holding period for financial foreign investment was eliminated and, in April 2001, the URR was suspended as an instrument, along with many other administrative controls: at that moment economic authorities claimed that Chile had reached the full openness of its capital account. However, capital outflows by residents are subject to some regulations and the policy tool of a reserve requirement on capital inflows is still available, albeit with some restrictions. If the Central Bank so decides, it can be reestablished to face the next capital surge with this effective counter-cyclical device.

3.5   Income distribution and poverty

Income distribution has become a major issue in Chile. Despite effective efforts made in the 1990s to reverse the deterioration of the 1970s and 1980s, poverty is still a fact of life for one in every five Chileans, and inequality in opportunities and income is still very evident. Lack of equity is a marked feature of the Chilean economy.

Distribution has changed significantly over the last thirty years (see Figure 3.2). There is clear evidence that the social situation worsened markedly in the 1970s and 1980s, with levels of both inequality and poverty rising. The standard measurement of poverty, with a poverty line in constant prices, documents that the number of people below that line fell sharply in the 1990s (see Table 3.4). The information regarding income distribution, however, is less conclusive. Some data, such as those from the National Socio-Economic Survey (CASEN), available since 1987, show some improvement in income distribution in the early 1990s, compared to the late 1980s, which remained relatively stable during the rest of the decade. Other information, such as the National Bureau of Statistics (INE) household budget survey, shows a substantial improvement between 1988 and 1997; but these INE data are only available for one year in each decade. The data we consider less weak, and that is available in a comparable basis since 1958, is the employment survey of Universidad de Chile for Santiago (the capital covers about 40 per cent of the Chilean population). The income data of that survey are depicted in Figure 3.2. There appears the ratio between the per capita income of the higher quintiles and the poorer ones. Figure 3.2 documents that income distribution in Santiago worsened sharply in the 1970s (from a ratio of 12–13 to 15) and then worsened still further in the 1980s (to 20 times). Only in the 1990s was there an improvement, to 15 times. What all the information signals, however, is a significantly worse distribution than in the late 1960s and a continuing high level of poverty. It can be said with certainty, then, that in the

Table 3.4   The 'indigent' and other 'poor' populations, 1987–2003 (percentage of the population)

	1987	1990	1992	1994	1996	1998	2000	2003
Indigent	17.4	12.9	8.8	7.6	5.8	5.6	5.7	4.7
Other poor	27.7	25.7	23.8	19.9	17.4	16.1	14.9	14.1
Total poor	**45.1**	**38.6**	**32.6**	**27.5**	**23.3**	**21.7**	**20.6**	**18.8**

Source: MIDEPLAN and national data from the CASEN surveys.

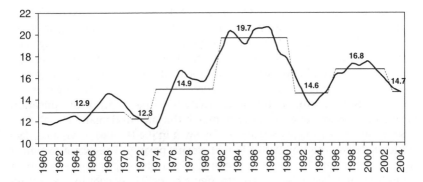

Figure 3.2 Income distribution in Santiago, 1960–2004 (Q5/Q1 ratio, moving averages of 3 years)
Source: Based on Ffrench-Davis (2002, chap. 9) and updated figures of Larrañaga (2001) and University of Chile employment survey for Greater Santiago.

1990s: (i) the deteriorating trend seen during the Pinochet regime was brought to a halt; (ii) poverty was reduced sharply; and (iii) income distribution became less unequal than in the 1980s. But despite this, the net balance indicates that Chile lost ground over the last thirty years rather than progressing toward greater equity. Equity is an essential ingredient of modernization.

The efficient approach for obtaining both growth and equity implies a comprehensive definition of macroeconomic equilibria. This includes far more than low inflation and structural fiscal balance (though both are necessary and convenient). It also requires of real economy equilibrium; that is, making full use of the available productive capacity, avoiding excessively fluctuating and outlier interest and exchange rates, and securing a favourable macroeconomic environment for productive investment.

The biggest setbacks in distribution and poverty have been caused by critical macroeconomic imbalances: the hyperinflation of 1973 and the recessions of 1975 and 1982. The recent 1998–2003 recession – though noticeably milder than those of 1975 and 1982 – represented a severe setback with social, economic and political costs. I argue that consistency between different objectives, which is essential if macroeconomic balances are to be sustainable over time and provide the required environment for socioeconomic development, was weakened.

The debate over which variables best determine distribution patterns and developments is also open. Here I shall mention four strong variables, which are ultimately the result of socioeconomic structures and public policies.

First, income levels have a highly positive relationship with years of schooling. Nonetheless, this relationship is subject to two qualifications, which have deep implications for public policy in this specific area. On the one hand, the quality of education and the matching of supply and the demand for skills are essential (Larrañaga, 2001). This is illustrated by the fact that, although the average worker had 3.5 years more schooling in 1992 than in 1970 (Hofman, 1999), the average real wage was similar, having been depressed in the intervening years. Furthermore, schooling is measured on the basis of the number of years of traditional education, without taking into account the training accrued during people's working lives. Training is essential as a way of enhancing the productivity of workers with little education or schooling whose quality does not match the current demand for labour.

Secondly, increasing participation of women in the labour force is a key factor for reducing the number of households in poverty. The extent to which women participate in the labour market determines which proportion of household members receives pay, the figure being 22 per cent in the bottom quintile and 51 per cent in the top one. Improving opportunities and facilities (such as day nurseries) for working women with lower incomes is a key factor in increasing equity.

Thirdly, unemployment is another very influential factor. In the CASEN survey of 1998, the unemployment rate was ten times as high in the first quintile as in the fifth, and its sensitivity to the economic cycle is very high. Unemployment is also substantially higher among young people and those with less schooling. Consequently, policies intended to strengthen the demand for labour and make the supply more flexible and better able to adapt to technological changes – with sustainable macroeconomic stability, vigorous physical capital formation, and increasing investment in people – play a very significant role in improving the distribution of opportunities.

Fourthly, social expenditure has a progressive incidence, representing a rising share of the access of the poor to goods and services in the 1990s.

Securing structural improvements in distribution is a long-term task. It has been addressed willingly since the return to democracy, albeit with some inconsistencies. Among other macro- and microeconomic aspects, the approach that needs to be taken includes: (i) Improving active macroeconomic management to make the economy less vulnerable to external shocks, the effects of which are always regressive; reactivating and improving regulation of flows in the face of the next capital surge; rebuilding an active exchange rate policy in order to provide greater predictability for the export sector; avoiding the two extremes of a fixed or totally free-floating exchange rate; and establishing a systematically counter-cyclical fiscal policy; (ii) Continuing to reduce legal tax avoidance (elusion) and illegal evasion, and reducing several highly regressive loopholes, which are detrimental to fiscal equity; (iii) Implementing a systematic educational reform, improving and standardizing educational quality (particularly reducing the huge quality gap that discriminates against poor children), and upgrading programmes and teaching staff, with the financing this requires; (iv) Making a real push towards an increase in the quantity, functionality and efficiency of labour training, in order to enhance the flexibility and adaptability of the labour supply; (v) A great pull up to the productive development of small and medium-sized enterprises (SMEs). Providing SMEs with significantly greater access to long-term domestic financing, modern technology, entrepreneurial and labour training, more stable domestic markets, which is most relevant for the overwhelming majority of them, and enhancing their ability to search for foreign markets, for the more successful ones; (vi) Strengthening the dynamism of non-traditional exports with greater value added. The essential ingredients for a renewed impulse of exports, more closely associated with domestic productive development, are: consolidating Latin American integration processes, promoting an active exchange rate policy, and an ambitious national programme for labour training.

3.6 Concluding remarks

Chile is frequently presented as a paradigmatic case of successful economic reforms. This has even been generalized to the idea that there is 'one' Chilean economic model. The fact is that there have been, at least, three different socioeconomic approaches since the military coup of 1973, with very different economic and social outcomes.

On the one hand, these brief accounts show that it is misleading to present both halves of the Pinochet regime as identical. They actually imply two different versions of how some markets work. The first half of *naïve neo-liberalism* was followed by a more pragmatic approach; however, with interventions heavily biased in favour of high-income sectors. We can term this *'regressive pragmatism'*. On the other hand, since 1990, under democracy, the country started significant *reforms to the reforms*, in order to improve the market model, strengthening the social component and correcting severe failures of the previous economic policies. There is neither only one model nor only one outcome.

The challenge of making growth consistent with distributive equity is of great importance, especially in light of the sharp drop in the standard of living of wide segments of population in the 1970s and 1980s, and the fact that three democratic governments have only partially met the expectations they aroused in the 1990s. Democracy and development require that growth and equity progress together.

Notes

1 The economic and social dimension is examined in CIEPLAN (1982, 1983); Foxley (1983); Larraín and Vergara (2000); Meller (1997). Texts of wide coverage, with abundant references, are Huneeus (2001); Moulián (1997).

2 The period covered by the dictatorship is longer than the three democratic governments that preceded it (Alessandri, Frei Montalva and Allende) and the three that followed it (Aylwin, Frei Ruiz-Tagle and Lagos).

3　Prices in 1973 rose 600 per cent.

4　This is the equivalent in terms of GDP of the difference between the terms of trade deterioration in 1975 and the improvement in 1973 and 1974, in 1977 prices. Copper prices began to rise in the third quarter of 1973.

5　In fact, switching policies in 1975–79 (excepting exchange rate policy in 1975), worked in the opposite direction to that required for reducing the output gap and increasing actual productivity.

6　Several indicators of this episode in Chile are similar, in sign and size, to those in the recent currency crisis of Argentina: negative inflation preceding the crisis; sharp GDP drop, huge unemployment, and a dramatic rise in the level of poverty.

7　Figures were calculated on the basis of the average exchange rate in 1976–78. With that very appreciated exchange rate of 1981, the deficit is 14.5 per cent of GDP. Notice that GDP in current US dollars was US$15 billion in 1978, US$33 billion in 1981 and US$16 billion in 1985. Given the enormous volatility, it is wise to 'normalize' the exchange rate used, in order to make intertemporal comparisons of GDP expressed in foreign currency.

8　This is the inflation rate for the twelve months ending in January 1990. Between August 1989 and January 1990 the annualized rate of increase in the consumer price index (CPI) was 31 per cent.

9　Collections of studies with diverse approaches can be found in Pizarro, Raczynski and Vial (1996); Cortázar and Vial (1998); Larraín and Vergara (2000); Ffrench-Davis and Stallings (2001).

10　We define macrosocial equilibria as the set of general social conditions like poverty levels, employment, social programmes, and the distribution of income, voices and opportunities.

11　It must be stressed that the tax rise was announced during the electoral campaign.

12　It can be argued that the increase in value-added taxes included in the reform would tend to impose a regressive effect as low-income families consumed a larger share of their income. Nevertheless, a comprehensive comparison also has to consider that most resources are transferred to these families through an increase in social spending. The net effect results evidently progressive.

13　Nevertheless, in 1998, it was established by law a strong additional triennial real adjustment. Minimum wages covered about 12 per cent of the labour force in the 1990s.

14　Notice that these figures are net from depreciation of capital goods in public firms; this depreciation is included in private savings. Moreover, the fiscal sector generated financing to cover the deficit of the public social security system. Under the social security reform, the public sector continued paying retired workers and financed part of the new pensions while income was shifted to the private system. The figures do not consider the quasi-fiscal deficit of the Central Bank – which was initially caused by the government intervention to face a massive bankruptcy of the domestic financial system in 1983.

15　A consulting committee named by the Ministry of Finance providing each year estimates of 'Trend GDP' for the next budget year, delivered figures averaging 4 per cent for the period 2001–04.

16　It is noteworthy that GDP growth also jumped in Latin America from 1.3 to 5.1 per cent during in that same period. The driving force was the same one of Chile. See Ffrench-Davis (2005, chaps. I and VII).

17　That domestic positive shock, which was highly successful for Korea and Malaysia in 1999 (see Mahani, Shin and Wang, 2006), in our view was available for Chile also.

18　As pointed out above, the convergence between the productive frontier and effect-ive demand is an essential element for efficient macroeconomic policies. The absence or weakness of this fundamental macroeconomic equilibrium has been characteristic of Latin American economies since the 1980s. See ECLAC (2000, chap. 8) and Ffrench-Davis (2005, chap. II).

19　In 1999, exports of goods and services represented 31 per cent of GDP (at 1996 prices) – that is, 13 points more than in 1980.

20　When firms issue ADRs, the prices of securities on the domestic and US markets tend faster towards one common price through arbitrage. In fact, equity price movements of Chilean firms that have issued ADRs on US markets are closely linked with movements on the Santiago stock exchange. This trend, evidently, implies con-verged prices of capital in economies whose factor intensity has not converged.

21　Good luck also played a role, with a sharp improvement in the terms of trade in 1995. Even so, the other factors provided strong macroeconomic insurance.

22　It is not difficult to impose URR on foreign portfolio investments. If funds to be invested are deposited in a Chilean bank, they remain subject to the reserve requirement there. For funds not using a Chilean bank as an intermediary, the reserve requirement can be enforced at the time the asset is registered to a party with a foreign address. Registration with the Central Bank is also necessary when converting securities into ADRs.

23　The 30 per cent rate was reduced to 10 per cent by the end of June 1998, and to zero in September, in order to accommodate to the new shortage of external financing associated to the Asian crisis.

24　It was argued that this would contribute to diversifying risk and increasing the profitability of the private pension system. See a critical view in Ffrench-Davis (2005, chap. VI).

25　References to the Chilean-style policy for dealing with capital flow instability are frequent in the main circles where these issues are discussed, for example in lec-tures and press interviews by Andrew Crockett, Stanley Fischer, Paul Krugman, Dani Rodrik, Joseph Stiglitz (also while he was vice-president of the World Bank), and John Williamson; see also *El Diario*, Santiago, 30 March 2000, which quotes Horst Köhler, then the Managing Director of the IMF.

26　Another potential source of real compensation for the Central Bank losses is the exchange rate band, which allows to buy cheap (near the floor) and to sell expen-sive (near the top). This would generate profits only if there is not an excessively strong revaluation of the band.

27　This only argues that the country is better prepared to cope with external shocks; it does not evaluate, however, whether the amounts involved are optimal or not.

28　The lack of coordination between the Central Bank and the government was evident. The Central Bank authorities expressed that they were not concerned about exchange rate real appreciation and stated that they did not perceive it as an imbal-ance in the external sector, while the Minister of Economics, for instance, held that 'it is necessary to intensify and strengthen policies such as the reserve requirement to reduce exchange rate appreciation.' *Estrategia*, September 26, 1997, Santiago.

References

Agosin, M. R. (1998) 'Capital Inflows and Investment Performance: Chile in the 1990s', in Ffrench-Davis and Reisen (eds), *Flows and Investment Performance: Lessons from Latin America*. Paris: OECD Development Centre/ECLAC.

Bitar, S. (1979) *Transición, socialismo y democracia: la experiencia chilena*. Mexico: Siglo XXI.

Coeymans, J. (1999) 'Determinantes de la productividad en Chile: 1961–97', *Cuadernos de Economía* 107, April.

Cortázar, R. (1996) 'A Labor Policy for a New Reality', in Pizarro, Raczynski and Vial (1996).

Cortázar, R. and J. Vial (eds) (1998) *Construyendo opciones: propuestas económicas y sociales para el cambio de siglo*, Dolmen Ediciones, Santiago.

ECLAC (2000) *Equity, Development and Citizenship*. Santiago: ECLAC.

ECLAC (2002) *Growth with Stability: Financing for Development in the New International Context*, ECLAC Books, No. 67. Santiago: ECLAC.

Edwards, S. and A. Cox-Edwards (1987) *Monetarism and Liberalization: The Chilean Experiment*. Cambridge, MA: Ballinger.

Ffrench-Davis, R. (1979) 'Exports and Industrialization in an Orthodox Model: Chile, 1973–78', *CEPAL Review* No. 9, December.

Ffrench-Davis, R. (2002) *Economic Reforms in Chile: From Dictatorship to Democracy*. Ann Arbor: University of Michigan Press.

Ffrench-Davis, R. (2005) *Reforming Latin America's Economies after Market Fundamentalism*. London: Palgrave Macmillan Press.

Ffrench-Davis, R. and B. Stallings (2001) *Reformas, crecimiento y políticas sociales en Chile desde 1973*. Santiago: LOM Ediciones/CEPAL.

Ffrench-Davis, R. and H. Tapia (2001) 'Three Varieties of Capital Surge Management in Chile', in R. Ffrench-Davis (ed.), *Financial Crises in 'Successful' Emerging Economies*. Washington: Brookings Institution Press.

Forbes, K. (2003) 'One Cost of the Chilean Capital Controls: Increased Financial Constraints for Smaller Traded Firms', *NBER Working Paper* No. 9777, June.

Foxley, A. (1983) *Latin American Experiments in Neoconservative Economics*. Berkeley, CA: University of California Press.

Hofman, A. (1999) *The Economic Development of Latin America in the Twentieth Century*. Aldershot, Great Britain: ECLAC, Edward Elgar.

Huneeus, C. (2001) *El régimen de Pinochet*. Santiago: Editorial Sudamericana.

Larraín, F. and R. Vergara (2000) *La transformación económica de Chile*. Santiago: Centro de Estudios Públicos.

Larrañaga, O. (2001) 'Distribución de ingresos: 1958–2001', in Ffrench-Davis and Stallings (2001).

Le Fort, G. and S. Lehmann (2003) 'The Special Reserve Requirement and Net Capital Inflows: Chile in the 1990s', *CEPAL Review*, No. 81, December, Santiago.

Loaysa, N. and R. Soto (2002) 'The Sources of Economic Growth: An Overview', in N. Loayza, and R. Soto (eds), *Economic Growth: Sources, Trends, and Cycles*. Santiago: Banco Central de Chile.

Mahani, Z., K. Shin and Y. Wang (2006) 'Macroeconomic Adjustment and the Real Economy in Korea and Malaysia since 1997', in R. Ffrench-Davis (ed.), *Seeking Growth under Financial Volatility*. London: Palgrave Macmillan.

Marcel, M. and P. Meller (1986) 'Empalme de las cuentas nacionales de Chile 1960–85. Métodos alternativos y resultados', *Colección Estudios CIEPLAN* 20, Santiago, December.

Marcel, M., M. Tokman, R. Valdés and P. Benavides (2001), 'Balance estructural del Gobierno Central, metodología y estimaciones para Chile: 1987–2000', *Estudios de Finanzas Públicas* No. 1, September.

Marfán, M. (1998) 'El financiamiento fiscal en los años 90', in R. Cortázar and J. Vial (eds), *Construyendo opciones: propuestas económicas y sociales para el cambio de siglo*. Santiago: Dolmen Ediciones.

Marfán, M. (2005) 'Fiscal Policy, Efficacy and Private Deficits: A Macroeconomic Approach', in José Antonio Ocampo (ed.), *Beyond Reforms: Structural Dynamics and Macroeconomic Theory*. Palo Alto, CA: Latin American Development Forum, Stanford University Press.

Marfán, M. and B. Bosworth (1994) 'Saving, Investment, and Economic Growth', in Bosworth, Dornbusch and Labán (1994).

Moguillansky, G. (1999) *La inversión en Chile: ¨el fin de un ciclo en expansión?* Santiago: Fondo de Cultura Económica/ECLAC.

Morandé, F. and R. Vergara (eds) (1997) *Análisis empírico del crecimiento en Chile*. Santiago: Centro de Estudios Públicos/ILADES.

Moulián, T. (1982) 'Desarrollo político y estado de compromiso, desajuste y crisis estatal en Chile', *Colección Estudios CIEPLAN* 8, July.

Pizarro, C., D. Raczynski and J. Vial (eds) (1996), eds., *Social and Economic Policies in Chile's Transition to Democracy*. Santiago: CIEPLAN/UNICEF.

Ramos, J. (1986), Neoconservative Economics in the Southern Cone of Latin America, 1973–83. Baltimore: Johns Hopkins University Press.

Robichek, W. (1981) 'Some Reflections About External Public Debt Management', Alternativas de políticas financieras en economías pequeñas y abiertas al exterior, *Estudios Monetarios* VII. Santiago: Banco Central de Chile.

Rodrik, D. And A. Velasco (2000) 'Short-term Capital Flows', *Conferencia Anual del Banco Mundial sobre Desarrollo Económico 1999*. Washington: World Bank.

Servén L. and A. Solimano (1993) 'Economic Adjustment and Investment Performance in Developing Countries: The Experience of the 1980s', in L. Servén and A. Solimano (eds), *Striving for Growth after Adjustment: The Role of Capital Formation*. Washington, D.C: World Bank.

Stiglitz, J. (2000) 'Capital Market Liberalization, Economic Growth and Instability', *World Development*, 28(6).

Titelman, D. (2001) 'Reformas al financiamiento del sistema de salud en Chile', in Ffrench-Davis and Stallings (2001).

Uthoff, A. (2001) 'La reforma del sistema de pensiones y su impacto en el mercado de capitales', in Ffrench-Davis and Stallings (2001).

Williamson, J. (1993) 'A Cost–Benefit Analysis of Capital Account Liberalization', in H. Reisen and B. Fischer (eds), *Financial Opening*. Paris: OECD.

Zahler, R. (1998) 'The Central Bank and Chilean Macroeconomic Policy in the 1990s', *CEPAL Review* No. 64, April.

Zahler, R. (2006) 'Macroeconomic Stability and Investment Allocation of Domestic Pension Funds in Emerging Economies: The Case of Chile', in R. Ffrench-Davis (ed.), *Seeking Growth under Financial Volatility*. London: Palgrave Macmillan.

4

A Case of Disruptive International Financial Integration: Argentina in the Late Twentieth and Early Twenty-First Centuries

Mario Damill and Roberto Frenkel
Centro de Estudios de Estado y Sociedad[1]

Abstract

In this paper we examine the evolution of the Argentine economy under the so-called second financial globalization, paying special attention to what happened from the early 1990s onwards, particularly to the processes associated with the macroeconomic dynamics under the convertibility regime. We also examine the main features of the phase subsequent to the 2001–2002 crisis. Particular attention is devoted to the fiscal accounts and the public debt in the 1990s, because there is an extended but incorrect explanation of the recent crisis and debt default that attributes the main responsibility to fiscal profligacy. A final section develops some prescriptive lessons from the previous analysis of policies and performance.

Keywords: Argentine economy, economic policy, financial globalization, Latin America, emerging countries markets, foreign debt, debt crisis, default.

JEL Classification: E44; E65; F32; F34; H62; H63; N16; N26.

4.1 Introduction

For a number of decades, the Argentine economy has been turning in very unsatisfactory performance in terms of macroeconomic stability, economic growth, income distribution and other social indicators. Since the mid-1970s, the country has experienced considerable fluctuations in gross domestic product, low levels of long-term growth, periods of high and very high rates of inflation, frequent oscillations in relative prices associated with successive attempts at stabilization and their failures. In the 1990s it also went through a prolonged period of exchange rate appreciation and low inflation. Special mention should be made of the unfavourable effects on economic growth and social conditions of the experiences of trade and financial openness accompanied by exchange rate appreciation in the late 1970s and the 1990s, as well as the several crises through which the country's economy has passed.

These features of Argentina's macroeconomic performance were the result of a combination of reform processes, stabilization policies, and major changes in the international situation. The adopted reforms and macroeconomic policies defined the particular way in which the economy fitted in with the new external financial framework during the phase known as the second financial globalization. In short, the above-mentioned disappointing macroeconomic performance observed in the period can be associated with the international integration path followed by the country from the mid-1970s.

Three main phases may be distinguished in the macroeconomic history of the period that ended in the 2001–2002 crisis and its defaulting on foreign debt. The first stage of active integration with the international financial market – one of deregulation and financial openness – extended from 1977 to 1982. It ended in a currency, financial and debt crisis and was followed by a period of closure of external financial markets or rationing of international credit, from 1982 to 1990. Then came a new phase of deregulation, trade and financial openness and active international financial integration, corresponding to the period in which the convertibility regime was in force, between 1991 and 2001. This phase too ended in crisis and payments defaults. A fourth phase, one of economic recovery and improvement in labour and social conditions, followed the 2001–2002 crisis and has lasted up to the present.

In this chapter we pay special attention to the analysis of what happened from the early 1990s onwards, particularly to the processes associated with the macroeconomic dynamics under the convertibility regime. We also examine the main features of the phase subsequent to the 2001–2002 crisis. It should be noted, however, that some of the most important broad features of macroeconomic behaviour in the 1990s are similar to what was observed in the previous period of openness in the late 1970s. Both these stages may be interpreted on the basis of a common model, as is also true of various comparable experiences in other economies, especially in Latin America. This common model, together with the comparative analysis of the experiences in question, has been developed elsewhere and we will succinctly describe them in section 4.2.

It should also be stressed that Argentina and other Latin American countries entered the 1990s burdened by heavy external debts, inherited from their early involvement in the financial globalization process. So, section 4.3 examines the evolution of the Argentine foreign debt from a long-term perspective, from the mid-1970s to the 2001–2002 crisis, relating its dynamics to the mentioned stages of the macroeconomic history. Particular attention is devoted to the fiscal accounts and the public debt in the 1990s, because there is an extended explanation of the recent crisis and debt default that attributes the main responsibility to fiscal profligacy. This is a false explanation whose refutation deserves a detailed analysis of the fiscal accounts.

Section 4.4 presents the main features of the macroeconomic evolution under the convertibility regime and in the recovery phase that followed its collapse. Special attention is put on what happened in the late 1990s in order to underline the main factors of the crisis and the debt default. The main conclusions of the analyses are presented in section 4.5.

4.2   An overview of Argentina and Latin America in the process of financial globalization[2]

The so-called second financial globalization process dates back more than three decades.[3] Its beginnings can be traced to between 1971 and 1973, the period when the United States broke the link between the dollar and gold and the currencies of the main developed countries were floated on the world's financial markets. The abandonment of the fixed exchange rate regime that had applied since the Bretton Woods agreements transferred currency risk to the private sector and stimulated the development of the currency and currency derivatives markets (Eatwell, 1996). Another early milestone was the oil price rise agreed by the Organization of the Petroleum Exporting Countries (OPEC) in 1973. The first oil shock resulted in large trade imbalances, which had to be financed. The Eurodollar market experienced a sharp rise in demand, while the surpluses of the oil exporting countries supplied it with ample liquidity.

Financial globalization is a historical process with two dimensions. One is the growing volume of cross-border financial transactions; the other is the sequence of institutional and legal reforms implemented to liberalize and deregulate international capital movements and national financial systems.

Financial integration has always been mainly a developed-country affair. It is notable, however, that the largest economies in Latin America were part of the globalization process from the start. First Brazil, and then Mexico, Venezuela, Argentina and Chile were large recipients of capital in the 1970s. These last two countries, along with Uruguay, then pioneered drastic liberalizing reforms, which anticipated those that were to be applied so widely in the 1990s. The increasing participation of Latin America in financial globalization was interrupted by the debt crisis of the 1980s. This caused a hiatus of about eight years, during which voluntary financing dried up. Then in the 1990s the region re-entered the process vigorously, carrying out drastic reforms and becoming a recipient of increasing flows (and ebbs) of capital. Just as the Mexican moratorium of 1982 is said to have marked the beginning of the debt crisis period, Mexico's signing of the first agreement under the Brady Plan may be cited as a landmark in the commencement of the most recent phase.

The first period of strong capital inflows into developing economies was cut short by profound internal and external financial crises in 1981 and 1982. These crises were followed by nationalization (through mechanisms that differed from country to country) of many external private sector debts and by the establishment of an institutional system whereby each country's external financing had to be settled by negotiation with lending banks and the International Monetary Fund (IMF). During this period, the regime under which the region operated was characterized by two stylized facts: (i) external financing was rationed; and (ii) negotiations with creditors and international financial organizations generally resulted in net transfers abroad on a scale that was substantial in macroeconomic terms. Consequently, it would be wrong to say that the region became 'detached' from globalization in the 1980s. What happened was that the region was practically debarred from obtaining new voluntary financing, but continued to be strongly tied to the international system by the negotiated service of debts contracted during the earlier period. Later, as a result of their early participation in financial globalization and the economic disaster this led to, a number of the region's economies, particularly the larger ones, went into the new financial boom of the 1990s with a large legacy of external debt.

4.2.1   The financial and currency crises

Argentina, in common with a number of other Latin American countries, has experienced domestic and external financial crises during the phase that began in the 1990s, and these have had dramatic effects on the real economy. Crises generally entail high economic and social costs and recession. Regional contagion is another striking effect, since a crisis in one country frequently has repercussions for financing costs and capital flows in others. This phenomenon first came clearly to light with the Mexican crisis of 1994–95. The 'Tequila effect' swept the region and other emerging markets and helped to trigger the 1995 Argentine crisis. Contagion effects were more pronounced in 1997 and afterwards. The effects of the 1997–98 Asian crises and the 1998 Russian crisis were universal, and not only Brazil and Argentina, but other Latin American countries that were more strongly placed, felt the impact of contagion (Ffrench-Davis, 2001). The crises in Mexico (1994–1995), Argentina (1995), Brazil (1998–1999) and Argentina again (2001–02) broke out in the very countries that had received the largest capital inflows during the preceding booms. They are also the largest economies in Latin America and the largest 'emerging markets' in the region.

A brief review of these cases will be enough to identify certain common features in the institutional and economic policy situation at the time of these crises: (i) the nominal exchange rate was fixed or semi-fixed; (ii) the real exchange rate had appreciated; (iii) there were virtually no barriers to the free movement of capital; (iv) capital inflows in the preceding boom had been large in relation to the size of existing local money and capital markets; and (v) the regulation of national financial systems during the boom phase was weak and permissive.[4]

In addition to the characteristics mentioned, more detailed analyses of these experiences reveal a cyclical macroeconomic dynamic in all cases, with an initial expansionary phase followed by a period of stagnation or recession and growing financial weakness domestically and externally, culminating in financial and currency crises. The Argentine economy went through this cycle twice in the decade, because the convertibility regime outlasted the 1995 Tequila crisis. After that year the Argentine economy went through another brief expansion, supported by a fresh rise in capital inflows that lasted until the Asian crisis. The turning point of this second cycle came in mid-1998.

The institutional and macroeconomic policy conditions whose characteristics are listed above resulted from the implementation of programmes that combined reforms such as trade and capital account liberalization (plus privatization, fiscal reforms and moves towards deregulation in other markets) with anti-inflationary macroeconomic policies in which fixed or semi-fixed exchange rates played a crucial role. Mexico implemented a program of this sort in 1988, Argentina in 1991 and Brazil in 1994.

4.2.2   The experiments in the Southern Cone

It was mentioned earlier that some of the region's early efforts to engage with the international financial system (Argentina and Chile in the 1970s) anticipated models that would be adopted widely in the 1990s. The 'Southern Cone liberalization experiments' combined drastic financial and trade reforms with macroeconomic arrangements involving pre-set exchange rates and passive monetary policy. The reforms included the liberalization and deregulation of capital flows, the liberalization of local financial markets and moves towards free trade. Fixed exchange rates were meant to bear down on inflation.

These policy experiments resulted in moves towards financial and trade liberalization and deregulation in situations of plentiful external funding and with appreciated fixed exchange rates (Fanelli and Frenkel, 1993; Frenkel, 2002).

These 1970s experiments display similar combinations of local conditions and surging capital inflows, as were seen in the critical cases of the 1990s. Furthermore, the processes to which the Southern Cone experiments gave rise were akin to those that subsequently led to the crises in Mexico, Brazil and Argentina during the 1990s. Although the 1970s experiences were shorter-lived than the recent cases, the macroeconomic dynamic displayed the same cycle of boom, bust and crisis.

Chile and, a little later, Argentina initiated their new currency programmes in 1978. By late 1979, when United States monetary policy raised interest rates, Argentina and Chile already had large external debts and substantial current account deficits. From then on, higher international interest rates contributed to further external fragility. The crises broke out shortly afterwards. The exchange rate regime collapsed early in 1981 in Argentina and in 1982 in Chile. In the latter year external financial markets closed to both these economies, and in both cases massive bail-outs of the local financial system were organized at great fiscal expense. As a result, both of these countries went into deep recessions. The rise in international interest rates in late 1979 accelerated the process. What the two countries experienced, however, had the hallmarks of an endogenous cycle, with a turning point and subsequent recessionary phase emerging independently of international interest rate movements. As in the more recent cases, this cycle involved the domestic financial system, movements in the external accounts and reserves, and a rise in borrowing.

There are a number of reasons for discussing the experience of the Southern Cone. Neither budget deficits nor government guarantees for bank deposits – a potential source of moral hazard – played significant roles in the crises. Both elements were present in Argentina, but Chile had a budget surplus and the bank deposit guarantee had been abolished with the explicit aim of making the financial system more efficient and less risky. The IMF strongly supported these policy experiments. In 1980 and 1981, when Chile was running large current account deficits, the IMF argued that this situation should not be a concern so long as it was not accompanied by a fiscal deficit, which at that time it was not in Chile.[5] The IMF subsequently took the same view of the situation in Mexico in 1994.[6] On both occasions, the basis of the diagnostic was that rational behaviour by the private sector would ensure that resources borrowed from abroad were allocated efficiently and would be repaid.

The crises to which the Southern Cone experiments led had a major intellectual impact. The Chilean case was particularly striking because it contained all the ingredients that ought to have guaranteed success and stability, according to the fashionable theory that were underlying the country's policies. The experiments were based on a modern version of the 'monetary approach to the balance of payments', the vision forged at the University of Chicago in the heat of the recent restoration of a world capital market. Studies and debates dealing with the experience of the Southern Cone gave rise to a body of economic literature, the so-called 'sequencing literature' (Fanelli and Frenkel, 1993). The main conclusion was that the crises had resulted from faulty sequencing of the reforms. Basically, it was argued that they were caused by premature financial liberalization. The resulting policy recommendation was that capital markets should be opened only once the economy had been stabilized and was open to international trade, with a robust financial system, i.e., only once a sequence of policies had been applied (the policies that would later form the core of the Washington Consensus) and the effects expected from the first reforms had fully manifested themselves.

What these observations show is that in the first half of the 1990s, when there was a new upsurge in capital inflows, there was no lack of historical experience, analytical studies or policy recommendations to provide a basis for examining the processes then going on in Mexico and Argentina. The Southern Cone experiments had taken place barely a decade before and had been repeatedly analysed. Yet the memory of these cases and the lessons drawn from them were not mentioned by the IMF, or in the work of market analysts, or in much of academic output.[7] Such was the degree of memory loss about the crises that the conventional interpretation, which became established after the Mexican crisis of 1994, treated this as though it were a bolt from the blue.

4.2.3   The cyclical dynamics following capital account liberalization and leading to crisis[8]

The starting point for the cycle that characterized the case of Argentina as well as the other mentioned experiences of the 1970s and 1990s was a combination of local programmes with an upsurge in capital flows to emerging markets. It is in fact the abundance of cheap international financing that provides the preconditions for the viability of such policy packages. The launch of these programmes is followed by massive capital inflows, an initial build-up of reserves and high rates of money and credit growth. Internal demand expands strongly and bubbles are inflated in real and financial assets such as land, real estate and shares. The effects on asset prices and on money and credit volumes are very substantial, because the capital flows are large in relation to the size of local markets. Local financial systems and capital markets are relatively small and barely diversified. The range of assets is limited and the degree of bank intermediation low. The local financial system, used to administering few resources, is not equipped to allocate a burgeoning mass of credit efficiently. Likewise, the authorities are not well equipped to supervise a system that is growing rapidly both in volume and in the number of intermediaries.

With a fixed or semi-fixed nominal exchange rate that initially enjoys strong credibility, investment in local assets yields high dollar returns. There are strong incentives to take positions in local assets financed by borrowings of international currency. The real exchange rate is already appreciated or tends to appreciate in the expansionary phase because inflation is higher than the sum of predetermined devaluation rates (zero in the case of a fixed exchange rate) plus international inflation. The pressure of rapidly expanding demand on non-tradable sectors contributes to currency appreciation. Currency appreciation, trade liberalization and growth in domestic demand cause imports to rise rapidly and the trade deficit to widen. The current account deficit also tends to grow, slowly at first but then more quickly as external debt mounts and the stock of foreign capital invested in the economy grows. Relative prices skew real investment towards non-tradable sectors. In the current account balance, consequently, rising international currency returns for FDI are not matched by export growth.

Movements in the external accounts and reserves define one aspect of the cycle. The current account deficit rises steadily, while capital flows can change abruptly. At some point the current account deficit is larger than capital inflows. Reserves then peak and decline, resulting in a money and credit crunch. However, this mechanical process does not exclusively determine the cycle: the scale of capital flows is not an exogenous factor.

The portfolio decisions of local and external agents regarding the proportion of local assets they hold – the portion of the agent's portfolio that is exposed to country or currency risk – are affected by developments in the country's balance of payments and finances. The domestic interest rate reflects the financial aspects of the cycle. It tends to fall in the first phase and rise in the second. Since exchange rate policy initially enjoys great credibility, arbitrage between local and external financial assets and credits causes the rate to fall. Low interest rates contribute to real and financial expansion. Under these circumstances, financial fragility[9] increases. In the second stage, the interest rate rises and episodes of illiquidity and insolvency begin to appear – first as isolated cases and then as a systemic crisis.

What accounts for the rise in both nominal and real interest rates? Because the financial market is open, there is arbitrage between local and external assets, as already mentioned. In these circumstances, the local-currency interest rate can be expressed as the sum of the international dollar rate which the country has to deal with, plus the devaluation rate allowed for by the exchange rate regime (zero in the case of a fixed exchange rate), plus a remainder answering to currency risk and local financial risk. The international rate that the country has to deal with, meanwhile, can be broken down into two terms: the interest rate paid by the United States Government bonds (this is the benchmark of the international financial market), plus a remainder to compensate for the risk of local dollar-denominated debt. Except in the case of some exceptional debt instruments, the floor for this remainder is the premium paid by the dollar-denominated bonds of the country's government, known as the country risk premium. The sum of the currency risk premium and the country risk premium – the aggregate price of devaluation risk and default risk – is the main factor determining local interest rates, so that when this variable rises interest rates tend upward as well.

A steadily increasing current account deficit (and, after a certain point, the tendency of reserves to shrink) undermines the credibility of the currency regime, while at the same time the likelihood of default on the debt issued increases. Increasing capital inflows are required to sustain the currency regime and enable external obligations to be serviced regularly. Consequently, risks tend to be priced upward. High risk premiums, and hence high interest rates, are required to balance portfolios and attract capital from abroad. Economic activity contracts and episodes of illiquidity and insolvency serve to undermine further the credibility of the currency regime. This dynamic proved explosive in the mentioned cases. By the end of the process no interest rate is high enough to sustain demand for local financial assets. There are runs on Central Bank reserves, leading eventually to the collapse of the currency regime. In the 1990s cases, the market was generally closed to new issues when the country risk premium reached a certain level.

The relative weight of the currency risk premium and the country risk premium was different in the 1990s from what it had been in the 1970s. This shift was due to the different forms taken on by external financing in the two decades. In the 1970s, financing came mainly from international bank credits. The country risk premium arose then the surcharge over the primary international rate charged by banks when lending to the country. The secondary debt market was insignificant. For Argentina and Chile in this context, the currency risk premium was the main factor driving interest rates higher in the second phase of the cycle, while the lending bank surcharge played only a minor role. This can be explained by the behaviour of banks. Any bank that already has part of its portfolio invested in a country's assets has an interest in preserving the quality of that portfolio and the borrower's ability to pay. Consideration of the sunk portfolio influences decisions about the scale and pricing of new lending. In the 1990s, on the other hand, most financing was raised by issuing bonds and other debt instruments in a primary market in which there were many different participants. The debt securities issued were traded daily in an active secondary market. The country risk premium was established by the continuous re-pricing of securities in this market. In that decade, rising country risk premiums, resulting from falling prices for the debt securities of the country traded on the global secondary market, were the main driver of higher interest rates in the contractionary phase of the cycle. The debt market in this recent phase of globalization is more volatile than the credit market of the 1970s. It is more vulnerable to contagion and herd movements.

4.2.4   Budget deficits and public debt

The above analysis identifies certain stylized facts that were present in all of the processes leading to the crises considered. The description of the stylized facts focuses on the linkage between the finances and the real economy of a country and the international financial system. It will be noted that in the description of national economies the private and public sectors are not analysed separately. Budget deficits financed with external capital are tacitly included among the local destinations for capital inflows and consolidated with the private sector deficits. The external debt of the public sector is part of the country's total external debt and is not examined separately. This approach is easily explained: fiscal sustainability did not play a notable role in creating the crises in Chile (1982), Mexico (1994–95), Argentina (1995) or Brazil (1998–99), or in the Asian crises of 1997–98.[10] Now, a rapidly growing public debt which comes to be viewed as unsustainable by the market that has been financing it *may* of course be the root cause and trigger for a crisis. Certainly, there was a substantial budget deficit and public debt in the Argentine crises of 1981–82 and 2001–02, and these crises have often been explained by reference to that circumstance. The origin of the Argentine crisis of 1981–82 is not to be found in the fiscal accounts, however. In this case, only half of the external debt was in the public sector prior to the crisis and the military regime seemed to be having little trouble adjusting the public finances. The fiscal deficit and its external financing were the result of government decisions which did not raise any special problems. Government policy was strongly endorsed by advisers who had signed up to the 'monetary approach to the balance of payments' and maintained, at that time, that monetary policy and monetary policy alone was what determined the balance-of-payments outcome and the level of reserves. It was argued that as long as discipline and control were exercised over domestic credit there would be no problem financing the public sector deficit. Furthermore, it was not the banks lending to the public sector that brought on the crisis by restricting the supply of financing or raising its price. The international banks carried on supplying financing to the public sector at a low premium until the last moments of the currency regime. In both the case of Argentina and also the parallel one of Chile, the domestic financial crisis began to manifest itself at least one year before the collapse of the currency regime.

In those aspects, the 2001–2002 Argentine crisis was different. On this occasion, the public debt was the main component of the country's external debt. Analysis of the case reveals the cyclical macroeconomic dynamic described earlier, but side by side with a fiscal deficit and a steadily growing public debt, largely financed from external resources, as will be shown in detail in the next section. This did not happen in the first cycle (1991–95) but in the second one, beginning in 1996, after the crisis triggered by the Tequila effect. The budget deficit deterioration had its origin in the social security system. This was partly because of the reform implemented in late 1994, whereby much of the system's revenue was transferred to the private financial sector[11] while public pension spending was maintained, and partly because the government reduced employers' contributions in an effort to improve competitiveness, which had been weakened by currency appreciation. However, in any event, in the second half of the 1990s the main component forcing current public spending upward was the interest on the public debt. The higher interest rates characteristic of the contractionary phase of the cycle directly impacted the growth of the public debt, contributing to a perverse dynamic of higher indebtedness and higher risk.

The rise in interest rates led, on the one hand, to an increase in the current account deficit and in the foreign debt, growing needs for capital inflows, and to the consequent rise in the external financial fragility of the economy as a whole. On the other hand, it also implied that, simultaneously with the process in the external sector, there was an increasing public debt and growing financial needs of the public sector. So, in the recent Argentine case, both the situation of the country's external accounts and the evolution of public finances weighted in the risk assessments of the market. However, this double perception of risk should not conceal the fact that the unsustainability of the public debt was an endogenous result of both the external unsustainability and the domestic financial crisis.

4.3 The evolution of the Argentine debt along the financial globalization process[12]

This section analyses the evolution of the debt since the mid-1970s. The main periods already referred to can be clearly distinguished in its evolution. As we have already mentioned, in the first stage, between 1977 and 1982, Argentina went through a phase of financial opening and accelerated indebtedness that ended with massive capital flight, an exchange rate crisis, devaluation and default.

The country showed low and stable debt indicators before the mid-1970s. The foreign debt, both public and private, was mostly owed to multilateral organizations and governments. It fluctuated in a range of 10 per cent to 15 per cent of GDP from the beginning of the 1960s to the mid-1970s, as can be seen in Figure 4.1. A deep liberalizing financial reform was implemented in 1977 and was followed by the progressive dismantling of foreign exchange controls to capital account private flows in the period 1978–80. These changes would jointly operate to completely change the country links with the international financial markets.

As can be seen in Figure 4.1, the foreign debt/output ratio showed a rising trend between 1976 and 2000. The ratio measured in purchasing power parity (PPP) exchange rate terms (the average 1935–2003 bilateral dollar real exchange rate) grew approximately 3 percentage points of GDP per annum in this period. The curve is more volatile when the ratio is measured at current exchange rates, with sharp rises at the beginning and end of the 1980s as well as in 2002, and a strong fall in the period 1990–93. These jumps are

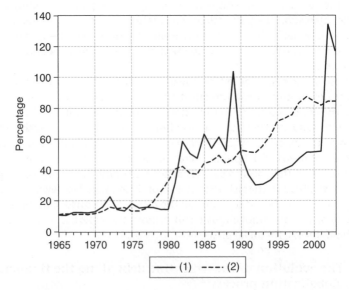

Figure 4.1   Total external debt/GDP ratio
Notes: (1) Debt in dollars multiplied by current exchange rate and divided by GDP at current prices. (2) Debt in dollars multiplied by PPP exchange rate and divided by GDP at current prices. PPP exchange rate was calculated as the 1935–2003 average real exchange rate, using US and Argentina Consumer Price Indexes.
Source: Authors' calculations based on the Ministry of Economy.

due to the real exchange rate instability experienced in the period, as can be seen in Figure 4.2.[13]

The total foreign debt/exports ratio, another standard debt indicator shown in Figure 4.3, complements the mentioned evidence. It rose abruptly after 1977, especially between 1977 and 1982, and never returned to the previous level.

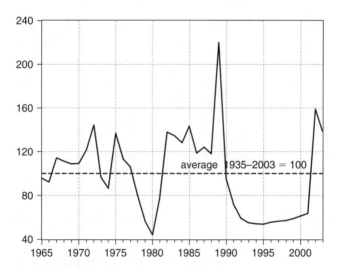

Figure 4.2   Real exchange rate: current and average of 1935–2003
Source: Authors' calculations based on the Ministry of Economy.

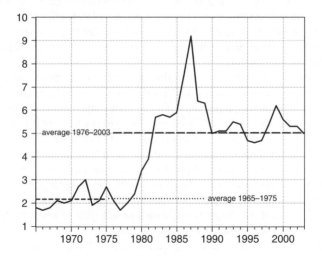

Figure 4.3   Total external debt/good exports ratio
Source: Authors' calculations based on the Ministry of Economy.

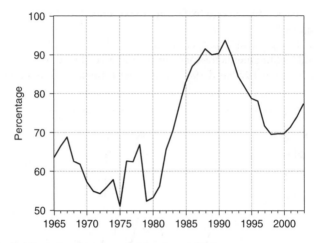

Figure 4.4 Public sector share over total external debt
Source: Authors' calculations based on the Ministry of Economy.

The 1976–2003 average much more than duplicates the level registered in the period ending in the mid-1970s.

Three stylized facts deserve to be stressed. The first is the role played by the private sector in the generation of external financial obligations. In both stages of accelerated indebtedness (the 1970s and the 1990s) this sector was initially the most dynamic one. The government's proportion in total obligations declines between 1978 and 1980, as can be seen in Figure 4.4. Something similar can be appreciated in the period starting in 1991, although in this case the process would be longer. Despite the strong rise in public external debt in the 1990s, its participation in total debt declined in more than 20 percentage points during that period.

The second important fact has already been mentioned: fiscal policies have not been the main factor of the debt growth and the fiscal disequilibrium has not been the main cause of the crises and defaults that followed both phases of accelerated indebtedness. We will consider this issue in detail below, when we focus the analysis on the 1990s' evolution.

A third relevant fact is that Argentina entered both phases of accelerated indebtedness in the context of stabilization programmes based on the fixation of the nominal exchange rate. High inflation was experienced in the mid-1970s and the same happened at the beginning of the 1990s. The opening of the capital account was in both phases adopted together with the launching of anti-inflationary programmes (jointly with other liberalizing-reform measures in goods and financial markets). In both cases, the key instrument of the stabilization policy was the fixation of the nominal exchange rate instrumented as an anchor for the stabilization of the prices.[14]

Table 4.1   Debt ratios variations and its sources

Period	External debt/GDP (in PPP) (variation in p.p.)	External debt/GDP (variation in p.p.)	External debt (variation in %)	Real exchange rate (variation in %)	Real GDP (variation in %)
75–80	19.2	−3.8	125.2	−67.8	11.8
80–82	9.9	44.1	37.2	212.8	−8.4
82–90	10.1	−8.3	4.9	−30.8	−2.7
90–01	29.4	2.1	66.6	−33.3	43.0
01–03	2.6	65.0	1.1	118.0	−3.1

Source: Authors' calculations based on the Ministry of Economy.

The mentioned stylized facts help to explain the features of the debt evolution presented in what follows. Table 4.1 presents the changes in the debt/GDP ratio, and the factors explaining them: the changes in the amount of the debt in dollars and the variations in both the real exchange rate and the GDP. It can be seen that between 1975 and 1980 the debt ratio rose by more than 19 points of GDP, measured by the PPP exchange rate (it rose from 13.2 per cent to 32.4 per cent). The figures in the same table show that this result was hidden by the strong appreciation of the exchange rate, since the debt ratio calculated using the current exchange rate not only did not rise but, in fact, fell by almost 4 points of GDP in that same period.

In 1981, the exchange rate anchor stabilization policy was abandoned, putting an end to the first phase of accelerated indebtedness in an appreciated exchange rate context. A new phase followed, characterized by a sequence of massive devaluations of the peso. These devaluations caused the foreign debt ratio, measured in current dollars, to reach a peak level close to 60 per cent of GDP in 1982. The figures in Table 4.1 show that the jump in the debt ratio at current prices between 1980 and 1982 (more than 44 GDP points) was to a great extent due to an increase of more than 200 per cent in the real value of the dollar.

Nonetheless, the debt in dollar terms rose 37 per cent between 1980 and 1982. An important factor behind this increase was the rise in the international interest rates that resulted from the policy carried out by the Federal Reserve since 1979.

An important jump in the public sector proportion in the country's foreign debt can also be observed during those years (Figure 4.4). In 1981–82, through the bail-out of domestic banks and debtors, the public sector ended up absorbing a considerable proportion of the private foreign debt, with the approval of the international banks. This, to a large extent, explains the jump in the participation of the public sector in total debt. It should also be stressed that no debt reduction provided relief to the public debt in the early

1980s default situation (it would only come later and in homeopathic doses, with the Brady agreement in 1992–93).

In the following period of international private credit rationing the debt measured by the PPP exchange rate kept on increasing, though at a slower pace. It increased the equivalent of 10 GDP percentage points between 1982 and 1990 (Table 4.1). The external obligations in dollars continued rising despite the lack of access to the international market (although at a much lower speed than in previous stages). The stagnant output trend also contributes to explain the mentioned rise.[15]

Later on, in the 1990s, the rate of growth of debt accelerated again, especially from 1992. As was mentioned, the Brady agreement did not provide significant relief to the debt inherited from the mistaken polices of the late 1970s. The achieved debt reduction was essentially insignificant.[16] The main favourable impact of the Brady agreement was on the banks' portfolios, since they could transform the defaulted credits, including the past due interests, into bonds.[17]

During the 1990–2001 period, the foreign debt/GDP ratio, measured by the PPP exchange rate, rose almost 30 percentage points (Table 4.1). This jump was completely due to the increase in the debt in dollars, which surpassed the accumulated GDP growth. However, it can be seen that the debt ratio measured with the current exchange rate barely rose, as a consequence of the important real appreciation that took place in the period.

4.3.1 The public debt in the 1990s

We have seen that the total foreign debt, measured by the PPP exchange rate, increased by almost 30 points of GDP between 1990 and 2001. About 60 per cent of that rise was generated by the private sector. The participation of the private sector was even more accentuated in the early 1990s: it originated approximately 70 per cent of the increase in the external financial obligations between 1990 and 1995.

The public sector debt issuing was more significant in the second half of the decade, when the international financial conditions had worsened. Besides, the placement of public debt in the domestic market started to play a more significant role in those years.

Figure 4.5 illustrates the public debt evolution in the period.

The series in Figure 4.5 and the figures in Tables 4.2 and 4.3 allow us to describe the main stylized facts of the Argentinean public sector indebtedness in the convertibility period

The fiscal accounts show three main periods in the 1990s. In the first one, a sharp adjustment in the public accounts is observed. The average deficit, which in the 1980s was about 7 per cent of GDP, decreased to less than one per cent of GDP in the 1991–94 period. As the figures in Table 4.2 show, this was mainly due to an improvement of 6 points of GDP in the national public sector balance, from which 90 per cent is explained by the primary balance result.

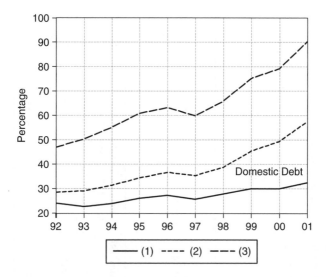

Figure 4.5 Total public debt/GDP ratio, 1992–2001
Notes: (1) External Public Debt. (2) Total Public Debt. (3) Total Public debt as a percentage of GDP calculated using the PPP exchange rate. *Source*: Authors' calculations based on the Ministry of Economy.

The year 1994 was a breakpoint in the last decade for three main reasons. In the first place, the social security reform that created the Private Pension Funds came into operation. One of the consequences of the reform was a considerable loss in the contributions to the public pension subsystem. In the second place, the expansion initiated in 1990 was then coming to an end: Argentina would go through the recession associated with the Tequila effect from the Mexican crisis in 1995. In the third place, the government took several measures aimed at compensating for some of the negative effects of the combination of commercial opening and exchange rate appreciation. It did that by lowering the tax burden on the tradable goods production sectors. All of the mentioned factors affected the public finances negatively. However, in spite of these negative effects, between 1995 and 1997 the average fiscal deficit was only two percentage points of GDP higher than the deficit in the early 1990s. This figure is almost equivalent to the increase in the public social security subsystem disequilibrium caused by the reform.

However, after 1997 the fiscal panorama would change significantly. The impact of the Russian and Brazilian crises in 1998 resulted in a new jump in the country risk premium, which had been rising since mid-1997, after the South East Asian crisis. This, on the one hand, negatively affected the internal demand and triggered a new recession trend. On the other hand, it increased the financial vulnerability of debtors, including the public sector as well as many private agents that were in a net debtor position.

Table 4.2 Consolidated fiscal balance (national administration and provinces) (as a percentage of GDP, annual average)

Period	National Administration				Consolidated Public Sector Balance (3)
	Primary surplus without Social Security (1)	Primary surplus	Interest payments	Total Balance (2)	
Average 1981–90	nd	−4.4	1.9	−6.2	−7.0
Average 1991–94	2.1	1.3	1.2	0.1	−0.6
Average 1995–97	1.7	−0.3	1.7	−2.0	−2.6
Average 1998–01	3.1	0.5	3.1	−2.7	−4.1
Average 1991–01	2.3	0.6	2.0	−1.5	−2.4

Notes: (1) Primary balance excluding receipts and expenditures of national security system.
(3) = (2) + Provinces and Buenos Aires City balances.
Source: Authors' calculations based on the Ministry of Economy, Cetrángolo and Jiménez (2003) and Gaggero (2003).

Table 4.3 Fiscal deficit and total public debt variation (in millions of dollars)

Period	Consolidated Public Deficit (1)	Gross Public Debt Variation (2)	Discrepancy (3)	'Skeletons' (4)	Brady Plan's Haircut (5)	Rescue of debt due to privatization (6)	Others (7)
1992–1994	3,247	25,094	21,847	22,859	2,323	7,111	8,422
1995–1997	20,815	22,659	1,844	3,892	0	40	−2,008
1998–2001	45,835	52,817	6,982	5,947	0	0	1,035
Total	69,897	100,570	30,673	32,698	2,323	7,151	7,449

Notes: column (2) does not include Central Bank's debt.
(2) − (1) = (3)
(3) = (4) − (5) − (6) + (7)
Source: Authors' calculations based on Ministry of Economy, Melconián et al. (1997), Cetrángolo et al. (2000) and Teijeiro (1996).

Before analysing this stage in more detail, let us consider the association between the fiscal results and the public debt evolution, using the figures in Table 4.3. A first important observation refers to the discrepancy between the variation of public sector's financial obligations and the accumulated fiscal deficit, which represents more than $30 billion in the 1990s. The figures show the main reason of this inconsistency: the recognition of debts incurred in previous periods but not registered in the fiscal results balance, especially debt with the public sector purveyors and with the social security system's beneficiaries ('skeletons in the cupboard'). There had been erroneous liquidations and payment delays, mainly during the 1989–90 period, when the economy experienced two short hyperinflationary episodes. The documentation of past debts was mostly concentrated in the initial stage, between 1991 and 1994. However, it should be noticed that the public debt ratio, measured as a percentage of GDP, was relatively stable up to 1994, in around 30 per cent in the case of total debt and 25 per cent in the case of foreign debt (Figure 4.5).

In comparison to the 1980s, the 1991–94 phase was generally characterized by a significant improvement in the public accounts and by the relatively ordered absorption of a considerable volume of debt mostly generated during previous periods, i.e. by the regularization of liabilities, many of which were litigious. It is clear from these figures that the standard financial vulnerability indicators did not show evidence of fiscal sustainability problems towards 1994, when the economy was reached by the shock resulting from the Mexican crisis contagion.

However, it is undeniable that the high debt burden inherited from the previous phase – a sort of original fiscal sin of the 1990s – is partially obscured by the real appreciation veil. Figure 4.5 shows the public debt/GDP ratio calculated with the PPP exchange rate. As can be seen, the curve intersects the 50 per cent line in 1993. The dollarization of the public debt establishes a direct link between the external fragility and the fiscal financial fragility, since taxes are paid in domestic currency. The relevance of this link is stressed by the exchange rate appreciation.

Between 1995 and 1997 the public debt/GDP ratio increased, in part as a result of the 1995 recession, and also because of the significant financial aid package led by the IMF, amounting to approximately $11 billion. This support enabled the country to recover quickly from the crisis that followed the Tequila effect. As can be seen in Figure 4.5, in the expansionary phase that followed the crisis, the debt ratio tended to stabilize again between 35 and 40 per cent of GDP, a relatively low level in comparison to international standards. Again, in spite of the rise in the current deficit and the disequilibrium in the social security system, the standard debt indicators did not suggest fiscal sustainability risk towards 1997, before the beginning of the depression. However, the debt ratio measured with the PPP exchange rate had already reached 60 per cent of GDP.

As pointed out earlier, Argentina's macroeconomic panorama would drastically change soon after, following the August 1998 Russian crisis. Table 4.4 helps

Table 4.4   Comparison between average public deficit of 1998–2001 and 1994 (in millions of dollars)

Consolidated deficit variation	7,112
Social Security deficit variation	4,867
National Administration's primary deficit variation (excluding Social Security)	−5,131
Provincial primary deficit variation	592
Consolidated interest payment variation	6,784

Source: Authors' calculations based on the Ministry of Economy and Cetrángolo *et al.* (2000).

us to understand some key features of the fiscal evolution during this period. Public sector's deficit took a significant rising path that would lead it to reach about six points of GDP in 2001, despite the many rounds of contractive fiscal policies instrumented to stop the trend.

In Table 4.4 we compare the average disequilibrium of the depression period to the deficit registered in 1994. In 1998–2001 the average accrued annual deficit (amounting to $11.5 billion) was $7.1 billion higher than the deficit registered in 1994. What were the sources of this increase? As can be seen, it was chiefly due to the rise in the interest payments (+$6.8 billion) and, secondly, to the amplification of the social security system gap (+$4.9 billion). Contrary to the standard interpretation, only a relatively minor figure (+$592 million) is accounted for by the disequilibrium in the result of the provincial administrations, though it is true that this figure was increasing.

The table also suggests that the pro-cyclical fiscal policies implemented were not ineffective: they produced a substantial increase in the primary surplus of more than a $5 billion annual average (without including the public social security results), though that was not sufficient to compensate for the rises in the interests item and in the social security system disequilibrium.

The explosive trend in the public debt interests account is also observed in Table 4.5.

The weight of interests on tax resources, which had increased slightly after 1994, exhibits a rapid upward trend after 1996. In 2000, that ratio was nearly 19 per cent, duplicating the ratio registered during the middle of the decade. This was in part due to the decrease in tax revenues caused by the recession, but it was fundamentally originated in the rise in the average interest rate paid by the public debt. The average interest rate of the total public debt rose from 5.8 per cent in 1996 to 9.4 per cent in 2001. Considering that this is an average rate, it is easy to see that the marginal rate rise was much higher than this.

The rising path of the interest rate is associated with the increasing trend in the country-risk premium (the two variables are narrowly correlated in the 1997–2001 period). These rising trends are the main factors behind both the consolidated deficit trajectory and the explosive path taken by the public debt.

Table 4.5 Total public interest payments, tax collection–GDP ratio and sovereign risk premium (in percentage)

Year	Tax collection as percentage of GDP (1)	Average interest rate on public debt (2)	Interest payments/tax collection ratio (3)	Sovereign risk premium (annual average)
1991	18.8	s.d	5.5	9.6
1992	20.8	6.6	8.3	6.9
1993	21.3	5.0	6.0	4.9
1994	21.1	5.5	6.9	5.9
1995	20.9	6.1	9.2	12.4
1996	19.6	5.8	9.7	6.5
1997	21.0	6.7	10.9	3.3
1998	21.4	7.6	12.2	5.8
1999	21.4	8.3	15.9	7.2
2000	21.9	8.9	18.5	11.5
2001	21.0	9.4	23.4	14.8
2002	19.2	5.2	13.3	—
2003	23.1	1.9	9.6	—

Notes: (1) Includes Security System receipts. (2) Calculated as a ratio between interest payment in period *t* and debt at the end of *t*−1, in percentages. (3) Tax receipts include those from social security system. The column figures are percentages.
Source: Authors' calculations based on the Ministry of Economy and Gaggero (2003).

This is illustrated in Figure 4.5. Between 1997 and 2001, in only four years, the public debt/GDP ratio increased by more than 20 percentage points.

4.4 Macroeconomic performance before and after the default

4.4.1 The balance of payments and the public debt under the currency board

In Figure 4.6 we present the results of the principal accounts of the balance of payments in the 1990s. They make it possible to complement our previous discussion of the macroeconomic cycle and the evolution of the public debt by illustrating some important aspects of the performance of the economy under the currency board regime.[18]

The macroeconomic performance of the 1991–95 period clearly fits the stylized cycle described in the first section. The capital inflows-led growth lasted until 1994. In early 1994 the Federal Reserve started to increase the discount rates affecting the capital inflows negatively and causing the foreign reserves stop growing, due to the continuously increasing deficit in the current account.

Then, the contagion of the Mexican crisis of December 1994 triggered a massive capital outflow at the beginning of 1995, with a sharp increase in

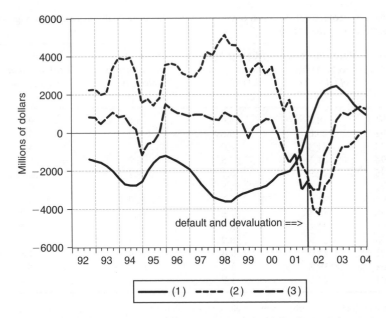

Figure 4.6   Balance of payments: current account, net capital inflows and variation of the stock of reserves (moving averages of four quarters)
Notes: (1) Current Account Balance. (2) Net Capital Inflows. (3) Foreign Reserves Variation.
Source: Authors' calculations based on the Ministry of Economy.

interest rates. Foreign reserves fell, as can be seen in Figure 4.6, and a contraction ensued. However, the recession of the mid-1990s was short-lived. A strong financial support package structured with the coordination of the IMF helped to change the negative expectations.

Due to the favourable effects of the external financial support, it was possible to preserve the monetary regime and in late 1995 a new expansion was already beginning. The elements of the cyclical dynamics were once again in motion.

The expansion phase that followed showed the same stylized facts of the first, although this time it was shorter in duration. The country risk premium jumped in mid-1997, after the devaluation in Thailand. Then, after the Russian crisis of 1998, a new contraction started.

4.4.2   Foreign debt, public and private

Beyond the mentioned similarities, the second cycle of the 1990s differed from the first one in many respects. We want to highlight here one of them: the dissimilar roles played by the public and private sectors in the generation of the capital inflows that fed the accumulation of reserves (a crucial variable under the currency board regime).

Table 4.6 Change in foreign debt and foreign assets by sector and period (in million of dollars)

Period	Changes in						
	External debt of				External assets of		Net external debt of
	Public sector (1)	Financial sector	Private sector (2)	Total	Financial sector	Private sector (3)	private sector (2)–(3)
1991:4 to 1994:4	8,529	5,726	10,321	24,575	1,728	566	9,755
1994:4 to 1995:4	5,924	2,952	4,361	13,238	821	11,174	−6,813
1995:4 to 1998:2	9,222	11,579	15,607	36,407	15,307	15,050	557
1998:2 to 2000:4	8,523	−555	3,139	11,107	−4,274	11,876	−8,737
2000:4 to 2001:4	2,975	−8,053	−688	−5,766	−10,665	12,865	−13,553
Total	35,173	11,649	32,740	79,561	2,917	51,531	−18,791

Note: (1) Including the Central Bank.
Source: Authors' estimations on the basis of data from the Ministry of Economy.

As already mentioned, during the first economic expansion, in the early 1990s, private inflows were predominant in spite of the fact that the privatization of the most important state-owned companies took place in that period. Capital inflows to the public sector became significant during the recession of 1995, thanks to the foreign financial support package we have already mentioned. Since then, capital inflows to the public sector were kept at a high level until the end of the period. Thus, the second expansion in the 1990s was bolstered mainly by capital inflows directed to the national government.[19] Meanwhile, net capital inflows directed to the private sector recovered only slowly and, from mid-1998 onwards, they stopped flowing in important amounts. Actually, an abrupt outflow started in late 2000.

As Table 4.6 shows, the increase in the foreign public debt surpassed $35 billion in the period. This amount is quite close to the increase in the foreign financial obligations of the non-financial private sector, which was more than $32 billion. If we add the increase in the external liabilities of the domestic financial sector, the amount jumps to more than $44 billion, but with a significant fall in the critical period 2000:4–2001:4. Thus, the rise in the amount of the public foreign financial obligations (including the Central Bank) explains about 44 per cent of the change in the total external debt during the period, or about 38 per cent if the year 2001 is excluded from the calculation. As we have just stated, the public sector played a crucial role in the financing of the accumulation of foreign reserves in the 1990s. Certainly, the increase in the foreign debt of the private sector was not less important, but a significant part of it had a counterpart in private outflows of funds. In effect, whether the private debt experienced a considerable increase, also did the external assets of this sector.

Table 4.6 shows that foreign assets grew more than foreign liabilities in the case of the non-financial private sector. As we have analyzed in other works, this sector's net demand for foreign currency was positive in the aggregate (Damill, 2000; Damill and Frenkel, 2005).

The accumulation of foreign assets by the private sector was small in the period 1991–94. It rose during the second half of the decade, after the Tequila shock. As can be seen in the table, in the expansionary phase which lasted from late 1995 to mid-1998, the level of private debt increased rapidly. It grew by more than $15 billion (for the non-financial sector). But private foreign assets rose by a roughly similar amount.[20] Furthermore, from this point onwards the net private foreign debt declined substantially. Over the whole period, it fell by about $19 billion, according to the figures in the table. In summary, in the late 1990s the level of reserves and the internal liquidity became more and more dependent on the access of the public sector to foreign funds.[21]

4.4.3   The late 1990s: from euphoria to depression

The basic plot of the macroeconomic story of the late 1990s was quite simple. To start with, the negative financial turnaround in the foreign environment experienced in 1997–98, after the South East Asian and Russian crises, found the Argentine economy a significant and growing current account deficit, a considerably appreciated currency and a visible lack of policy instruments to deal with this problem, given the rigidities of the macroeconomic rule adopted. It was no surprise that, in these conditions the country-risk premium jumped upwards and the access to foreign funds became more and more problematic. As explained in the previous section, the subsequently increased interest burden had a negative impact on all borrowers, including the public sector.

Given that the government lacked other policy instruments, restrictive fiscal policies had to bear the main burden of the adjustment to the new situation. The official story used to say that fiscal discipline would entail stronger confidence, and consequently the risk premium would fall, bringing interest rates down. Therefore, domestic expenditure would recover, pushing the economy out of the recession. Lower interest rates and an increased GDP would, in turn, improve the balance of the public sector, thus closing a virtuous circle. De la Rua's administration borrowed the entire argument from Menem's administration and the IMF gave its seal of approval. All of them failed.

Hence, the macroeconomic story of the late 1990s is about this failure. Despite the strong adjustment in the primary result of the public sector we have already mentioned in the previous section, the virtuous circle was never attained. Worse still, the increases in taxes and the cuts in public expenditures reinforced the recessionary trend, thus feeding the negative expectations that prevented the much-anticipated fall in the country-risk premium. Fiscal policy alone was impotent to compensate for the strong macroeconomic unbalances, which lay mainly in the external sector of the economy. Under this self-destructive fiscal policy orientation, the economy got trapped into a vicious circle for several years, and suffered from the longest recession since the First World War.[22]

4.4.4 The efforts to prevent the default and the end of the currency board regime

As usually happens during a crisis, its development involved a complex succession of events, including many contradictory policy decisions (especially throughout 2001) and steps back and forward. We will only mention here some of the crucial aspects of these processes.

In December 1999 the newly elected government of President De La Rúa took office. As already mentioned, the new administration adhered to the belief that the main cause of the economic depression was not the exchange rate appreciation and the financial vulnerability to external shocks, but fiscal mismanagement. This vision led the government to adopt a tight fiscal policy as a way to, quite paradoxically, take the economy out of the recession. We have presented these arguments and the expected results above.

However, the failure of this policy orientation should not hide the fact that huge efforts were made to balance the public accounts and to prevent any defaulting on the government's financial obligations. Indeed, aiming at re-establishing the bridges to the international financial markets, successive packages of tight fiscal measures were applied during 2000 and 2001, grounded on the fiscal consolidationist view of the crisis. Some of these episodes deserve to be mentioned as examples of the actions oriented to fulfil the commitments with creditors, both foreign and domestic.

The efforts to prevent the default included, among other measures, a Fiscal Responsibility Law approved in late 1999 that set a mandatory declining trend for the public deficit that should bring it to zero in a few years. Tax increases and expenditure cuts were adopted with that purpose. Later on, when the credit constraint had become very hard, a 'zero deficit' policy was approved, by mid-2001, determining that the public accounts had to be immediately balanced (so that total expenditures had to be adjusted to total cash receipts). The norm intended to guarantee some basic payments of the state, including interests on the public debt, and making endogenous the rest of the expenditures subjected to the evolution of public receipts. The other 'protected' items were legally established transfers of tax receipts to provinces, and wages and pensions amounting to less than 500 pesos per month (or dollars at the ruling parity). The package included an unprecedented 13 per cent across-the-board cut in public wages and pension benefits, which hardly contributed to either the social approval of the government policy or the social peace. It should be kept in mind that these measures were taken when the economy had already experienced three years of recession. These decisions exemplify the huge efforts made to prevent the default of the public debt.

In any case, the expected 'confidence shock' never materialized. With the economy suffering from a deep recession and caught into a debt trap, these rounds of contractionary fiscal policies only reinforced the deflationary scenario and the pessimistic expectations, as we have already explained.

During 2000 and 2001 the government attempted to complement the fiscal measures with some initiatives on the financial front. It obtained foreign support and implemented important debt swaps aiming to convince the public that there was no risk of default. Thus, at the end of 2000 an important package of local and external support, for about $40 billion, was announced: (the '*blindaje*', financial shield). The IMF led the operation with a $13.7 billion extension of the stand-by credit in force since March 2000. Local agents (a group of banks and the private pension funds) also played a significant role. The beneficial effect of this action was very short-lived. Two months after its announcement, and following the development of a new crisis in Turkey, the country-risk premium began to climb again.

Later on, an important voluntary debt swap (the 'mega-*canje*') was implemented in mid-2001 to seduce private creditors (local and foreign). The transaction amounted to about $30 billion in public bonds (24 per cent of the total debt of the national public sector at the time) and had the IMF's support. The operation made possible some extension in the duration, but involved an increase in the nominal debt (of about $2 billion) as well as a heavy interest burden, because the newly issued bonds committed dollar interest rates of about 15 per cent per year. Instead of alleviating the financial constraint, these high interest rates contributed to a consolidation of the perception that the debt path had become unsustainable.

Finally, there was another voluntary swap of public debt in November (although it would be better to call it 'induced', semi-voluntary). This was directed to domestic bondholders (mainly banks and the private pension funds), who agreed to swap more than $42 billion in public bonds for the same amount in loans of lower yield but insured by tax revenues. The operation could not stop, however, the ongoing divergent processes.

The withdrawal of bank deposits and the contraction of international reserves had started in October 2000, with the resignation of Vice-President Alvarez. In March 2001, after the ephemeral recuperation that followed the announcement of the '*blindaje*', this process became more intense and lasted until mid-June, when the government again issued a new signal aiming at changing the expectations: the already mentioned 'mega-*canje*'. At the beginning of July, the deposits withdrawal and the run against the reserves started again. The intensification of these processes could neither be stopped with the announcement in August of a new extension of $8 billion of the current IMF stand-by credit, nor with the debt swap in November.

From the beginning of December onwards the government established hard restrictions on capital movements and on cash retirements from banks (the so-called 'corralito'). One of the purposes of the measures was to avoid either the generalized bankruptcy of the banks or the violation of the currency board monetary rule. No bank, domestic or foreign owned, complained about that. But the main objective of the measures was to hold back the demand for foreign currency, preserve the stock of reserves and avoid the devaluation (i.e. the formal abandonment of the convertibility regime). It was also the last drastic move attempting to prevent the default. Yet, the measures actually did represent the end of the regime.

The December financial restrictive measures contributed to a deepening of the already strong social and political tensions. After a few days of social unrest and political commotion the country experienced the resignation of the government, followed by a series of ephemeral presidents. One of them announced to the Congress the decision of defaulting the public debt, and resigned a few days later. In the first days of 2002, with a new president, the economic policy officially abandoned the currency board regime and the one-to-one parity of the peso to the US dollar.

4.5   The macroeconomic performance after devaluation and default

After three years of recession, the economic activity suffered from an additional abrupt fall after mid-2001. The massive flight to external assets that took place in the second semester precipitated the collapse of the convertibility regime and ended up in the devaluation of the peso and the default. Figure 4.6 shows the strong fall in reserves experienced along that year that rapidly reduced the level of liquidity. The payments chain collapsed after the 'corralito' was established. The output and employment followed the abrupt contractionary trajectory showed by the reserves and liquidity. Social indicators such as the unemployment rates and the poverty and indigence indexes, which had considerably worsened along the nineties, suffered from an additional deterioration, adding to the social tensions and the politic crisis that brought the government of the Alianza to an end (Damill, Frenkel and Maurizio, 2003).

4.5.1   The economic recovery

The large fall in output and employment continued after the end of the convertibility regime, but only for a very short period. Certainly, in opposition to most opinions and beliefs – including those of the IMF's officials – the traumatic episodes that brought the convertibility regime to an end were not followed by a deeper depression. Moreover, an extraordinary quick recovery started only one quarter after the devaluation and default, as can be seen in Figure 4.7.

In the figure, the 'V-shaped' trajectory can be seen, consisting of the economic collapse phase of the last quarters of the convertibility regime and the following quick recovery. As just indicated, the GDP recovery started soon after the exchange rate depreciation (around three months later, as can be

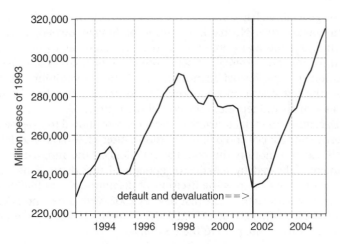

Figure 4.7   Real GDP, Quarterly values, seasonally adjusted, 1993:1–2005:4
Source: Authors' calculations based on figures from the Ministry of Economy.

seen in the available monthly activity indicators). The recovery was triggered precisely by the sudden change in the relative prices in favour of the tradable goods sectors. In the beginning of this phase the recovery was led by the local production of previously imported goods.

It is remarkable that the beginning of the new phase began to be perceptible when the country was still immersed in a context of accentuated economic instability and political uncertainty, and when the services payments of part of the public debt were interrupted.[23] In other terms, the 'rebound' took place in spite of this extremely complicated setting and also despite the short-term recessionary effects of the depreciation.

4.5.2   Despite the IMF

Apart from the shift in the relative prices, the rapid economic recovery that followed the crisis is also a consequence of a set of policies that, albeit still with flaws and ambiguities, aimed to recover the basic macroeconomic equilibria.

It should be stressed that many of the policies that played important roles at this stage were opposed by the IMF. Firstly, the imposition of exchange controls. This measure compelled the exporters to liquidate in the local market a considerable part of the international currency generated by the exports and also restricted capital outflows. Secondly, the establishment of taxes on exports (retentions), which absorbed part of the devaluation's favourable effect on the exporters' incomes (thus contributing significantly to the recovery of the fiscal equilibrium), and attenuated the impact of the devaluation on domestic prices and, consequently, on real wages. Thirdly, a flexible monetary policy that initially enabled the assistance to banks in the crisis phase and later

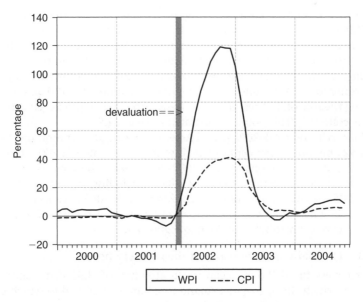

Figure 4.8 Consumer (CPI) and wholesale (WPI) price indexes: Monthly year-to-year variation
Source: Authors' calculations based on figures from the Ministry of Economy.

allowed for the revitalization of money demand, thus helping the economic recovery. Fourthly, when the exchange market started to show an excess supply of international currency, an exchange rate policy attempted to avoid the peso appreciation throughout the interventions of the Central Bank (and of the Treasury later on).

The IMF put particular insistence on the free flotation of the peso. For a short period the government adopted this regime. Once the exchange rate was free to float the parity rose sharply, reaching levels close to four pesos per dollar. The following reintroduction of exchange controls was crucial to contain the exchange rate bubble. By mid-2002 the government managed to stabilize the nominal exchange rate by compelling the exporters to liquidate the international currency in the local exchange market and also by limiting the currency outflows.

Soon after, when the exchange rate was stabilized the demand for pesos started to recover and the exchange market begun to show an excess of supply of dollars. The stop of the exchange rate bubble decisively contributed to stop the rise in the domestic prices. The freezing of the public utilities prices[24] as well as the high unemployment rates – that kept constant the nominal wages – also contributed to stop the rise in prices. The quick decline of inflation in the second half of 2002 can be seen in Figure 4.8.

Another important point involving the tense relations of the country with the IMF refers to the net flows of funds between Argentina and the multilateral organizations. In this regard, a substantial change can be seen after the end of the convertibility regime. Actually, in the post-default phase the net funding of the IMF and the multilateral organizations became negative. According to the Argentinean Minister of the Economy the IMF passed from playing the role of 'last-resort lender' to play the role of 'privileged debt payments collector'. This point is illustrated in Figure 4.9.

Whereas in the 1994–2001 period Argentina received a net funding of more than $23 billion (40 per cent of which were concentrated in 2001) from the multilateral organizations, in the 2002–2005 phase the country made net payments amounting more than $14 billion (including interest payments).

In 2005 the government of President Kirchner decided to cancel the whole outstanding liabilities with the IMF, and that explains the significant size of the negative bar attributed to 2006 in Figure 4.9.

4.5.3   The main characteristics of the recovery phase

The recovery in GDP that began in the first half of 2002 had a short first phase in which the aggregate demand rose hardly at all and in which every internal component of domestic expenditure (private consumption, public consumption, investment) kept on shrinking, as it happened along the previous depression, though at a lower pace. Therefore, it was not the aggregate demand that stopped the decline in the level of activity. The expansive factors were mainly the international trade variables – exports and imports – and

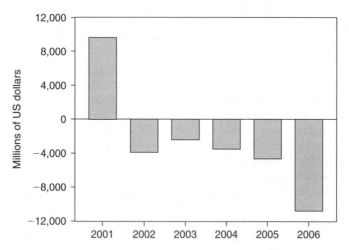

Figure 4.9   Annual net disbursements from IFIs
Source: Ministry of Economy.
Note: The figure of 2006 corresponds to the first quarter of the year.

especially the latter. Local production started to provide an increasing proportion of aggregate demand. This imports substitution particularly favoured the manufacturing sector. After that short initial stage, the activity level recovery was led by the increase in the domestic demand components, and, in particular, investment – which grew at an yearly rate close to 40 per cent between 2002 and 2004 – and by private consumption.

It is frequently mentioned that the favourable external context is an important element behind the economic recovery. In some analyses the main part of the rebound is usually attributed to a set of positive 'exogenous' factors. In those interpretations, this recovery would be taking place in spite of what is interpreted from this perspective as an economic policy full of mistakes and omissions. Although the contribution of external factors to recovery has been undeniable (in particular some commodities' high prices) the fact that the substantial part of the expansion's dynamism derives from internal demand sources weakens that interpretation.

It should also be stressed that the consumption and investment recovery took place in a context of accentuated credit rationing, both external and internal. The investment was apparently financed by higher profits retained by firms, although the 'wealth effect' resulting from the significant external assets holdings of the private resident sector, surely contributed as well. These assets – which today reach about $130 billion – increased their value in pesos with the exchange depreciation, and also rose in relation to the prices of domestic assets such as real estate and land. This was also a factor that fed the recovery of the private consumption expenditure.

4.5.4   External and fiscal adjustment

The adjustment experienced by the Argentinean external sector in recent years took place to a great extent before the devaluation, as shown in Figure 4.6, where the improvement in the current account since 1998 can be seen.

Actually, the abrupt contraction that characterized the end of the convertibility generated an important trade surplus. The trade balance exhibited a deficit higher than $3 billion in 1998. It rapidly decreased from then on and turned into surplus, due to the reduction in the volume of imports. In 2002 the balance was higher than $17 billion, and it remained over $16 billion in 2003 (and over $12 billion in 2004 and 2005). The trade surplus caused the change of sign in the current account balance. In recent years it has shown positive results even taking into account the interests accrued by the debt in default (as it is shown in the figures in Figure 4.6). In fact, the macroeconomic policy has been facing the problem of sustaining the real exchange parity in order to preserve the incentives to investment in the tradable goods sector in a context of international currency excess supply.

As can be seen from Table 4.7, a strong adjustment in the public accounts has been also taking place together with the external adjustment process we have just mentioned.

Table 4.7   Fiscal adjustment: results of the consolidated public sector (CPS) (as a percentage of GDP)

Concept	2001	2005	Variation (2005–2001)
Tax receipts	13.8	19.2	5.3
Taxes on exports	0.0	2.3	2.3
Financial tax *	1.1	1.5	0.4
VAT	3.1	3.5	0.4
Income tax	2.5	3.6	1.1
Other taxes **	5.3	6.7	1.4
Other receipts	5.0	4.5	−0.5
Total receipts	18.8	23.8	5.0
Total expenditures	22.0	22.0	0.0
Primary expenditures	12.1	14.9	2.9
Interest services	3.8	2.4	−1.4
Primary result	0.5	4.2	3.6
Total result of the NPS	−3.2	1.8	5.0
Provinces ***	−2.4	0.2	2.5
Total result of the CPS	−5.6	1.9	7.6

Notes: * Tax on bank debits and credits. ** Includes taxes shared with provinces, which are included as expenditures in the Primary expenditures item as transfers to provinces.
*** Including the City of Buenos Aires.
Source: Authors' calculations based on the Ministry of Economy.

The improvement in the Consolidated Public Sector global result that took place between 2001 and 2005 was equivalent to 7.6 points of GDP. This result passed from a global deficit of 5.6 per cent of GDP in 2001 to a 1.9 per cent surplus in 2005.

Which are the factors explaining the adjustment in the fiscal cash flow results? About a third of it derives from an improvement in the provinces' balances. This improvement comes from the increase in tax collection facilitated by the recovery and the rise in nominal prices, together with the restraint in expenditure. Meanwhile, more than 70 per cent of the five percentage points adjustment in the national public sector's budget is explained by the improvement in the primary result (+3.6 per cent of GDP). The contraction of interest payments, basically resulting from the default of the sovereign debt and the debt restructuring of 2005 accounts for the rest (−1.4 per cent of GDP).

The rise in the national primary surplus is mainly explained by an improvement in tax revenues (+5.3 per cent of GDP). It is interesting to observe that although the receipts from traditional taxes such as the VAT and income tax rose significantly, they did not increase substantially when measured as a proportion of GDP. Between 2001 and 2005 they increased by 1.5 per cent of GDP as a whole. The tax on exports is the item that mostly explains the rise in tax revenues (+2.3 per cent of GDP). The exports of soy-bean and its derived products generated almost one half of the taxes on exports.

Hence, the public sector absorbed part of the effect of the devaluation on the profitability of the tradable goods sector, and it also benefited from the high prices reached by some of the exportable goods, such as soy-bean and oil. The tax on financial operations established in 2001 also contributed to the increase of tax collection (+0.4 per cent of GDP).

The interest payments on the public debt deserve a separate paragraph. As can be seen in Table 4.7, this flow passed from representing almost 4 per cent of GDP in 2001 to 2.4 per cent in 2005.[25]

However, the fiscal effects of the suspension of part of the debt services payments in the 2001–2004 and the debt restructuring of 2005 are significantly higher than what is shown in the mentioned account. It cannot be calculated with precision because a significant amount of new debt was issued after the suspension of debt payments. We have estimated that the amount of interest accrued on the public debt in 2004, the year before the restructuring, valued at the 2004 exchange rate, would have represented in that year between 9 and 11 points of GDP. This is approximately equivalent to one half of the total tax collection for the year. These payments would have been certainly incompatible with the economic recovery. As was pointed out above, a crucial aspect of the fiscal financial vulnerability derived from the extremely high proportion of debt in foreign currency, with the consequent exposure to the impacts of the exchange rate variations. The 2002 substantial exchange rate depreciation would have had a harsh impact on the public sector's financial equilibrium. Taking this aspect into account, it can be said that the payments suspension and the following debt restructuring enabled a considerable amount of fiscal savings – either measured in domestic currency or as a proportion of GDP.

However, the most important effect of the default and the end of the convertibility regime was the re-establishment of the effectiveness of the instruments of macroeconomic policy which had crucial importance to take the economy out of the abyss generated by the final collapse of the convertibility regime.

4.5.5   Debt restructuring and fiscal consolidation

As already mentioned, a key step to fiscal consolidation after the crisis was the partial restructuring of the public debt. It involved a significant haircut in the nominal amount of the public financial liabilities, as well as an important reduction in interest rates and a considerable extension of average maturity.[26]

A first proposal was made to creditors in 2003. The government recognized a defaulted debt stock of about $87 billion, to be reduced later to $81.8 billion. This amount left aside an important volume of past due interests.[27] In the restructuring proposal of the government a 75 per cent reduction was imposed to the amount of eligible debt. The issuing of three bonds called Par, quasi-Par and Discount was announced. It was established that the issuing date would be 31 December 2003 and that the bonds would accrue interest after that.[28] The offer included a coupon tied to GDP growth. It was announced that the Par and Discount bonds could be issued in inflation-adjusted pesos, US dollars, euros and yens. The quasi-Par bond – tailored to the needs of some domestic bondholders, pension funds in particular – was exclusively issued in inflation-adjusted pesos. The government announced that in order to guarantee the offer's financial consistency it would commit to maintaining a 2.7 points of GDP primary surplus target during the first five years – when the service of the post default issued debt is concentrated – and stabilize the primary surplus around 2.3 per cent of GDP from 2014 onwards. The bondholder's organizations rejected the proposal, claiming that the country should pay more than was being offered. By mid-2004 the financial analyses showed that the new offered debt value, including the coupons tied to the GDP-growth, was between 20 and 27 cents. This signified a present value reduction of between 73 per cent and 80 per cent, which was considered unacceptable by the market's participants. The discount rate used in these calculations was crucial. Most of the analysts considered reasonable to use the yield of assets of similar-risk emerging market countries, which at that moment was around 12 to 14 per cent.[29]

By late 2004 the international capital markets evolution unexpectedly started to play in favour of the Argentinean offer. The level of world liquidity stimulated the appetite for risk, which turned into an increasing demand from emerging markets debt and into a reduction of the developing countries' risk premium.[30] In this new context, the swap looked more attractive. The present value of the offered bonds calculated with the discount rate settled by the new financial conditions (for instance 10 per cent, the Brazilian debt yield) was between 30 and 35 cents. This present value represented a 65–70 per cent cut and was similar to the market price of the defaulted bonds.[31]

The swap finally started on 14 January 2005. As minister Lavagna said, 'it has come the moment for the markets to talk'. Six weeks later the restructuring operation was closed. On 3 May 2005, the government announced that the acceptance had reached 76.15 per cent of the debt in default. This meant that $62.3 billion of the old bonds would be exchanged for about $35.3 billion of new instruments, plus the corresponding GDP growth-linked coupons. The maximum amount of the issuing would be $15 billion in the case of the Par bonds, $8.33 billion in the case of the quasi-Par bonds and about $11.9 billion in the case of the Discount bonds. The government expressed satisfaction at the swap outcome. The operation signified a reduction in public debt stock of about $67.3 billion and attenuated the exposure of the public finances to the exchange risk, since around 44 per cent of the new bonds are denominated in local currency.

As already mentioned, by the end of the same year the government had decided to redeem the whole outstanding debt to the IMF by a payment close to us $10 billion.

4.6 Summary and conclusions

We have argued that the Argentine economic history of the last thirty years can be told as a story of the country's insertion in the financial globalization process.

Certainly, the Argentine case has been one of the worst experiences of insertion in the globalized financial system. This phase exhibited the poorest economic performance since the country began to integrate into the world economy as an exporter of agricultural goods and importer of manufactures and capital. This can be illustrated by the fact that the per capita income at constant prices in 2001 was almost the same reached in 1975, but its distribution was considerably more unequal then than before.

We have indicated that in the two periods of active integration, the late 1970s and the 1990s, the country's insertion took place in contexts of exchange rate appreciation and led to large current account deficits. Hence, significant amounts of debt were accumulated, which eventually became unsustainable. The public sector participated in this debt process either as a direct recipient of external funding or as a result of the socialization of private debts in the crises. Even though the Argentine history in the financial globalization constitutes an extreme case, it has not been unique.

Some normative conclusions can be derived from these observations. In the first place, international financial integration should be administered: the use of external savings is to be kept within the range in which they make a positive contribution to economic growth. Macroeconomic policies – that is, fiscal, monetary and exchange rate policies – play a key role in the administration of financial integration.

Furthermore, if external savings are to be carefully administered the real exchange rate policy plays a strategic role in the development process. Among other objectives, a real exchange rate policy has the purpose of keeping external savings within limits that are sustainable in the long run, which are the same limits within they make a positive contribution to economic growth.

In some recent studies we have put the accent on the competitive real exchange rate policy as an instrument to promote growth and employment (Frenkel, 2004, Frenkel, 2006; Frenkel and Ros, 2006; Frenkel and Taylor, 2006). It is also worthwhile highlighting the preventive nature of the exchange rate policy. The Argentine case that we have examined in the previous chapters shows – by its opposite experience – that exchange rate policy must coordinate trade and financial insertion so as to ensure that the balance of payments and external debt perform in a way that is sustainable in accordance with the objectives of the development strategy.

The need to manage the exchange rate through exchange rate policy brings in an alternative macroeconomic policy regime that is in conflict with the IMF orientation. The latter consists of unlimited opening to capital flows, pure floating exchange rate and a monetary policy exclusively focused on inflation.

On the contrary, given the need for consistency within macroeconomic policies, in a managed exchange rate regime with a competitive real exchange
rate target, fiscal and monetary policies must be formulated in coordination
with the exchange rate policy, simultaneously managing multiple objectives of
exchange rate, inflation and activity level and employment. If it is necessary,
financial opening may have to be regulated through capital controls in order
to preserve the policy regime.

Notes

1 The authors wish to thank the co-operation of Julia Frenkel and Marcela Fraguas.
2 This section is based on Frenkel (2003).
3 The first financial globalization took place in the last quarter of the nineteenth
   century and with ups and downs lasted to the crisis of 1929.
4 System regulation was reformed and strengthened in Argentina after the 1995 crisis, so that it had become more robust by the time of the 1996–97 upsurge in capital inflows. In Argentina, however, there was systemic currency risk owing to the
   partial dollarization of the domestic financial system. While banks had matched
   their local dollar assets and liabilities and did not seem to face any currency risk
   individually, much of their dollar lending was to agents with local-currency
   incomes from non-tradable activities.
5 See, for example, Robichek (1981), cited in Díaz Alejandro (1985).
6 Michel Camdessus took a similar position on Mexico when he visited that country
   in 1994.
7 We have drawn attention to the way the issue of reform sequencing was 'overlooked' in writings reflecting mainstream economic opinion. Perhaps less striking
   (because it is more common) is the total ignorance displayed of studies published
   in the Southern Cone countries and by less conventional analysts, such as Frenkel
   (1980, 1983a and 1983b) and Damill and Frenkel (1987) in Argentina, and Arellano
   (1983), Ffrench-Davis and Arellano (1983) and Díaz Alejandro (1985) in Chile.
8 This account is based on a model inspired by the early experiences of Argentina
   and Chile which is presented in Frenkel (1983a). The model was synthesized and
   presented in English in Williamson (1983) and Taylor (1991). It was also used in
   explaining the 1990s crises by Taylor (1998), Eatwell and Taylor (2000) and
   Frenkel (2002).
9 As defined by Minsky (1975).
10 If the public sector has some deficit to finance and has issued some debt, the
   increase in interest rates during the contractionary phase tends to widen the deficit
   and cause debts to accumulate faster, as it happens in the case of the private sector
   as well. As their crises neared, Mexico in 1994 and Brazil in 1998 had trouble
   administering the public debt. But this is not the point. What matters is the mechanism causing risks and interest rates to rise, i.e., whether the original source of
   uncertainty is to be found in the dynamic of the public accounts and financing
   needs or in the dynamic of the external accounts and financing needs. In Brazil
   and Mexico, the second phase of the cycle was not brought on by fiscal problems.
11 To the Pension Fund Administrators (AFJP).
12 This section is based on Damill, Frenkel and Rapetti (2005).

13 Note that the debt ratio is defined as: $(d.P^*E/y.P)$, where d is the debt measured in real dollars, P^* is the international price level, E the nominal exchange rate, y the real GDP, and P the domestic price level. Therefore, this ratio is affected by variations of the real exchange rate (EP^*/P). Ceteris paribus, a real depreciation increases the debt ratio and a real appreciation reduces it.

14 We are referring to the 'tablita', the programme of prefixed devaluations implemented from the end of 1978, and the convertibility regime that established the free convertibility of the peso to the dollar at a one-to-one fixed parity.

15 Although the access to voluntary international funding was ended, part of the interest flows accrued in the 1980s were accumulated as new debt, i.e. as bank credit involuntary funding, and would end up being recognized and instrumented in bonds with the Brady agreement.

16 The haircut can be estimated in slightly more than $2.3 billion, equivalent to less than 4 per cent of the total debt of the public sector at the end of 1992.

17 In 1992, before the agreement, the bonds in circulation were only 17 per cent of total public debt, whereas in 1993 they had reached almost 65 per cent of it. On the other hand, foreign currency-denominated bonds represented less than 13 per cent of the public debt in 1992, but approximately 57 per cent in 1993.

18 A formal model of the dynamics of the Argentine economy under the currency board regime as well as its econometric estimation can be found in Damill, Frenkel and Maurizio (2002).

19 Notice that the main channel was not the foreign financing of public expenditures, but a monetary mechanism: the issuing of new foreign debt by the government surpassed its payments in foreign currency. By selling this surplus to the Central Bank, the Treasury covered the net foreign currency needs of the private sector and fed the accumulation of reserves, essential for the expansion of both the money and credit supplies at the domestic level. The mechanism is discussed in Damill (2000).

20 Capital flights and the dollarization of private portfolios had also been a central feature of the crisis of the financial opening experience of the late 1970s. Thus both policy experiments ended, among other aspects, in a strong de-nationalization of private wealth.

21 Note, in Table 4.6, the important fall of the financial sector external assets in the crisis phase (that adds up more than $10 billion in 2001 only). However, this is basically a reflection of the capital flight of the rest of the private sector. In effect, banks then held the main part of their reserves ('liquidity requirements') in liquid deposits abroad. Facing the withdrawal of deposits, the banks were forced to use those funds, hence their external assets declined while the external assets of the rest of the private sector increased.

22 We have emphasized here, in the explanation of the negative trends that would bring the economy to the crisis, the aspects related to the design of the macroeconomic programme and policies and the impact of the strong negative financial shocks suffered from mid-1997 onwards. But Argentina was also hit by a number of other negative foreign shocks in the late 1990s. On the one hand, the recessions in Southeast Asia, and then in Russia and Brazil, reduced the external demand for export goods. Argentine exports, which had been growing at a significant pace during the 1990s, stopped growing in that negative context. On the other hand, the average price of Argentine exports decreased significantly: in early 1999 it was nearly 25 per cent lower than in early 1997. An additional negative impact resulted from the exchange rate variations in different economies. While the Argentine peso was pegged to the US dollar, the latter appreciated in relation to other currencies. The Argentine multilateral real exchange rate declined by more

than 10 per cent between early 1997 and late 1998; later on, it abruptly decreased as a consequence of the Brazilian currency depreciation at the beginning of 1999. In 2001, the average multilateral real exchange rate was almost 25 per cent lower than the one registered at the beginning of 1997. Some explanations of the 2001–02 crisis saw these exogenous shocks as the main cause of it.

23   When the floating regime was adopted, soon after the initial devaluation that had taken the parity to 1.40 pesos per dollar, the exchange rate was weakening; the depreciations pushed up the nominal prices, the financial system was going through a deep crisis, etc.

24   Many of which were dollarized and subject to automatic adjustment with the US rate of inflation, as established in the privatizations' contracts subscribed in the 1990s.

25   After the 2005 public debt restructuring the amount of interest payments will increase, but reaching levels well below those observed before the crisis.

26   These issues are extensively discussed in Damill, Frenkel and Rapetti (2005).

27   This set of obligations was denominated the 'eligible debt'. It consisted of 158 instruments, issued in seven different currencies (Argentinean peso, inflation-adjusted Argentinean peso, US dollar, euro, yen, sterling pound and Swiss franc) and eight jurisdictions (Argentina, United States, Great Britain, Japan, Germany, Italy, Spain and Switzerland).

28   This issuing date enabled interest payments immediately after the closing of the swap. This aimed at including a sweetener in the proposal to incentive the bond-holders' participation.

29   Brazil's debt was commonly used as a benchmark. Its yield then oscillated around 12 per cent. The debt of Ecuador, a country that had recently restructured its external liabilities, yielded a rate close to 14 per cent. High yields were a consequence of the unfavourable funding conditions that the developing countries faced at that time. The JP Morgan EMBI + index, which measures the emergent market risk weighted average, showed an average value of 502 basic points in May–June. In the same period Brazil's country risk-premium averaged 691 basic points.

30   The EMBI + index decreased to an average of 375 basic points in the final quarter of the year, whereas the Brazilian country risk premium fell down to 417 basic points. The yield of Brazilian debt was about 9–10 per cent and the yield of Ecuador bonds was about 11–12 per cent.

31   Some financial analysts opined that lower discount rates should be used, since after the restructuring, the Argentinean debt would turn out to be less risky than many of the countries' debts used as a benchmark for the calculation.

References

Arellano, J.P. (1983) 'De la liberalización a la intervención. El mercado de capitales en Chile, 1974–83', *Estudios CIEPLAN*, No. 11, Santiago de Chile.

Cetrángolo, O., M. Damill, R. Frenkel and J.P. Jiménez (2000) 'La sostenibilidad de la política fiscal en América Latina. El caso argentino', in: E. Talvi and C. Végh (eds), *¿Cómo armar el rompecabezas fiscal? Nuevos indicadores de sostenibilidad*. Washington DC: IDB.

Cetrángolo, O. and J.P. Jiménez (2003) 'Política fiscal en Argentina durante el régimen de convertibilidad', *Serie Gestión Pública* No. 108. Santiago de Chile: CEPAL.

Damill, M. (2000) 'El balance de pagos y la deuda externa pública bajo la convertibilidad', *Boletín InformativoTechint* No. 303, Buenos Aires.

Damill, M. and R. Frenkel (1987) 'De la apertura a la crisis financiera. Un análisis de la experiencia argentina de 1977 a 1982', *Ensayos Económicos*, No. 37. Buenos Aires: BCRA.

Damill, M. and R. Frenkel (2005) 'Argentina: Macroeconomic Performance and Crisis', in R. Ffrench-Davis, D. Nayyar and J.E. Stiglitz (eds), *Stabilization Policies for Growth and Development*. New York: Initiative for Policy Dialogue, Macroeconomics Task Force, forthcoming.

Damill, M., R. Frenkel and R. Maurizio (2002) 'Argentina: A Decade of Currency Board: An Analysis of Growth, Employment and Income Distribution', *Employment Paper 2002/42*. Geneva: International Labour Office.

Damill, M., R. Frenkel and R. Maurizio (2003) 'Políticas macroeconómicas y vulnerabilidad social. La Argentina en los años noventa', *Serie Financiamiento del Desarrollo*, No. 135. Santiago de Chile: CEPAL.

Damill, M., R. Frenkel and L. Juvenal (2003) 'Las cuentas públicas y la crisis de la Convertibilidad en Argentina', *Desarrollo Económico-Revista de Ciencias Sociales*, No. 170. Buenos Aires.

Damill, M., R. Frenkel and M. Rapetti (2005) 'The Argentinean Debt: History, Default and Restructuring', Initiative for Policy Dialogue (IPD), Columbia University. Working Paper, 15 April.

Díaz Alejandro, C. (1985) 'Good-bye Financial Repression, Hello Financial Crash', *Journal of Development Economics*, 19(1).

Eatwell, J. (1996) 'International Financial Liberalization: The Impact on World Development', *ODS Discussion Papers Series*. New York: ODS.

Eatwell, J. and L. Taylor (2000) *Global Finance at Risk: The Case for International Regulation*. New York: The New Press.

Fanelli, J.M. and R. Frenkel (1993) 'On Gradualism, Shock Treatment and Sequencing', *International Monetary and Financial Issues for the 1990s: Research Papers for The Group of Twenty-four*, Volume II. New York: United Nations.

Ffrench-Davis, R. (2001) *Crisis financieras en países 'exitosos'*. Santiago de Chile: ECLAC–McGraw-Hill.

Ffrench-Davis, R. and J.P. Arellano (1983) 'Apertura financiera externa: la experiencia chilena entre 1973–1980', in R. French-Davis (ed.), *Las Relaciones Financieras Externas. Su Efecto en las Economías Latinoamericanas*. Mexico: Fondo de Cultura Económica.

Frenkel, R. (1983a) 'Mercado financiero, Expectativas Cambiarias y Movimientos de Capital', *El Trimestre Económico*, vol. L (4), No. 200, Mexico.

Frenkel, R. (1983b) 'La apertura financiera externa: el caso argentino', in R. French-Davis (ed.), *Relaciones Financieras Externas y su Impacto en las Economías Latinoamericanas*. Mexico: Fondo de Cultura Económica.

Frenkel, R. (2002) 'Capital Market Liberalization and Economic Performance in Latin America', in J. Eatwell and L. Taylor (eds), *International Capital Markets: Systems in Transition*. Oxford: Oxford University Press.

Frenkel, R. (2003) 'Globalization and Financial Crises in Latin America', *CEPAL Review*. No. 80. Santiago de Chile: CEPAL.

Frenkel, R. (2004) 'Real Exchange Rate and Employment in Argentina, Brazil, Chile and Mexico'. Paper for The G-24, Washington DC, September.

Frenkel, R. (2006) 'An Alternative to Inflation Targeting in Latin America: Macroeconomic Policies Focused on Employment', *Journal of Post-Keynesian Economics*, 28(4), 573–91.

Frenkel, R. and J. Ros (2006) 'Unemployment and the Real Exchange Rate in Latin America', *World Development*, 34(4), 631–46.

Frenkel, R. and L. Taylor (2006) 'Real Exchange Rate, Monetary Policy, and Employment', *DESA Working Paper*, No. 19. New York: United Nations.

Gaggero, J. (2003) 'La cuestión fiscal bajo la convertibilidad.' Buenos Aires, mimeo.

IEO (2004) 'Report on the Evaluation of the Role of the IMF in Argentina, 1991–2001', *Independent Evaluation Office*. Washington, DC: IMF.

Melconián, C., R. Santángelo, D. Barceló and C. Mauro (1997). 'La deuda pública argentina entre 1988 y 1996'. *Programa de Consolidación y de Reforma Administrativa y Financiera del Sector Público Nacional*, Buenos Aires.

Minsky, H. (1975) *John Maynard Keynes*. New York: Columbia University Press.

Robichek, W. (1991) 'Some Reflections about External Public Debt Management', in Banco Central de Chile, 'Alternativas de Políticas Financieras en Economías Pequeñas y Abiertas al Exterior', *Estudios Monetarios VII*. Santiago de Chile.

Taylor, L. (1991) *Income Distribution, Inflation, and Growth*. Cambridge, MA: MIT Press.

Taylor, L. (1998) 'Lax Public Sector and Destabilizing Private Sector: Origins of Capital Market Crises', in United Nations Conference on Trade and Development, *International Monetary and Financial Issues for 1990s*, vol. 10. New York: UNCTAD.

Teijeiro, M. (1996): *La política fiscal durante la convertibilidad*. Buenos Aires: Centro de Estudios Públicos.

Williamson, J. (1983) *The Open Economy and the World Economy*. New York: Basic Books.

5
Recent Political Economy in Venezuela

Carolina Pagliacci and Jorge Portillo
*Central Bank of Venezuela**

Abstract

As with most oil-producing countries, Venezuela's income depends heavily on the upheavals of the oil market, which not only affect economic decisions, but also impact the dynamic of political transactions among policy makers. In this paper, we describe the political economy of the recent Venezuelan policy-making process in the appropriation and delivery of oil rent, providing coherent hypotheses about the strategic government behaviour and taking into consideration the prevailing political, historic and institutional conditions.

Keywords: political economy, policy-making process, oil bargaining game, social programmes, rent seeking, clientelism.

JEL Classification: P16, H5, Q33.

5.1 Introduction

One could argue that, in general, Venezuelan governments face the dilemma of how to allocate the oil rent received by the state – which economic or social groups to favour and what type of expenditure or investments to undertake.[1] The current administration of President Hugo Chávez does not escape this dilemma, especially during the recent oil boom, but it also copes with the additional complication of facing a non-cooperative political landscape

*Both authors work in the Economic Research Department at the Central Bank of Venezuela. Opinions expressed on this chapter are personal and do not represent those of the Central Bank. We thank, in particular, Daniel Barráez, León Fernández, Francisco Vivancos and Francisco Sáez for insightful comments, and Harold Zavarce for suggestions in the preliminary stages of the work. All errors are our own.

147

characterized by a series of confrontations between political actors. This political instability has its origin in the process of substitution of the traditional political elite (based on a two-party system ruling the country since 1958) by a new political class emerging from the anti-party discourse advanced by Chávez. This substitution has also induced a continuous change of institutions and policies that allow asserting that major transformations have taken place in the recent Venezuelan policymaking process.

In this chapter, we describe the political economy of the policy-making process in the appropriation and delivery of oil rent, providing coherent hypotheses about strategic government behaviour and taking into consideration the prevailing political, historic and institutional conditions.

The major challenges in laying down these hypotheses are: (i) that those institutions and policies under consideration are still experiencing major changes; (ii) that there is little available information about the impact of policies, either because there has not been a systematic collection of their results or, in the majority of cases, because it is too early to measure their full effect; and (iii) there is not a long enough historical perspective of events to develop a sufficiently impartial analysis. Nevertheless, we attempt to evaluate the incentives faced by the government in the management of the oil rent, assuming that observed actions are the result of strategic behaviour in respect to other relevant actors. Analytically, we divide the oil rent allocation mechanism into two main processes: the generation or appropriation of the oil rent by the state; and its distribution among society members through a set of public policies, among which we distinguish the ones devoted to distributive ends.

In the process of the state appropriation of oil rent, we believe that the implicit bargaining game existing after the nationalization of oil has now turned into a different bargaining game with new political actors. The main hypothesis is that the government's gain of control over the state oil industry, and the favourable international conditions have improved the negotiation power of the government, domestically and with foreign oil companies, all of which has increased the state discretion over oil resources.

In the political dynamic, the collapse of the party system and the under-representation of opposition sectors to the Chávez government in state institutions have characterized an asymmetrical non-cooperative political interaction between two actors:[2] Chávez (with strong political power), and the opposition (a gathering of diverse political factions facing collective action problem). The performance and outcomes of both sets of actors have been affected by the lack of reconstruction of political parties. However, in the case of Chávez, this condition has induced a direct relationship between him and the electorate that explains the emergence of a distinctive type of policy actions (called polarizing actions). These actions, more than being directed against opposition groups, have tried to bring about the cohesion of Chávez's core constituency in order to cope with the political confrontation observed during most of his administration.

The sequence of political events that emerged from the non-cooperative interaction of political actors has also affected the timing of the process of distribution of oil rent among society members. In Chávez's administration this allocation has mainly occurred through social programmes, which have been articulated around three recurrent themes: (i) 'endogenous development' as an answer to neoliberalism and globalization; (ii) rights-based social policies as an alternative to residual or compensatory social policies; and (iii) participatory democracy instead of representative democracy. However, the most emblematic of these programmes have been the 'misiones', specialized social programmes with an emphasis on providing goods and services to the poor. After the launch in 2003 of the first three of these initiatives, in the areas of health care, education and food security, a wide variety of other 'misiones' have appeared with the intention of satisfying many different social needs.

Nonetheless, along the complete history of creation of social programmes, particular initiatives have failed to fulfill their announced objective, have been redefined within other programmes or have simply lost intensity through time. We provide two main hypotheses in order to explain this dynamic.

In the provision of social programmes, as in other policies financed with resources from oil exploitation, there is always room for the appearance of rent-seeking behaviour. In particular, we describe two main mechanisms to best characterize rent-seeking practices in association with clientelism in Venezuela. We believe that, although the private sector is receiving a significant part of the oil rent, the government might discretionally promote rent seeking with clientelistic purposes, i.e. with the intention of receiving political support.

Since there is no evidence that social programmes are created solely for electoral purposes, we cannot disregard the hypothesis that such programmes could satisfy both objectives of redistribution of the oil rent towards more vulnerable groups and also electoral objectives. This might imply that, if social policies do not fulfil their objectives of accumulating human, physical and social capital to increase economic productivity and development, then high levels of private appropriation of oil rent could be very important to explain an impaired future development. Unfortunately, in the short run, these two effects are strongly intertwined, making it difficult to make any kind of forecast about future economic performance. Nonetheless, there are some medium-term outcomes that can be expected over the next few years, if policies are actually producing their expected consequences. These results, which will finally reveal the quality of institutional and policy transformations currently happening, should relate not only to the improvement of growth and certain basic social indicators, but also to the spread of new economic relations, where communities and informal networks of social protection will gain significant importance.

This chapter is structured as follows: first, we describe the dynamic of the state appropriation of oil rent, highlighting the more important legal and institutional changes occurred in the recent Venezuelan history. Then we describe the political dynamic, separating events before and after the Fifth Republic, the one emerging with the 1999 Constitution. Later, we describe the structure an intentionality of social programmes, relating them with political events. Finally, we address the problem of rent seeking in the provision of social goods in association with practices of clientelism. Although no direct references are made to development, we hint the relationship between rent seeking, clientelism and development.

5.2   The oil policy-making process: the state appropriation of oil rents

The exclusive property right that the Venezuelan state exercises over the oil and the market power coming from the world market structure generate a significant state-owned rent. On the other hand, a policy-making process refers to the procedures or means by which policies are approved, discussed and implemented (Stein *et al.* 2005). For the oil industry in countries like Venezuela, the 'oil policy-making process' can be understood to be a repeated bargaining game between the government and other economic actors to divide oil revenues, given the constraints imposed by the inherited legal framework. However, this bargaining game might change in time because of the transformations that may occur to the institutional framework or to the key actors involved, as has indeed happened in Venezuela.

In this section we will describe the evolution through time of the outcomes of these bargaining games according to the changes occurred in the institutional framework and the specific events that altered the interaction between the government and other economic agents. It will be argued that the bargaining game that existed between the state oil industry and the government after nationalization has been transformed into a new bargaining game between the government and foreign companies, which has granted the state more discretion and negotiation power for the appropriation of oil rent.

5.2.1   The bargaining game before Chávez

The state ownership of oil reserves was established in Venezuela as early as 1922 following the passage of the first Petroleum Law, but only after 1976, with the nationalization of the oil industry, did the state exercise exclusive rights of oil extraction.

Prior to the nationalization, concessions for oil exploitation were granted to multinational foreign companies, which repaid the state with a part of the oil income they received. However, the split of the oil income between multinational companies and state was subject to the particular conditions negotiated in each concession, and, according to the experts, these contracts explicitly favoured foreign investors.[3] Only after the Hydrocarbons Law in 1943 did a unification of the legal framework of all contractual concessions take place, and a split in equal parts of the total oil income was implemented (the 50–50 deal) along with the creation of a special oil taxation for the oil industry

Table 5.1 Summary of changes in the oil institutional framework

Year	Institutional change	Impact
1922	1st Petroleum Law: state ownership of reserves.	Creation of the initial oil infrastructure.
	Several reforms to the fiscal contribution. Reforms were applied only to new contracts.	Proliferation of foreign operators.
1943	Hydrocarbons Law: 50–50 deal. Unification of all contractual concessions. Creation of a special Income Tax Rate for oil activities (66.7 per cent) and Royalty Tax (16.6 per cent of gross revenues). Renovation of concessions for 40 years. Recognition of legal property rights for all concessions.	Significant increase of oil production and investment in capital stock.
1959	Increase in oil Income Taxes: break of the 50–50 deal.	Government share of revenues increased from 51 per cent to 65 per cent. Reduction of foreign capital investment.
1967	Increase in oil Income Tax Rate. Creation of the *Fiscal Reference Price* (FRP) for income tax calculations: the price could be modified every 5 years.	Further increase in the government revenue share.
1970	Congress approved a yearly discretionary modification to the FRP by the Executive Power.	Further increase in the government revenue share. Decline in oil production.
1976	Nationalization of the oil industry and creation of PDVSA.	Reduction of the effective tax rate. Increase in capital investment to broad available oil reserves.
1983	PDVSA's investment fund of $5.5 billion is used to finance the ongoing currency crisis.	Elimination of PDVSA's foreign investment funds.
1983–85	PDVSA starts the Internationalization Policy: acquisition of shares of international refineries (VEBA and CITGO); utilization of *Transference Prices* to compute Income Taxes.	Slow down of the investment in domestic net capital.
1990	PDVSA associates with foreign companies to produce synthetic crude.	
1991	Proposition of the PDVSA's Expansion Investment Plan partially financed by foreign companies: creation of Operational Service Agreements, Strategic Associations Agreements and Sharing Risk Exploration Agreements, all under	Increase in capital investment and oil production. Reduction in fiscal contributions through the income tax.

(Continued)

Table 5.1 (Continued)

Year	Institutional change	Impact
	art.5 of the Nationalization Law, which reserved to the state the possibility of limited foreign associations whenever approved by the Congress.	
1999	Creation of the Natural Gas Law: minimum Royalty Tax of a 20 per cent and Income Tax rate of 34 per cent. It is allowed the private exploration and exploitation of gas, prior government approval. Litigation processes are not subject to foreign arbitration.	
2001	Reform to the Hydrocarbons Law (passed through a presidential decree and implemented in 2002): reduction in the Income Tax rate (from 66.7 per cent to 50 per cent) and increase in the Royalty Tax (from 16.6 per cent to 30 per cent); requirement of separate fiscal tax declaration by activities; elimination of *Transference Prices*; elimination of foreign arbitration in litigation processes; establishment of a minimum domestic capital requirement for operating companies in 'down water activities'. Significant profit transfers to the government through *dividends*.	Increasing tension between the executive and PDVSA.
2002	Oil Strikes (April, August and December)	
2003	Deepening of the general Oil Sector Strike. Firing of PDVSA's employees and managerial staff by the executive power.	Temporary plunge in oil production.
2005	Creation of the operational regulation of the Hydrocarbons Law of 2001: increasing monitoring of the state (Ministry of Energy and Oil) over operating companies in all areas of the oil business (exploration, exploitation, transportation, refinement and commercialization)	
	Announcement of the creation of Mixed Capital Companies in substitution of the Operational Service Agreements. Increase of the Royalty Tax Rate for Strategic Association Agreements.	
2006	Implementation of Mixed Capital Companies. Announcement of the reduction of foreign capital participation in Strategic Association Agreements.	

Sources: Monaldi (2001), Mommer (2003), Mora-Contreras (2004) and author's own calculations.

(see Table 5.1). This element, although less favourable to multinationals, still fostered the increase of oil investment and the growth of the net capital stock of the industry.

After democracy was established in 1958, political sectors believed that fiscal resources were needed to satisfy the many social demands repressed by the previous military regimes (Betancourt 1978; Fuenmayor 1979). This idea encouraged the extraction of additional rents to multinational companies, and in 1959, the government's share of operating profits rose to 65 per cent, representing a break of the '50–50' rule that had been agreed in 1943. This event clearly marked a more confrontational form of extraction of rents that would continue up to the nationalization in 1976. This confrontation also reflected a disincentive to increase oil investment by multinationals, causing a slow decline in the net value of the oil capital stock (see Figure 5.1). Part of this tendency of the capital stock is also explained by the fact that in 1970 multinational companies were already anticipating the nationalization of the industry, which not only had a diminished productive capacity but also faced a very low level of proven reserves (Monaldi 2001).

After nationalizing the oil industry, the state had to compensate foreign companies for the cost of expropriation, since concessions were supposed to last in most cases until 1983.[4] Also in 1976, the current state oil company (PDVSA: Petróleos de Venezuela, S.A.) was created. The oil boom in the 1970s and the reduction of the industry effective tax rate caused an expansion of reserves and of the net capital stock of the industry. However, redistributive tensions between the government and PDVSA over the allocation of the oil income among fiscal programmes and the industry investments did arise with years, and deepened in 1983 during the currency crisis faced by Venezuela. In particular, the Executive Power forced PDVSA to withdraw $5 billion from its investment fund in order to finance the ongoing currency crisis. According to Mommer (2003), the reaction of the state company to the 'government expropriation' of its investment fund was to avoid accumulating profits in cash funds (since eventually expropriation could be repeated), and directly invest profits in international assets through what was called the 'internationalization of PDVSA', which started with the acquisition of shares of foreign refineries. Mommer also states that 'transfer prices' were created, as part of the strategy of the industry to divert profits out of the hands of the Venezuelan government,[5] while members of the industry argued that such prices were a mean to lock the provision of oil to their foreign partners throughout favourable long term contracts.

It would seem that under the internationalization strategy PDVSA had already started increasing its oil production during the years of 1988 and 1989. In 1991, PDVSA formally proposed what was called the 'oil opening', which was a ten-year expansion investment plan in association with foreign companies to increase production capacity of heavy oil and to transform extra-heavy oil into synthetic crude. This idea was coupled with the belief that in

Billions of 1997 Bs.

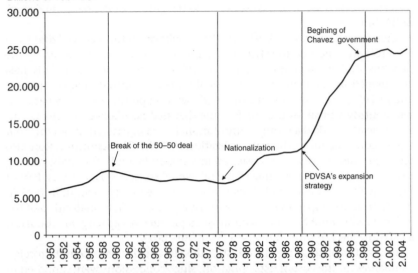

Figure 5.1   Net capital stock of the oil industry in real terms (Base 1997)
Source: Palacios *et al.* (2005) and own calculations.

the following years OPEC would face difficulties in satisfying the increasing
world demand and that low prices would lock the provision of oil to markets
such as the US market. This investment plan used mainly two different forms
of association with foreign capital (OSA: Operational Services Agreements and
SAA: Strategic Association Agreements).[6] The evident consequences of the plan
were an accelerated increase in the net capital stock of the industry, a sustained
increase in oil exports, and a progressive reduction of the fiscal participation
on oil revenues (see Figures 5.1 and 5.2).

An interesting characteristic of the expansion investment plan was that
PDVSA, in order to ensure foreign participation in an environment of potential
risks of rent expropriation, provided investors with institutional guarantees
based on the assets that PDVSA had outside Venezuela, and the commitment
that any litigation process caused by a government's violation to the established contracts might be resolved in international (and not local) courts
(Monaldi 2001; Mommer 2003).

In a retrospective analysis, Mommer (2003) points out that the expansion
investment plan constituted the means by which PDVSA historically acquired
more power *vis-à-vis* the central government, attempting to autonomously
control the design of the oil policy and explicitly bypassing the state control,
represented legally in the figure of the Ministry of Energy and Mines. This
assertion is sustained by the argument that the oil-opening strategy, based
on the expansion of production in a non-OPEC world, and the recurring

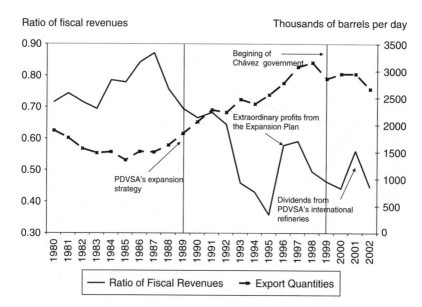

Figure 5.2 Ratio of fiscal revenues to oil exports and PDVSA's exports
Source: B.C.V. Annual Economic Bulletin and own calculations.

reduction of fiscal participation in oil revenues were both practices that did not consider the best interest of the nation and privileged the oil industry bureaucracy's preferences above the rest of society.

5.2.2 The current state of the bargaining game

It is clear from the preceding discussion that by the time President Chávez was sworn into office in 1999, there was likely to be a tension between the policy endorsed by PDVSA's bureaucracy, and any policy change that the entering government had tried to impose. In fact, under this premise, one could analyze the period 1999–2002 as a period of confrontation between the Executive Power (trying to regain control of the industry) and PDVSA's bureaucracy (trying to maintain the levels of independency exercised during the past decade). In fact, one of the first government decisions of President Chávez was to promote OPEC agreements in which the production quotas were observed in order to cause a recuperation of oil prices[7] (Mora-Contreras 2004). This strategy within the OPEC, already signed a change of direction in the way oil policy was conceived in Venezuela during the last ten years.[8]

At the level of observable variables, in the period, 1999–2002 there was a slow down in the rate of accumulation of the capital stock (Figure 5.1), a reduction in PDVSA's export quantities (Figure 5.2), an increase in the average oil price,[9] and a relatively constant 33 per cent participation of fiscal

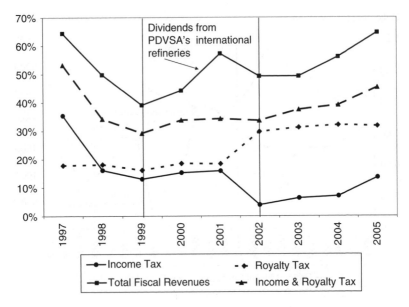

Figure 5.3   Ratio of fiscal revenues to oil exports
Note: Cash-based figures. Total Fiscal Revenues include PDVSA's disbursements for FONDESPA and FONDEN.
Source: Banco Central de Venezuela.

revenues coming from the income and royalty taxes (Figure 5.3). At the level of the legal framework, during this period two important modifications occurred: the creation of the Natural Gas Law, and the reform of the Hydrocarbons Law.

Because of the limited production of gas in Venezuela, the creation of the Natural Gas Law in 1999 had no immediate economic impact, but it signalled important changes in the conception of the oil business (Mora-Contreras 2004). The participation of private investments was promoted by establishing an income tax rate of only 34 per cent, but a minimum royalty tax of 20 per cent. However, in the contingency of disputes between the state and private agents, litigation processes necessarily were subject to local (not international) courts.

In certain aspects, the reform to the Hydrocarbons Law in 2001 follows the path of the Gas Law, since it establishes the reduction in the income tax rate (from 66.7 per cent to 50 per cent) and the increase in the royalty tax (from 16.6 per cent to 30 per cent). This change in the composition of tax is interpreted by some analysts as a way of improving tax monitoring and collection, since royalty taxes require a smaller supervising bureaucracy than income taxes (Mora-Contreras 2004). In terms of incentives, the new tax structure favours the realization of greater profits by oil companies when operative costs remain constant and oil prices are high.[10] However, it is important to stress that, by the time of the implementation of this reform in 2002, only PDVSA's fiscal contribution was affected, since the existing joint capital ventures between PDVSA and foreign companies (the SAA) had special tax conditions that followed their own contractual clauses.

Another important aspect of the reform to the Hydrocarbons Law was the reversion of some institutional practices of PDVSA that, according to the government, were undermining the fiscal participation in oil revenues. In particular, the imposition of separate fiscal tax declarations by activities (exploration, production and refinement) in order to improve monitoring in tax collection, and the elimination of Transfer Prices to avoid under-reporting of profits were both reforms in the above direction (Mommer 2003). Another measure of the reform was the elimination of foreign arbitration in litigation processes, more in the direction of recovering national sovereignty, as some analysts would argue.

The implementation of the Hydrocarbons Law in 2002 came together with key political events that made evident the conflict between the government and PDVSA's bureaucracy. In particular, in April 2002, PDVSA joined in the first general strike called by the major labour union (CTV), the Federation of Industry and Commerce (FEDECAMARAS) and the political opposition to the government, arguing that the new PDVSA's president and directive board appointed by the government jeopardized the scheme of incentives and meritocracy operating in the industry. The chain of events unleashed by this strike ended in a military coup against President Chávez, who was restored to power after only three days. In October of the same year, the government hired an international consulting company to audit the financial statements of the industry. In December 2002, a longer general oil strike started, which lasted 62 days, with the backing of the government's political opposition. The result of this series of incidents was the dismissal of almost all industry managerial staff and employees, and the gain of total control of the industry by the government (for more details see Mora-Contreras 2004).

The oil strike had enormous consequences for the rate of growth in the economy in 2003, and oil production fell sharply for a few months. As the immediate economic impact of the strike was overcome, it was clear that this event allowed the government to establish a new form of relationship with the industry bureaucracy in which past tensions between the state supervision organ of the industry (the Ministry of Energy and Oil) and the industry had disappeared.[11] The gain of complete control over the design and implementation of the oil policy by the government, redefined the dynamic of the existing bargaining game after the nationalization toward a new game in which the focus of attention shifts to another actor: foreign oil companies.

The sequence of oil policy events since 2003 with respect to foreign oil companies provide a mixed signal regarding the actual strategy followed by the

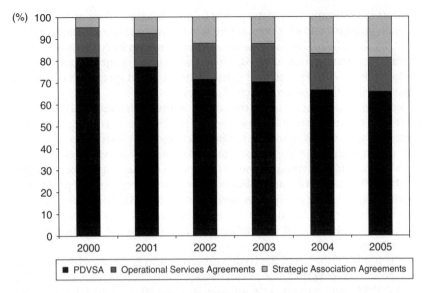

Figure 5.4   Domestic oil production by PDVSA, OSA and SAA
Sources: PDVSA, MEP and authors' own calculations.

government on this matter. On the one hand, the production of the Strategic Association Agreements (SAA) has been increasing as a proportion of domestic oil production, which is indicative of the significance gained by foreign companies and the space granted by the Venezuelan state[12] (see figure 5.4). In this same direction, the investment plan announced by PDVSA for the years 2006–2012 estimates that the participation of private capital (presumably mostly foreign) will represent around 26 per cent of total resources. On the other hand, some of the guarantees provided by PDVSA in the past to foreign investors were reversed. In fact, in 2005 the royalty tax rate for Strategic Association Agreements (SAA) was raised from one per cent to 16.66 per cent, which represents a modification of the contractual conditions under which these agreements were signed.[13] In March 2006, the government substituted the figure of the Operational Services Agreements (OSA), some of which were supposed to operate until 2017, with the figure of 'Mixed Capital Companies', giving PDVSA 51 per cent of the shares and foreign companies the remaining 49 per cent. The tax structure applied to these mixed companies is the one established in the 2001 Hydrocarbons Law, which, in scenarios of elevated oil prices, creates better investment incentives for foreign companies in terms of their potential benefits. Recent government announcements (the second quarter of 2006) have stated that state capital participation through PDVSA in SAA (currently with less than 50 per cent in all of agreements) will be increased against private capital participation.

The above narrative indicates that although foreign companies have been gaining increasing importance, these last modifications to the legal framework might be understood as a signal for a form of expropriation by the government, as the literature on sunk cost investments would indicate. If this is the case, a puzzling question would be why most of the foreign companies continue to run businesses in Venezuela and seem willing to engage in further negotiations with the government. At the time of writing (the third quarter of 2006), foreign oil companies have remained in the country and only three of them did not accept the conversion of OSA to Mixed Capital Companies,[14] while all SAA are still carrying out operations.

One possible hypothesis is the following: the centralization of domestic policy-making decisions in the figure of the Minister of Energy and Oil, the active negotiation positions of Venezuela in OPEC, the elevated oil prices and the estimated amount of Venezuela's oil reserves with respect to other competing producer countries[15] seemed to have granted the Executive Power, at least temporarily, some negotiation power that explains the compliance of foreign companies to the changes described above. Partially, this is because the new institutional and tax framework, under high oil prices scenarios, have put forward better incentives in terms of expected benefits to foreign companies.

Domestically, the government has also been able to access a greater amount of resources during 2004 and 2005 by undertaking three actions: (i) increasing the formal fiscal participation in oil revenues through PDVSA's income tax; (ii) creating two new investment funds (FONDESPA and FONDEN) with direct disbursements of PDVSA to finance productive investments designed by the government[16] (see Figure 5.3); and (iii) involving PDVSA in the sponsorship of social programmes. These later two actions are possible because PDVSA has explicitly declared the improvement of social welfare as one of the industry's legal objectives.

The conclusion that can be drawn is that, domestically, the government has increased its discretion over oil resources in the context of elevated oil prices, which enlarges the amount of fiscal revenues destined to be distributed among society members. From the point of view of the relationship with foreign oil companies, the government seems to have gained negotiation power, which however could be reversed, if oil prices conditions deteriorate or future investment plans are redefined.

5.3 The political dynamics

Most analyses point out that the election of Hugo Chávez represented a major transformation in the political arena that marked the definitive rupture of the political agreement existing in Venezuela since 1958 (named the Punto Fijo Pact). In this section we explain how this change occurred, and how it has fostered the current non-cooperative interaction among political agents.

5.3.1   The collapse of the Punto Fijo regime and the emergence of the Fifth Republic

After an interrupted democratic experience of only three years (from 1945 to 1948), the longest democratic history of Venezuela starts in 1958 with the overthrowing of the dictatorship of General Marcos Perez Jimenez and the celebration of free national elections. In this election the winning party was AD (Acción Democrática), a social democratic party with a very strong anti-communist bias in foreign policy. AD also secured the largest share of seats in Congress. To consolidate the incipient democracy, the leaders of the main political parties (AD, COPEI and URD[17]) subscribed to a political cooperation agreement called the Punto Fijo Pact.[18] As a mean of ensuring stability, this pact introduced a set of political arrangements such as: compliance with election results, independently of the winning party; the power sharing of executive positions between signing parties; and the implementation of common social and economic policies regardless of the presidential and legislature electoral outcomes (Monaldi *et al.* 2004).

An early expression of this agreement between parties was the Constitution of 1961, which was designed by a constitutional committee in which the opposition to AD (COPEI, URD and PCV) was over-represented with respect to their congressional performance in the 1959's elections (Corrales 2003). Among the constitutional rules emerged to induce cooperative behaviour between competing parties were: the impossibility of immediate presidential re-election; the use of proportional representation for legislative elections;[19] and the distribution of public funds to finance political parties according to their share of votes in the previous election (Monaldi *et al.* 2004).

In a stylized fashion, analysts argue that until the late 1970s the Punto Fijo regime produced the desired political stability, which also promoted a good economic performance, especially when measured in terms of a rising real per capita GDP.[20] This stability was characterized by the alternation in power of the main political parties (AD and COPEI), and the strong influence exercised by party leaders over appointments at the legislative, state and municipal level.[21]

The 1980s are typically described as the beginning of the deterioration of the Punto Fijo regime, but there are diverse emphases regarding which were the triggering factors. Corrales (2003) claims that the rise of instability, street protests, electoral apathy and military discomfort that characterized this period and the early 1990s was due to the deterioration of economic performance and the failure of the main parties to provide solutions to the economic crisis. This incapacity of response of political parties was mainly due to the lack of incorporation of technical expertise and the inadequate representation of people interests. Monaldi *et al.* (2004) stress that the excessive control of political parties in most spheres of social life and the fact the governorships and local bureaucracies were used as instruments to foster patronage and clientelistic networks, introduced serious accountability problems that deteriorated as a whole the existing institutional framework.

Monaldi *et al.* (2004) and Di John (2005) both point out that the first evident sign of the collapse of the Punto Fijo party system was the victory of the presidency by Carlos Andres Perez in 1988, without the support of most members of his party (AD) ruling elite.[22] Another factor that opened the gate to fragmentation of the main parties discipline was the initiation of the process of decentralization,[23] since it provided the opportunity for minor parties to compete electorally at the state and municipal level and encouraged politicians within the two main parties to develop local alliances and assert autonomy from national party bosses. Most of these emerging parties only developed their organization at regional level and did not expanded at national level. Main parties in fact increased their alliance strategies in order to maximize their chances of electoral representation. At a more general level, 'there was a substitution of political parties by loose coalitions conformed by political movements with superficial tag-names and little organizational structure or capacity, which was instrumental in the growing volatility of the period' (Di John 2005).

Another emblematic fact that had serious consequences for the cohesion and legitimacy of the party system was the winning of 1993 presidential elections by the ex-president Rafael Caldera, without the support of the party he founded (COPEI), but with a loose coalition of small parties.[24] This event signalled that 'the presidency could be obtained by running outside traditional party affiliation' (Di John 2005). During his electoral campaign, Caldera capitalized the discontent with traditional parties (AD and COPEI) by arguing that such parties had abandoned the people and were transformed into corrupted structures (Monaldi *et al.* 2004). These same arguments were used by Caldera as an explanation for the popular riot occurred in 1989 (the so-called 'Caracazo') and as a justification for the failed military coup attempt commanded by Hugo Chávez in 1992. However, the administration of Rafael Caldera (1994–1998) produced bad economic outcomes, and was characterized by a large rotation of ministers and changes of directions in the economic plans implemented.

The poor economic performance of Caldera's administration and the growing discontent with the traditional parties, because of their unwillingness to undertake political and institutional changes, set the stage for Hugo Chávez to win presidential elections in 1998. His campaign was run using an anti-party, anti-corruption and anti-neoliberal discourse that called for the transformation of the political system and the Constitution (Di John 2005). In this context, Chávez refused to make any alliances with traditional parties, and instead constructed a broad alliance with new and alternative movements and small left-oriented parties, all of which became known as the Polo Patriótico (PP). Among its members, the PP included the party MVR (Movimiento V República), which was a party conceived to serve as an electoral front and whose only concern was the support of Chávez's presidential candidacy (López-Maya 2003).[25]

After his victory in the presidential election, Chávez faced a Congress dominated by opposition parties, chiefly the AD and the COPEI, which also controlled important state and municipal assemblies, the Supreme Court, the Judicial and the National Electoral Council (Di John 2005). Under this scenario, in April 1999, Chávez managed to call upon a referendum to approve the reform of the Constitution through a Constituent Assembly, and in July 1999, to call for the election of the Constituent Assembly. Given the nominal representation rule approved in 1998 for upcoming elections, Constituent Assembly appointments did not used the proportional representation rule but used a majority system that helped dramatically over-represent the Chavismo, which obtained 96 per cent of the seats with about 55 per cent of the votes.

At a more general level, the resulting Constitution allowed Chávez to change the institutional framework without negotiating with the Punto Fijo traditional parties, representing the definitive breakdown of the Punto Fijo regime and the emergence of the Fifth Republic (the way Chávez himself has named his government for considering it a rupture with the previous political regime: the Fourth Republic).

What concerns us next is to explain the conditions that have characterized the new political game during the Fifth Republic.

5.3.2   The Fifth Republic: a new political game

The meagre representation of non-Chavista groups in the Constituent Assembly had several consequences. On one hand, it allowed the Chavismo to re-write the Constitution unilaterally[26] and signalled the unwillingness of Chávez to negotiate with political opposition groups. As Corrales (2003) claims, any incumbent would not have any incentive to negotiate with opposition forces if there is an evident asymmetry of political power that favours the incumbent.[27] This was exactly the case for the balance of power emerged from the composition of forces in the Constituent Assembly. As a response, despite the wide popularity of Chávez in his first year, traditional political parties and diverse civil organizations arranged street demonstrations seeking the inclusion of their demands and aspirations in the new Constitution (López-Maya 2003). In this sense, one could argue that these informal mechanisms of manifestation might have taken place because of the lack of formal devices to incorporate these demands into the Constitutional discussion.

On the other hand, the resulting Constitution granted the president increased power in several aspects: it augmented his ability to legislate over diverse legal subjects (not only financial and economic) upon the previous approval of a special law (Enabling Law); it gave the president the possibility to call for popular referenda, and therefore to abrogate laws or to convoke a Constitutional Assembly; it provided him with the option to dissolve the legislature and call for a new election if the vice-president were recalled more than three times by the legislature; it increased the presidential term from five to six years; and it allowed presidential re-election (Monaldi *et al.* 2004; Corrales 2003; López-Maya 2003). These constitutional features contributed to formally strengthen the figure of Chávez as the protagonist of all political events since his election up to today.

Another element that probably stemmed out from the under-representation of the opposition was the elimination of public funding to political parties, which certainly increases the operational costs of political parties, and therefore diminishes the chances for the incumbent to face competition for votes (López-Maya 2003). In addition to this economic disincentive, the new Constitution has contributed to undermine the figure of political parties by not formally acknowledging their legal nature, which denotes the intention of the Constituent Assembly to suppress the hegemony of political parties within the State (Álvarez 2003). Furthermore, to break the political practices of distributing the representatives of the Supreme Court and other high-level state positions among political parties, the new Constitution instituted general mechanisms of appointments based on a more direct participation of citizens (Álvarez 2003).[28]

The above elements, summarized as the exercise of an increased presidential power and the lack of appearance of a political opposition not related to the Punto Fijo parties, created a political environment that was highly unstable, characterized by multiple confrontations between government and opposition, not very frequent at the beginning of Chávez's administration, but more often as political events unravelled.

Among the events that contributed to the hostile political environment, the increase of Chavismo control over political institutions at the expense of their political opponents stands out. In particular, at the end of 1999 (in the midst of the discussions for reforming the Constitution), using the thesis of 'legal transition', the Legislative Commission of the Constituent Assembly designated temporary magistrates to the Supreme Court, which were mostly government sympathizers (Álvarez 2003). Similarly, representatives of the Electoral Power were appointed without following the general procedure prescribed in the Constitution (Álvarez 2003). At the end of year 2000, the majority in the National Assembly (the Chavista coalition, with 65.5 per cent of the seats[29]), designated the Committee of Postulations for the Citizen Power (a new Power created in the 1999 Constitution) and endorsed as definitive the magistrates of the Supreme Court, using procedures that favoured the government control of these institutions (Álvarez 2003).

As well as the Supreme Court and other high-level state positions, during the Punto Fijo regime, the major labour union of Venezuela (the CTV) had been tightly controlled by political parties, in particular AD, which refused to approve internal reforms to democratize the union (Roberts 2003). In an attempt of Chavismo to gain control over the CTV, in late 2000 the National Assembly approved a referendum to temporarily remove CTV's leading representatives from their positions. However, the alternative Chavista labour union could not take proper advantage of the favourable outcome of the referendum to secure their representation within the CTV, which lately turned in one important member of the opposition to Chávez (Ellner 2003).[30]

The above instances of 'power grabs' by the Chavismo and the progressive radicalization of the opposition started a chain of political actions that deepened the confrontation between the two groups and strongly divided public opinion into Chavista or anti-Chavista stands during 2001 and 2002. On the one hand, Chávez started increasing what we call 'polarizing actions', which are basically any kind of speeches or events that intend to produce (but not necessarily succeed in doing so) extreme reactions in the public opinion (approval or disapproval).[31] Among the most emblematic polarizing actions during this period, we found: the announcement of the legislative initiative for the creation of the Land Law, which was used recurrently from the end of 1999 until the end of 2001 as a flag for a land reform against powerful economic elites;[32] the pronouncement about the close cooperation with Cuba at the end of 2000, which caused street protests against the 'cubanization' of Venezuela; the creation of popular organizations named the 'Bolivarian Circles' in June 2001, interpreted by the opposition as violent groups against the non-Chavistas;[33] the introduction of the law project on mass media management during the third quarter of 2001 (Ley Resorte), which was taken by the opposition and mass media owners as a direct restraint to the freedom of speech; and the television announcement of the dismissal of several of PDVSA's managers in March 2001 as a product of the confrontation between the government and the state company bureaucracy. For a complete time-line representation of polarizing actions and major political events, see Figure 5.5.

On the other hand, during the period 2001–2002, the opposition actions pointed in the direction of overthrowing Chávez. In December 2001 there was the first general strike organized by the Federation of Industry and Commerce (FEDECAMARAS) to protest openly against Chávez's policy and Land Law for considering them a detriment to private property rights (García-Guadilla 2003). In April 2002, the CTV (the major labour union) and the FEDECAMARAS joined in the opposition street protests that led to the brief military coup against Chávez (Roberts 2003). In December 2002, PDVSA participated in the general strike organized by the opposition, turning it into an oil strike that lasted more than sixty days and that had important consequences on the economic performance.

Presumably, these confrontational events had important impacts on the government. Chavista groups that were not willing to cope with the more radical compromises implied by the political speech, defected from the Chavista coalition at the National Assembly.[34] As for the public opinion, confrontation and the poor economic performance[35] probably had a negative effect on Chávez's popularity.[36] Nonetheless, from this observation is very difficult to infer if this loss of popularity also entailed a reduction in the support from Chávez's core constituency.

After the oil strike was resolved by the government assuming control of PDVSA in 2003, the opposition focused on pursuing the removal of Chávez from the presidency through the use of a popular recall referendum. The strategic

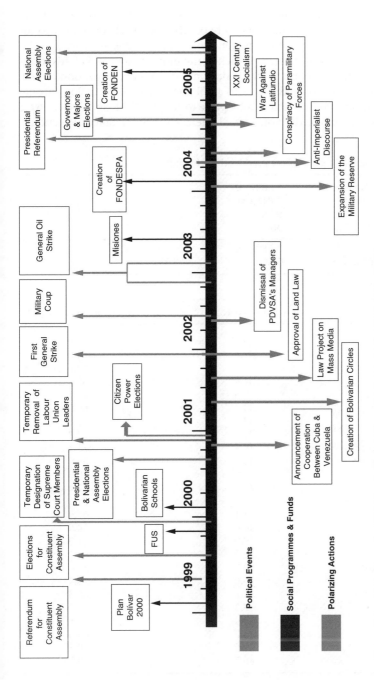

Figure 5.5   Time-line of political events, social programmes and polarizing actions
Source: Ministry of Planning and Development and data compiled from database of local newspapers.

response of the government consisted in delaying the occurrence of the event as long as possible in order to boost the low levels of popularity of Chávez after the oil strike.[37] Consistent with this strategy, as early as in the second quarter of 2003, Chávez launched the more symbolic of all his social programmes (the 'misiones'), which not only revived the generation of new social programmes, but also tried to fulfil the expectations of low-income classes.[38] The referendum finally took place in August 2004, and Chávez won it with 59 per cent of the votes (see Table 5.2 for the detailed referendum

Table 5.2   General results of the presidential referendum

Electoral population	14,027,607	
Number of voters	9,815,631	
Valid votes	9,789,637	
Abstention rate (%)	30.2	
Against Chávez	3,989,008	40.5%
In favour of Chávez	5,800,629	59.3%

Results by State

	Against Chávez (%)	*In favour of Chávez (%)*
Amazonas	29.1	70.9
Anzoátegui	45.8	54.2
Apure	32.2	67.8
Aragua	31.9	68.1
Barinas	30.5	69.5
Bolívar	33.4	66.6
Carabobo	43.2	56.8
Cojedes	32.8	67.2
Delta Amacuro	28.9	71.1
Distrito Capital	44.0	56.0
Embajadas	90.0	10.0
Falcón	42.4	57.6
Guárico	28.9	71.1
Lara	35.1	64.9
Mérida	46.0	54.0
Miranda	49.0	51.0
Monagas	38.9	61.1
Nuevas Esparta	50.0	50.0
Portuguesa	26.6	73.4
Sucre	32.7	67.3
Táchira	49.3	50.7
Trujillo	33.4	66.6
Vargas	35.7	64.3
Yaracuy	39.5	60.5
Zulia	46.7	53.3

Source: National Electoral Council.

results). International figures and organizations present during the event, such as the OEA, the Carter Center and European observers, certified that the referendum results were consistent with their own scrutiny of votes.[39] The reactions of the opposition were mixed: while some claimed fraud and promoted from then on the abstention to participate in any future electoral episode, others tried to achieve electoral representation in state and municipal governments or at the legislature level. While the elections for governors and mayors elections in December 2004 had a moderate participation of opposition candidates, the elections of the National Assembly in December 2005 totally lacked of opposition electoral representatives.[40] The slim participation of opposition voters played an important role in governors and mayors elections, causing that all governorships, except two, were won by the Chavismo. The current National Assembly only has the Chavista coalition representation.

In addition to continuing the creation of social programmes, 2004 and 2005 seem to be years in which polarizing actions were renewed.[41] In fact, in the first quarter of 2004, Chávez announced the expansion of the 'military reserve', stating that this is a group of urban reservists whose principal assignment is to face and overcome possible attacks of the imperialism against the Venezuelan sovereignty.[42] During the second quarter of 2004, Chávez informed on 'the conspiracy of the opposition with paramilitary forces' to overthrow him, and publicly stated that the Bolivarian revolution had an 'anti-imperialist' character.[43] In the fourth quarter of 2004, Chávez emphasized his intention of deepening the 'war against the latifundio'.[44] In the first quarter of 2005, Chávez declared the insertion of Venezuela in the 'XXI century socialism' (see Figure 5.5).

In a stylized way, the still ongoing political game could be described as non-cooperative interaction between two main actors, one in a position of considerable political power (Chávez), and other (the opposition) with fewer possibilities of representation in state organizations. Confrontation between the two players probably has its origins in the under-representation of opposition sectors in the Constituent Assembly of 1999, which allowed for a non-balanced appropriation of institutions by the Chavismo. The game has taken place in an environment characterized by the collapse and fragmentation of the party system, which has affected the performance and outcomes of both actors.

On the opposition side, strong internal diverging stands have been publicly expressed on frequent occasions, and important actions have emerged from the imposition of one stand over the others after long struggles. This constant difficulty to reach agreements seems to be the result of a collective action problem, in which each individual or group within the opposition looks for his interest and tries to free ride the others. This phenomenon has either precluded: (i) the conformation of a stable coalition – that is, one in which the different political factions can collaborate for long periods of time;[45] or (ii) the emergence of new political parties that revive political representation through a party system.

On the government side, the anti-party discourse maintained by Chávez in his electoral campaign has permeated the actual dynamic of his own party (the MVR). In fact, as Eller and Hellinger (2003) point out, the MVR does not have the solid organization exhibited by other parties such as AD (the main party during the Punto Fijo regime), which incorporated the participation of workers through their links with unions and had a well defined internal structure. We believe that this lack of organization has favoured Chávez by strengthening his figure as the protagonist of all domestic political events and has induced a direct relationship between Chávez and the electorate (almost without the intermediation of his political party).

This direct interaction with voters has allowed Chávez to exploit three types of benefits for his policy making. The first one is that Chávez has had enough freedom to innovate in terms of policy actions.[46] This is because the government party exercises no kind of veto over Chávez initiatives, which are, in most cases, explained directly to the citizens. The second benefit is that when announced policy actions have not had the desired effect, Chavistas have tended to justify the lack of delivery of the government by completely blaming the surrounding bureaucracy to Chávez (but not Chávez himself).[47] The third benefit is that this direct interaction with voters has allowed Chávez to employ polarizing actions as the instrument to bring about the cohesion of his core constituency, which is the group that would deter any attempt of removing him from power. In this same line of reasoning, one could argue that polarizing actions, more than being directed against opposition groups, intend to feed the bond between Chávez and his supporters through the development of 'ideological' links that induce loyal behaviour. In some sense, these polarizing actions supply among Chávez sympathizers the cohesion that a sound political party structure should have typically provided.

Instead of being a political instrument, one could contend that polarizing actions are simply a mechanism to obtain votes from more vulnerable social groups because of the confrontational discourse used along. Although we do not deny this possibility, we think that it is unclear that a polarizing action is an effective mechanism to win the adhesion of central voters (those people that claim belonging neither to the Chavismo nor to the opposition), because, by definition, polarizing actions tend to be radical while central voters do not.[48]

5.4   Oil rent distributive mechanism: social programmes of the Chávez administration

Typically, oil states such as Venezuela can distribute the oil rent received through the direct state production of private goods (the entrepreneurial activity of the state) or through the production of social goods.[49] In this section we describe the provision of social goods by the Chávez administration through social programmes, and discuss them under the perspective of an innovative process.

5.4.1   Description of social programmes

According to Chávez's political platform, poverty is a social problem that has its origins in the unbalanced spatial distribution of the country's population and economic activity (concentrated mainly along the northern shoreline), and in an excessive dependence on oil production; all features that have been reinforced by globalization. The proposed solution to this quandary is first and foremost political: to substitute the old political establishment and to create, via a Constitutional Assembly, a new institutional framework that puts the state at the service of the people. This would allow, among other things, the implementation of a new model of economic development (humane, participative and sustainable) that promotes more democratic modes of production (like cooperatives) and calls for a more active role by the State.

Some of these ideas found their way into the new Constitution and were developed later, with varying degrees of success, into specific laws and government programmes. More precisely, there are three recurrent themes that, although vague at times, underlie Chávez's discourse and policy prescriptions throughout the period: (i) endogenous development as an answer to neoliberalism and globalization; (ii) rights-based social policies as an alternative to residual or compensatory social policies; and (iii) participatory democracy instead of representative democracy.

At the risk of oversimplification, endogenous development can be understood as building the capacity of communities or territories to withstand social exclusion by reorienting their development efforts around local resources; by promoting active citizen participation; and by implementing sustainable context-specific policy alternatives. The idea is to build social capital and connectivity among the poor and disadvantaged – even at the expense of economic efficiency.

Rights-based social policies seem a departure from traditional poverty relief programmes, which typically target 'vulnerable groups' and mitigate fluctuations in household income as the economy adapts to global competition. Instead, the new approach sees poverty as a political and social issue, and emphasizes social inclusion as a universal right.

Finally, participatory democracy is intended to go beyond political participation and to encompass the economic sphere. Cooperatives and other forms of participatory management are seen as an extension of the individual's right to take part directly in the design and control of public policies. Technical assistance is also a priority for the government, to the extent to which scale economies and liquidity constraints are a barrier to self-employment initiatives and access to credit.

Historically, one can distinguish several stages in the evolution of Chávez's social programmes strategy (see Figure 5.5). During the first stage, from the beginning of 1999 through mid-2000, Chávez created the Plan Bolívar 2000 (PB-2000) as a quick response to the 'social emergency' affecting the poor. The PB-2000 had the objective to provide health and education services directly to the poor, to organize workfare programmes and to build basic community infrastructure. Given Chávez's military background and the direct connection he had with his constituency, the army served as a trusted agent to deliver on his electoral promises. In addition, the PB-2000 intended to foster a closer partnership between the military and the civilian population, in light of the enhanced role given to the army in economic matters in the new constitution. Later, accusations of corruption and fraud practically dismantled the PB-2000 (Norden 2003). Unfortunately, this first stage also saw a reduction in some poverty alleviation programmes inherited from the previous government, including a national programme of conditional transfers targeted to households with children attending public schools (Penfold-Becerra 2005). During this period a social fund named Fondo Único Social (FUS) was also created to intend the concentration of most of the ongoing social programmes into a single one in order to improve efficiency in their execution. In practice, the FUS had the opposite effect and was characterized by implementation delays, poor coordination and lack of transparency.

The next stage, from mid-2000 through early 2003, was characterized by heightened political tension and a less clear course in economic policy and social programmes. The PB-2000 was scaled down and its more promising initiatives were given a more permanent status within the armed forces' bureaucracy and budget. Policy innovation during this period was mostly confined to the creation of public development banks[50] and several micro-lending institutions intended to support small and micro enterprises.[51] However, most of these institutions had operational constraints that limited their initial economic impact.

Given the possibility of a mid-term recall referendum and the limited impact of Chávez's social programmes up to that point, from mid-2003 through 2005, Chávez devoted considerable time and effort to the implementation of a new policy strategy that would help in busting his popularity. In this third stage, Chávez launched the 'misiones', specialized social programmes that were fostered by the availability of oil resources, the effectiveness of Cuba's technical assistance, and a combination of self-selection and geographic targeting methods. In fact, during 2004 and 2005 PDVSA's contributions to the newly created funds (FONDESPA and FONDEN[52]) greatly increased the government's availability of extra-budgetary resources, exclusively destined for carrying out social investment plans. Indirect effects of the creation of these funds were the relative reduction in PDVSA's operational and investment expenditures, and the smaller participation of social expenditure within the formal budget approved by the National Assembly (see Table 5.3 for details).

Among the several existing 'misiones', the most emblematic are basically the initial ones. The first 'misión', created by Chávez with the help of Cuban physicians in the poor neighbourhoods, constructed a network of popular clinics that provided basic health care services free of charge (Misión Barrio Adentro). The second initiative, Misión Róbinson, was a massive literacy programme, based on Cuban teaching methods that helped the country to push literacy rates from 93.6 per cent to 95.0 per cent in less than two years. Thirdly, the government set a food security initiative, Misión Mercal, that combined

Table 5.3 Relative figures of PDVSA's and government expenditures and funds

	PDVSA's Fiscal Contribution as % of Oil Exports[1]	PDVSA's Operational Expenditures as % of Oil Exports	Social Expenditure as % of Total Budget Expenditure[2]	Extra-Budgetary Funds as % of Oil Exports[3]
1990	65	30	30	0
1991	81	43	36	0
1992	64	58	40	0
1993	54	58	40	0
1994	43	56	34	0
1995	41	58	37	0
1996	38	48	32	0
1997	53	61	39	0
1998	34	98	35	0
1999	29	58	49	0
2000	34	41	46	0
2001	34	66	47	0
2002	34	69	57	0
2003	37	47	55	0
2004	39	43	47	12
2005	45	32	43	31

Notes: (1) Refers to income and royalty taxes. (2) Social expenditure corresponds to programmed figures in the National Fiscal Budget plus additional credits. (3) Refers to the disbursements of PDVSA and the Venezuelan Central Bank to FONDESPA and FONDEN.
Source: Own calculations.

traditional food subsidies and agricultural intermediation programmes with the deployment of a government-owned retail distribution network intended to reach poor neighbourhoods. After these three initiatives, others, from sports promotion to vocational training, transformed into an important number of social programmes, all of which intended satisfying a wide array of needs, but always under the crafted 'misión' brand name.

Having won the presidential referendum held in August 2004, Chávez defined a strategic roadmap that has shaped his policies to date (Chávez 2004). Thus, in November 2004 he outlined the ten strategic goals of the 'next phase' and suggested the means to achieve them. On the economic front, the strategy pursues laying down the foundations of a more humane and egalitarian economic system. Specifically, this roadmap includes the following goals:

- Promoting cooperatives and other forms of participatory management by giving them special tax breaks, preferential treatment in government contracts, and comprehensive financial aid and technical assistance.

- Reducing the country's geographic imbalances through the consolidation of special endogenous development zones, and the elimination of large unproductive estates (*latifundios*).
- Strengthening the social programmes, and particularly the 'misiones', integrating them into the government's formal bureaucracy, and reaching out to 'the poorest of the poor' with the help of participatory (community-based) poverty assessments.
- Empowering communities through the implementation of participatory budget initiatives and the municipalization of government social programmes.

These goals, although spelled out only recently, reflect adequately the intentionality of the diverse social programmes created between 1999 and 2006. As shown in Tables 5.4 and 5.5, 65 per cent of the programmes intend to endow communities with the organizational skills required to build up participatory activities. Similarly, 34 per cent of programmes include the provision of some form of financial aid, usually destined to the development of communitarian projects. Around 60 per cent of the social programmes try to cover the education and/or health care requirements of the communities.

One could argue that, rhetoric aside, these social proposals resemble, in some respects, those ones lately circulating in academic circles and multilateral organizations. Nevertheless, the number and scope of the ongoing initiatives, if implemented successfully, might contribute to the delivery of a comprehensive answer to the multidimensional problem of social exclusion. For example, it is expected that the resources devoted to funding social programmes will reach $4.5 billion in 2006. Unfortunately, it is too early to assess the full effect of this wave of government interventions and the available statistical evidence is sketchy.[53]

5.4.2   Innovation in social programmes?

Chávez's policy-making style could be characterized as a continuous policy process in which the themes of endogenous development, rights-based social policies and participatory democracy have appeared relentlessly in a series of policy initiatives. Nonetheless, on several occasions, particular initiatives associated with these themes have failed to fulfil their announced objective, have been redefined within other programmes or simply have lost intensity through time. For example, during the period 2000–03, the government tried implementing a whole range of labour market initiatives: emergency workfare programmes, temporary payroll subsidies, financial and technical assistance to small and micro enterprises, job-training programmes, and labour market intermediation services (see Table 5.6 for details). Some of these initiatives have ceased to exist, while others are now being implemented in a different fashion. Yet it was only in 2004, with the creation of Misión Vuelvan Caras, that some form of consistent welfare-to-work programme began to take shape.

Table 5.4 Social programmes (1 of 2)

Social programmes	Purpose area	Economic classification
1999		
Gestión Comunitaria del Agua	Organizational, Environmental	Public
Manejo de residuos sólidos	Housing, Education, Health Care	Private-Club
	Food Security, Health Care, Education,	
Plan Bolívar 2000	Organizational, Housing, Infrastructure, Financial Aid, Income Transfer, Recreational	Club-Private-Public
Programa de Alimentos Estratégicos	Food Security, Organizational, Financial Aid	Club-Private
Programa de Asistencia Médica y Hospitalaria a los Estudiantes de Educación Superior	Health Care, Education, Income Transfer	Public-Private
Programa de Financiamiento de Microcréditos	Financial Aid, Organizational	Private
Programa de Formación de Cooperativistas para la Economía Popular	Organizational	Club
Programa de Inversión y Desarrollo Social	Infrastructure, Organizational, R&D	Public
Programa de Modernización y Fortalecimiento de la Educación Básica	Income Transfer, Education, Food Assistance, Health Care	Private-Club
Programa Nacional de Accidentes y Hechos Violentos	Organizational	Public
Programa Nacional de Compensaciones al Transporte Terrestre	Income Transfer	Private
Programa Nacional de Oncología	Education, Organizational, Health Care	Public
Programa Nacional de Salud Mental	Organizazional, Health Care	Public
Programa Nacional Integrado de Control de la Tuberculosis y Enfermedades Respiratorias	Health Care	Public
Programa Nacional Tabaco o Salud	Health Care	Public
Programa Nacional VIH/SIDA	Health Care, Education, Organizational	Public
Proyecto Educativo Nacional	Organizational	Club

(Continued)

Table 5.4 (*Continued*)

Social programmes	Purpose area	Economic classification
2000		
Atención a pobladores de la calle	Infrastructure, Health Care, Food Assistance	Club
Habilitación Física de las Zonas de Barrios	Urbanism, Infrastructure, Housing	Club-Private
Mejoramiento y Ampliación de Casas en Barrios y Urbanizaciones Populares	Housing, Financial Aid, Urbanism, R&D	Private-Club
Nuevas Urbanizaciones y Viviendas en Desarrollo Progresivo	Housing, Infrastructure, Organizational, Urbanism, R&D	Private-Club-Public
Plan de Rehabilitación de Viviendas en Barrios	Organizational, Housing	Club-Private
Programa de Innovación para el Desarrollo Endógeno Local	Financial Aid, Organizational	Private-Club
Programa de Protección y Atención Nutricional y Alimentaria	Nutritional Care, Food Assistance, Income Transfer	Club-Private
Programa Nacional de Educación Física y Deporte Escolar	Organizational, Recreational	Club
Programa Nacional de Salud Escolar	Health Care	Public
Programa Nacional de Salud Sexual y Reproductiva	Health Care, Education	Public
Programa Nacional Deporte para Todos	Education, Organizational, Financial Aid, Infrastructure, Recreational	Public-Private
Programa Petróleo, Gas y Energías Alternas	Education, R&D, Organizational	Public
Rehabilitación de Urbanizaciones Populares	Urbanism, Financial Aid, Infrastructure, Housing, R&D	Club-Public-Private
Urbanizaciones y Viviendas Regulares	Financial Aid	Private

2001

Atención Convencional y No Convencional en Educación Inicial (a niños)	Infrastructure, Education, Health Care, Organizational	Club
Centro de Oportunidades de Negocio de la Pequeña y Mediana Industria	Organizational, Financial Aid	Club-Private
Misión Zamora	Organizational, Financial Aid, Infrastructure	Club-Private

2002

Plan Nacional de Lectura Todos por la Lectura	Organizational, Recreational	Public
Programa de Articulación entre el Sistema Educativo y el Sistema de Producción de Bienes y Servicios	Organizational, Financial Aid	Club-Private
Programa de Capacitación para el Desarrollo Rural (indígena)	Organizational, Education	Club
Programa de Educación de Adultos	Organizational, Education	Club
Programa de Educación para el Trabajo	Infrastructure, Organizational, Education, Financial Aid	Club-Private
Programa de Salud Pública	Health Care	Public
Programa de Soberanía Alimentaria	Financial Aid, Organizational, Education, R&D	Private-Club
Proyecto de Infraestructura Social	Infrastucture, Organizational	Public-Club

2003

Atención Integral en Calidad de Vida y Salud a las Comunidades Afectadas por Desastres Naturales	Infrastructure, Health Care, Food Assistance	Public
Canasta Familiar	Tax exemption, Organizational	Club

(Continued)

Table 5.4 (Continued)

Social programmes	Purpose area	Economic classification
2003		
Empresas o Unidades de Producción Primaria	Organizational, Financial Aid	Club-Private
Misión Barrio Adentro I	Health Care, Infrastructure	Club
Misión Cristo	Food Assistance, Health Care, Education, Housing	Club
Misión Guaicaipuro	Housing, Health Care, Education, Organizational, Income Transfer	Private-Club
Misión Miranda	Organizational, Education, Infrastructure, National Security	Club-Public
Misión Piar (mineros)	Organizational, Financial Aid, Environmental	Club-Private-Public
Misión Ribas	Education, Income Transfer	Club-Private
Misión Robinson I	Education, Income Transfer	Club-Private
Misión Sucre	Education, Income Transfer	Club-Private
Programa Barrio Adentro	Health Care, Education	Club
Programa de Comercialización y Fortalecimiento Industrial	Organizational, Financial Aid	Club-Private
Programa de Conservación y Protección de Parques Nacionales	Environmental, Recreational	Public
Programa de Suministro de Medicamentos y Tratamientos a toda la Población	Financial Aid, Organizational	Private-Club
Programa Nacional de Cirugía Ambulatoria	Health Care, Infrastructure	Public
Programa Nacional de Extensión Agrícola	Organizational, Financial Aid	Club-Private
Programa Nacional de Financiamiento de Microcréditos para la Mujer	Financial Aid, Organizational	Private-Club
Programa Nacional de Salud Oral	Health Care, Education	Public
Programa Transectorial de Protección, Promoción y Apoyo a la Lactancia Materna	Health Care, Organizational, Education	Public-Club

2004

Program	Categories	Type
Fianzas Agrícolas	Financial Aid, Organizational	Private-Club
Fondo Autónomo para la Preinversión, Asistencia Técnica e Inversión en Proyectos Económicos y Sociales	Financial Aid, Organizational	Private-Club
Formación Básica en Gerencia Social Comunitaria	Organizational, Education	Club
Misión Alimentación	Assi	Club-Private
Misión Cultura	Organizational, Education, Recreational	Club-Public
Misión Hábitat	Housing, Financial Aid	Private
Misión Identidad	Identification	Public
Misión Milagro	Health Care, Income Transfer	Club-Private
Misión Vuelvan Caras I	Organizational, Financial Aid, Infrastructure	Club-Private
Programa de Rescate, Transformación y Distribución de la Tierra	Organizational, National Security	Public
Programa de Tecnologías de Información y Comunicación	Organizational, Education, Infrastructure	Public
Programa de Visibilidad y Promoción Social de la Ciencia y la Tecnología	Organizational, Financial Aid	Club-Private
Programa Nacional de Capacitación para Medios Alternativos y Comunitarios	Organizational, Education, Financial Aid	Club-Private

2005

Program	Categories	Type
Aprovechamiento de Recursos Hídricos	Infrastructure, Organizational, Education	Public
Asistencia Habitacional Indígena	Housing, Organizational	Private-Club
Haciendo Turismo desde Nuestros Juegos Tradicionales	Organizational, Recreational	Club
Inclusión de Personas con Discapacidad en Actividades Turísticas Recreativas	Organizational, Recreational	Club

(Continued)

Table 5.4 (Continued)

Social programmes	Purpose area	Economic classification
Inclusión para el Adulto Mayor en Actividades Turísticas Recreativas	Organizational, Recreational	Club
Iniciativa Cardiovascular, Renal, Endocrinometabólica	Health Care	Public
Misión Barrio Adentro II	Health Care, Infrastructure	Club
Misión Barrio Adentro III	Health Care, Infrastructure	Club
Misión Robinson II	Education, Income Transfer	Club-Private
Plan Nacional de Modernización del Transporte Público	Financial Aid, Infrastructure, Organizational	Private-Public-Club
Programa Cultural para el Desarrollo Humano	Organizational, Financial Aid, Education, Recreational	Private-Club-Public
Programa de Economía e Industrias Culturales	Organizational, Education, Financial Aid	Club-Private
Programa de Fianzas Técnicas	Financial Aid, Organizational	Private
Programa de Financiamiento para el Desarrollo Agropecuario, Pesquero, Forestal y Afines	Financial Aid, Organizational	Private
Programa Hábitat y Desarrollo	Organizational, Infrastructure, Environmental	Public
Programa Nacional de Planificación Académica Universitaria	Organizational	Public
Programa Nacional de Políticas Estudiantiles Universitarias	Organizational, Financial Aid	Club
Programa Nacional de Rehabilitación Médica	Health Care, Organizational	Club
Programa Nacional Diálogo Social para la generación de un Nuevo Modelo Diversificado, Incluyente y Socio Productivo	Financial Aid, Organizational	Private-Club
Programa para la Democratización de las Organizaciones de Trabajadores	Organizational	Club
Programa para la Promoción de la Responsabilidad Sociolaboral de los Trabajadores	Organizational	Club

Programme	Purpose area	Economic Classification
Programa Patrimonio e Identidad Cultural	Recreational, Organizational, Financial Aid	Public-Club-Private
Regularización de la Tenencia de la Tierra	Organizational	Club
Sistema de Crédito por Ley de Política Habitacional	Financial Aid	Private
Venezuela Móvil	Financial Aid	Private
2006		
Misión Árbol	Environmental	Public
Misión Ciencia	Organizational, Education, R&D, Financial Aid	Club-Private
Misión Justicia	Organizational, Education	Club
Misión Madres del Barrio	Income Transfer	Private
Misión Negra Hipólita	Health Care, Education, Organizational, Infrastructure	Club
Misión Vuelvan Caras II	Organizational, Financial Aid, Infrastructure	Club-Private
Programa Avanzado de Capacitación para el Desarrollo Tecnologías de Negocios en la WEB	Organizational, Education	Club
Programa de Becas Gran Mariscal de Ayacucho	Education, Income Transfer	Club-Private

Purpose area is inferred from the formal description of the objectives of social programmes. Economic Classification refers to the type of goods produced by the social programme.
Source: Fundación Escuela de Gerencia Social and own.

Table 5.5   Classification of social programmes

	Purpose area	%
Organizational	70	65
Financial aid	37	34
Education	36	33
Health care	28	26
Infrastructure	23	21
Income transfer	13	12
Housing	11	10
Recreational	10	9
R&D	7	6
Food assistance	5	5
Environmental	4	4
Urbanism	4	4
Food security	3	3
National security	2	2
Identification	1	1
Nutritional care	1	1

	Economic classification	%
Club	72	67
Private	54	50
Public	40	37

Year	No. of social programmes	% of programmes per year
1999	17	16
2000	14	13
2001	3	3
2002	8	7
2003	20	19
2004	13	12
2005	25	23
2006	8	7
Total	108	100

Note: Purpose area is inferred from the formal description of the objectives of social programmes. Economic classification refers to the type of goods produced by a social programme. Categories according to Purpose area and Economic classification are not mutually exclusive: a social programme can satisfy several categories simultaneously.
Source: Table 5.4 and own calculations.

Table 5.6   Active labour market policies in Venezuela, 1999–2004

1. *Workfare programmes[†]*
   - Plan de Empleo Rápido: launched in late 1999.
   - Plan de Trabajo Ocasional: part of the Proyecto País, it was launched in 2001. Army units organize seasonal workfare programmes.
   - Plan Avispa: part of the Proyecto País, it was launched in mid-2001. Army units provide temporary jobs in the construction of housing for low income families.
   - Plan de Empleo Simón Rodríguez: launched in late 2001 by the Ministry of Labour.
   - Plan Juana La Avanzadora: launched in 2004 by PDVSA. It targets communities in the vicinity of petroleum facilities, providing temporary jobs in non-petroleum activities.

2. *Subsidies to private job creation*
   - Plan de Empleo Concertado: a nine-month programme launched in May 1999. The government would pay half of the salary of a new apprentice trough a corporate income tax credit.
   - Plan de Incentivo al Empleo: an 18-month programme launched in September 2002. The government would pay for new employees a percentage of the employer's social security.

3. *Support to small and micro enterprises*
   - Low interest lending through:
   - Banco del Pueblo Soberano (2000)
   - Banco de la Mujer (2001)
   - Fondo de Desarrollo Microfinanciero (2001)
   - Programa Monta tu Negocio (2003)
   - Programa Fábrica de Fábricas: launched in late 2003. The government would provide start-up capital and/or credit guarantees for small manufacturing plans in key sectors.
   - Programa Plan Zamora: launched in early 2002, later to become Misión Zamora. The government would provide land, credit and technical assistance to rural cooperatives.

4. *Job training programmes*
   - Plan Pescar 2000: part of the Proyecto País. Provides credit to small fishing enterprises.
   - Unidades Especiales de Reservistas para el Desarrollo Social: part of the Proyecto País, it was launched in mid-2001. Provides job training for unemployed members of the army reserve.
   - Misión Vuelvan Caras: launched in early 2004. It targets those graduating from Misión Róbinson and other educational 'misiones', combining job training with technical and financial assistance.

5. *Labour intermediation services*
   - Servicio Nacional de Empleo: part of the Ministry of Labour, it provides job placement services, mainly for those in the formal sector.

Note: † Does not include local funding through: Fondo Intergubernamental para la Descentralización (FIDES), Fondo de Inversión Social de Venezuela (FONVIS), Fondo Único Social (FUS), and Autoridad Única de Vargas.
Source: Compiled from databases.

In this sense, one could argue that rather than a continuous and increasing building up of social programmes, what has been observed is a sort of mutation process in which unsuccessful initiatives have been re-launched with operational variations and under different names. From Chávez's perspective, this practice might imply a learning process with a 'trial and error' dynamic. As already mentioned, we believe that the ability of Chávez to innovate in terms of social programmes without experiencing a significant reduction in his popularity reflects the very direct relationship he has cultivated with his constituency.

From the point of view of efficiency, the natural question that arises is why the rate of innovation in terms of policy initiatives has been so high during Chávez's administration. A possibility lies in asserting that, because of the nature of the political process, i.e. one dominated by non-cooperative relations between political actors, Chávez has preferred to assign the implementation of these programmes to loyal – rather than effective – agents. This has led to the design of several programmes that, not being fully developed, are lately substituted by better ones. This hypothesis would also be consistent with the high turnover rate of ministers observed during Chávez's administration.

A different hypothesis in terms of Kingdon's (1984) streams model of policy formulation is that it was only after 2003, and not before, that an opportunity window brought together the three different favourable streams required to make possible the implementation of a successful social programme: the problem, the policy and the political stream. Thus, Misión Barrio Adentro and Misión Robinson can be understood as suitable proposals in health care and education that, on the one hand, were both technically and financially feasible, and on the other hand, politicians found it advantageous to approve. In this case, the technical expertise was provided by the exchanges with Cuban specialists, while the financially favourable conditions were granted by greater government control over oil resources. At the political level, although in 2003 the government coalition held around half of the seats in the National Assembly, it was still able to control key committees to implement the Misión Barrio Adentro.[54]

5.5 Rent seeking and the government's provision of social goods

Economies dependent on the exploitation of natural resources, like that of Venezuela, have always been characterized by a relatively large public sector in which rent-seeking behaviour may arise. As a logical consequence of this premise, one of the political economy theses on the natural resource curse exploits the negative impact of rent-seeking behaviour on economic growth and development. In this section, we propose a definition of rent-seeking behaviour that intends to be closer to the practices observed in Venezuela. We also argue that the spreading of rent seeking might impair development because of the scarce and low quality production of social goods, especially in economies in which growth relies upon the state provision of goods.

5.5.1 A definition of rent seeking

In this chapter, we define rent seeking as the broad process – undertaken by private agents, but promoted by state intervention – that intends to secure the reception of a rent and to extract extraordinary private pecuniary returns by diverting resources from activities that are meant to produce social goods.

This definition, although inspired by the classical concepts provided in Tullock (1967, 1980) and Bhagwati and Srinivasan (1982), has several caveats that extend it and modify the accounting of the costs associated.

In the first place, we emphasize that the process of rent seeking can only exist when there is a discretional state intervention (say, the implementation or an announcement of a policy) that creates the incentives for private agents to initially, use resources to guarantee the appropriation of a rent, and latter, to appropriate extraordinary profits that otherwise would have been used to produce social goods and services. For example, the state property of oil determines the existence of an oil rent that can be allocated to society by producing goods, or in the form of transfers to their members. If the state allocated the oil rent through an announced rule (and assuming there is no time inconsistency), private agents would have no incentives to use resources to compete for this rent because there would be an assignment mechanism that ex-ante determines who the recipients are. However, because there are problems such as time inconsistency, lack of commitment to distributional rent rules, asymmetries of information or the impossibility of perfect monitoring of rent-rights, then rent seeking can arise.

The second important element of discussion refers to the description of the mechanisms by which private agents appropriate 'extraordinary pecuniary returns' originally destined for the production of social goods. For instance, to provide these goods, the government needs to acquire supplies or to hire specialized services produced by the private sector. This process usually takes place through the auction of government contracts, which hand in to private agents a sort of patent or exclusivity right in the provision of supplies and services that generates a monopolistic profit. However, to appropriate extraordinary returns, private agents would need to perceive profits higher than those of the technically efficient monopolist. We argue that these extra returns might be obtained by either of the following two actions: first, by arbitrarily reducing the quality of the supplies and services provided; or secondly, by charging an extremely high price for such supplies and services, which ultimately the government is willing to accept.[55] In the limit, the rent seeker might appropriate the complete value of the good as a private profit, if he does not fulfil his contract with the government and does not deliver the good he was paid for. There is also an extraordinary private appropriation of pecuniary returns when subsidies, income or lump sum government transfers are assigned to individuals that do not employ these resources according to the intended policy objectives. For example, when a government assigns a subsidy – in other words, a financial compensation to induce the production of a particular good – if the good delivered does not conform to the standards of the policy, then part of the subsidy becomes a private appropriated rent.[56]

The relevant question is, then, which are the government incentives to allow rent seeking by the private sector.

5.5.2   Rent seeking and clientelism

We believe that the incentives for the government to allow rent seeking are basically found in the political arena. That is, a government might promote rent seeking discretionally as a way to favour particular individuals or social groups with the intention of receiving political support in exchange. This implicit contractual arrangement between the politician and the rent seeker is simply a form of 'clientelism' that arises in the process of oil rent allocation. There are basically two ways in which rent seeking occurs in association with clientelism. The first one is when the government acquires supplies or hires services from the private sector: the extraordinary pecuniary returns obtained by individuals providing such supplies and services could be regarded as the payment for political support. The second one is when, according to an electoral objective, the government assigns the oil rent through subsidies, income or lump sum transfers: the privately appropriated part of these resources could also be regarded as the payment to individuals for political support.[57] In these two mechanisms, the private agents might try to secure the reception of the rent either through lobbying activities or bribery, both of which grant to the state bureaucracy a portion of the assigned rent. However, we believe that the private sector is the one collecting the larger share of the oil rent by diverting resources meant to produce social goods.

Related to the above description, in the analysis of Chávez's educational 'misiones', Penfold-Becerra (2005) explains that such programmes could have been used as clientelistic instruments because cash transfers (scholarships) are allocated discretionally to participants and seem to be more common to geographic areas that have typically supported Chávez electorally. He also contends that individuals participating in the programmes might be potentially excluded, if the government does not receive the expected anticipated level of political support. One could generalize that when 'misiones' are uniquely used as clientelistic instruments, the gains (appropriated rent) of the clients are the scholarships provided by the social programme, while the fulfilment of the clientelistic contract is enforced by the fact that consumption of the social good (education) can be discretionally taken away (it has the excludability property[58]).

Following the excludability criterion, in our economic classification of social programmes between 1999 and 2006 (see Table 5.5), we observe that 67 per cent provide club goods and 50 per cent provide private goods, indicating that social programmes could indeed be used potentially as clientelistic instruments, since these types of goods are by definition excludable. In addition, 46 per cent of the programmes incorporate income transfers and/or diverse forms of financial aid, making these programmes possible candidates for the emergence of rent seeking and clientelism.

Another element that has led to signal the clientelistic potential of social programmes is their connection with political events (see Figure 5.5). In the first quarter of 1999, Chávez launched the Plan Bolívar 2000, the same year of the referendum and elections for the Constituent Assembly. In the fourth quarter of 1999, the government created the Fondo Único Social (FUS), and in the first quarter of 2000, began the construction of Bolivarian Schools. These two initiatives and the Plan Bolívar 2000 were the scenario for the Presidential and National Assembly elections in year 2000. During 2001 and 2002, years with no electoral events, the numbers of social programmes created were significantly lower than those in any other year (see Table 5.5 for more information). In the second quarter of 2003, Chávez started launching the 'misiones' jointly with an important publicizing campaign and significant efforts to delay the realization of the presidential referendum. The public emphasis in these programmes and the creation of important funds to finance social investments and programmes (FONDESPA in 2004 and FONDEN in 2005) conform the context of several electoral events: the presidential referendum, the elections for governors and majors, and the National Assembly elections.

The former ideas suggest that, although there is no evidence that social programmes are created solely for electoral purposes, we cannot disregard the hypothesis that such programmes could satisfy both objectives of redistribution of the oil rent towards more vulnerable groups and electoral objectives. This implies that while part of these social policies accumulate human, physical and social capital, which eventually increases economic productivity and development, another part can be used with clientelistic ends and affect development negatively. In the short run, these two effects are strongly intertwined, preventing making any type of forecast for the future economic performance.

5.5.3   Rent seeking and development

From the description of rent seeking provided it should be clear that social costs include not only the resources devoted by the private sector to attempting capture to a rent (through lobbying activities or bribery), but also the rent appropriated by the rent seeker while fulfilling his contract with the government or when receiving government subsidies and transfers in exchange for political support.

We claim that diverting resources into the pocket of the rent seeker is a social waste, since it brings about producing low quality or extremely few and expensive social goods, all of which precludes development and causes very low levels of social welfare.[59] This is because, in an oil economy such as the Venezuela's, the oil allocation decisions of the state are crucial in fostering private investment. In this sense, we are emphasizing that high levels of private appropriation of oil rent might be more important in explaining impaired development than is the behaviour of private capital investment itself.[60]

In a similar direction, Sáez and Zavarce (2005) provide a stylized model of growth for the Venezuelan economy in which the total productivity of factors diminishes when rent-seeking behaviour arises. Because the model's simulated GDP is relatively close to the observed path, they conclude that the data are not inconsistent with the hypothesis that rent-seeking behaviour might cause negative externalities that reduce economic growth. This association occurs as long as these externalities are sufficiently persistent in time.

It is important to stress that the connection through which rent-seeking behaviour leads to a poor state production of social goods, and therefore to less development in this paper, is different from other mechanisms pointed out by Bjorvatn and Selvick (2005) and Rodríguez (2004). In these two works, rent seeking and also corruption cause transferences from private agents to the government bureaucracy, leading instead to private capital underinvestment and, therefore, to less development.

In terms of concrete achievements in development, the statistical evidence is very limited. Looking at the country's poverty rate, there has been a steady improvement in living standards in terms of cash income over the past two years. As shown in Figure 5.6, the percentage of households living below the normative poverty line decreased steadily – from 42.8 per cent in early 1999 to 39.0 per cent in late 2001. This was followed by a sharp increase in poverty rates during 2002 and 2003 (up to 55.1 per cent in late 2003) and then a decrease during the following years, so that the percentage of households below the poverty line in late 2005 reached 37.9 per cent. A similar story can be drawn from the country's Human Development Index (Figure 5.7): an improvement during 1999–2001 is followed by a decline during 2002–03 and a rapid recovery in 2004–05.[61]

5.6   Final remarks

The available information about the impact of the current set of policies is scant, either because there has not been a systematic collection of results or, in most cases, because it is too early to see their full effect. Nevertheless, there are some medium-term outcomes that can be expected during the next three to five years, if such policies are actually producing their expected consequences.

First, if much of the social investment is actually devoted to productive activities rather than to clientelism and rent seeking, one should expect sustained levels of growth in the non-oil sector of the economy. Secondly, cooperatives and endogenous development zones should be able to consolidate their growth, and stay in business once the government subsidies are phased out. Thirdly, the spatial distribution of the country's economic activity should improve or, at least, traditionally marginalized regions should start receiving an increased proportion of the national budget in order to develop. Fourthly,

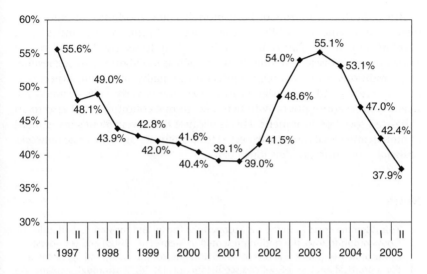

Figure 5.6   Percentage of Venezuelan households under the poverty line
Source: Venezuelan National Statistics Institute (INE).

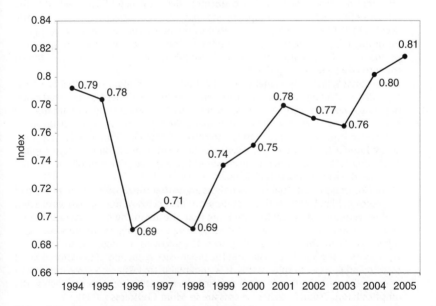

Figure 5.7   Venezuela's Human Development Index
Source: Venezuelan National Statistics Institute (INE).

health indicators, in terms of both mortality and morbidity, should show steady improvement. Specifically, the network of primary care clinics being developed by Misión Barrio Adentro should help to reduce the incidence of readily treatable diseases among the poor, such as food-borne diseases, respiratory conditions, and birth-related infections. Finally, one would expect that poverty rates – and, more significantly, extreme poverty rates – should fall steadily, in response not only to better economic conditions, but also to an enhanced social environment. This is because the government's investment in human and social capital is expected to strongly enhance informal networks of social protection not developed before.

Notes

1   This dilemma arises from the state property of the oil and the national oil industry.
2   Cooperation follows the notion presented in Stein *et al.* (2005) and is understood as the ability of political actors to reach and enforce intertemporal agreements.
3   For a political analysis of policies see Betancourt (1978). A thorough explanation of changes in the institutional framework for the oil industry during the period 1920–98 can be found in Monaldi (2001).
4   An evaluation of the nationalization process can be found in Mendoza-Potellá (2006).
5   Transfer prices were the formal (accounting) prices at which PDVSA sold oil to the refineries in which they had capital participation. These prices were discretionally decided by PDVSA, and could reduce its profits when set under international prices. According to Mommer, these overseas refineries never distributed the corresponding profits to the headquarters in Caracas, until 2001, when President Chávez forced them to (see Figures 5.2 and 5.3).
6   Operational Services Agreements (OSA) extract oil from marginal oilfields, which typically need a large operation investment. Companies under OSA received a pre-negotiated fee from PDVSA, were subject to regular non-oil taxes and did not pay royalty taxes. Strategic Association Agreements (SAA) upgrade heavy crude throughout the construction of highly capital intensive refineries in Venezuela. Projects were created under the figure of joint-ventures between domestic and foreign capital. According to their contract, projects should pay the regular non-oil income tax rate, but the royalty tax is contractually determined.
7   Mora-Contreras points that some analysts argue that the recovery of oil prices had its origins in March 1998 with a pact signed in Riad between representatives of Saudi Arabia, Venezuela and Mexico, implying that already in the pre-Chávez PDVSA a change in strategy was being considered. However, he stresses the importance of other events in the boost of oil prices: the recovery of demand in emergent economies of the Southeast Asia, and the progressive reduction of inventories faced by USA and Europe. In spite of this, it is undeniable that Chávez's government had a very active participation in implementing the new OPEC agreements, such as the oil price band. Details on these events are in Mora-Contreras (2004).
8   This policy represents indeed a return to the oil policy promoted by the first governments of democracy.
9   While the average Venezuelan oil price during the period 1989–1998 was $15.5 p/barrel, during 1999–2002 it was $21 p/barrel.

10 Using a simple simulation to compute profits per barrel of oil under the old and new tax structure, assuming different unit costs and oil prices per barrel, it can be shown that for a cost of $5 per barrel, prices as low as $12 per barrel would already produce a greater profit than the one that had been perceived under the old tax structure. Greater oil prices simply increase the benefit per barrel.

11 The clearest example of this new form of relationship is the fact that the current president of PDVSA (Rafael Ramírez) is also the Minister of Energy and Oil.

12 For 2005, the production of associations with foreign capital (OSA and SAA) represented almost 35 per cent of total domestic production.

13 Some analysts assert that this change is consistent with the current Hydrocarbons Law that reserves to the state the faculty of modifying tax rates if market conditions vary.

14 According to Luhnow and Córdoba (2006), Exxon, Total and Eni did not accept the conversion of OSA to Mixed Capital companies.

15 According to Luhnow and Córdoba (2006), Venezuela estimated reserves might be higher than Saudi Arabia's, if heavy crude is jointly accrued with conventional oil reserves.

16 FONDESPA, Fondo de Desarrollo Social del País, was created in 2004 and received the equivalent to 12 per cent of oil exports in 2005. This fund is intended to mainly finance social and capital investment projects. FONDEN, Fondo de Desarrollo Nacional, was created in 2005 with both, disbursements of PDVSA and a transfer from Central Bank's International Reserves. Its objective is to finance mainly capital investments. PDVSA's contribution to this fund in 2005 represented around 4 per cent of oil exports.

17 COPEI is a Christian socialist party and URD is a social democrat party originally formed around the figure of Jóvito Villalba.

18 It is important to mention that this political agreement excluded the communist party (PCV), which had a significant political representation at the time. After few years from its signature, the Punto Fijo Pact practices exclusively reduced to AD and COPEI.

19 The proportional representation rule allowed minority parties to gain access to Congress seats. Up to 1993, this rule was implemented through the use of a ballot in which there was a single vote for the two legislative chambers. Legislative representatives were chosen from 'single closed and blocked party lists', which gave party leaders a great deal of control over nominations and order of election of party members. For details of the characteristics of the electoral and institutional framework prevailing in Venezuela for the period 1958–2003, refer to Monaldi *et al.* (2004).

20 As the result of the strong anti-communist bias of the AD governments and the exclusion of the communist party from the political agreement, from the early 1960s until 1968, left-oriented guerrilla groups emerged. However, this episode seemed not to have influenced economic performance and ended with a pacification process that allowed the incorporation of these groups to the formal political practices through the creation of new parties.

21 It can be stated that the alternation in office of AD and COPEI was the reflection of the power sharing at all levels of political life, since parties' control permeated also unions and the judiciary power. Moreover, the support of the different important economic groups was also allocated among these two parties.

22 Monaldi *et al.* (2004) describe in detail how the nomination of Carlos Andres Perez as presidential candidate was the result of the confrontation between two factions of AD.

23 Decentralization consisted in the direct election of governors and mayors, the reform of the legislative electoral system from a 'proportional representation with closed lists' to a 'mixed' system, and a greater administrative independence for the regions. Decentralization was partially applied for the 1988 election and completed by the 1993 elections (Monaldi *et al.* 2004).

24 Simultaneously, in this 1993 election, the candidate Andrés Velázquez obtained an important share of votes by using a strong anti-party and anti-puntofijismo discourse.

25 The MVR was controlled by the MBR-200 (Movimiento Bolivariano Revolucionario) that incorporated diverse types of groups and personalities. The MBR-200, founded in 1994 by Chávez and others, was based on a civic–military alliance that included left-wing intellectuals, academics and ex-guerrilla activists. The creation of the MVR was rationalized as a mean to protect the MBR-200 from the obstacles of the electoral campaign and to separate the electoral activity from the ideological one (López-Maya 2003).

26 The fact that the Constituent Assembly was mostly dominated by the Chavismo did not ensure a unified programmatic thinking to re-write the Constitution. As indeed many people have pointed out, the Constituent Assembly represented, as well as the MVR, a collection of different views and conceptions whose only cohesive factor was the figure of Chávez.

27 Corrales specifically refers to the 'asymmetry of power' as the numerical difference between the representatives of the incumbent and the opposition forces.

28 Alvarez (2003) claims that this constitutional treatment to political parties is consistent with the concept of 'participative democracy' introduced in the 1999 Consitution, which has changed most of the political process of appointments in the 1961 Constitution. In a participative democracy, the 'people' are the protagonists of public decisions through mechanisms that do not involve the intermediation of political parties and that incentive the direct organization of citizens. Theoretically, appointments of important positions are implemented through the creation of 'Postulation Committees' conformed by citizens, which nominate potential candidates for the positions. Appointments are finally made by the National Assembly.

29 After the 1999 Constitution was written, in the third quarter of 2000, Chávez was ratified as President and a new National Assembly was elected.

30 Refer to Ellner (2003) for a detailed explanation of the transformations and struggles within the labour unions during the Chávez administration.

31 A polarizing action might also try to achieve a concrete objective (to approve a law for instance), but its characterization is based on its communicational strategy. Typically, a polarizing action goes along with a discourse that exploits some type of confrontation between groups.

32 In a newspaper of national circulation (*El Universal*), the number of articles regarding the Land Law is: 111 in 1999, 189 in 2000 and 536 in 2001, indicating that the major discussion in the public opinion occurred during 2001.

33 For more references on Bolivarian Circles, see García-Guadilla (2003).

34 Corrales (2005) documents that by the early 2003, the shares of Chavista seats at the National Assembly reached around 52.1 per cent (down from 65.5 per cent in 2000).

35 For years 2002 and 2003 economic growth was − 9.0 per cent and − 7.7 per cent respectively, while inflation reached rates of 31.2 per cent and 27.1 per cent (the highest of Chávez's administration).

36 Corrales (2005) states that, in July 2003, Chávez's support among low-income groups hovered around 39 per cent (down from 94 per cent at the beginning of his administration).

37 For the presidential referendum to take place, the opposition had to collect twice the number of signatures required by law (in the first and third quarters of 2003). Also, the process of validation of signatures by the Electoral National Council was a very long process subject to several public discussions.

38 More on this discussion is developed in the sections concerning social programmes, and rent seeking and clientelism.

39 For a discussion on the referendum results, see Lander (2004).

40 In the struggle between forces within the opposition, the ones promoting the 'no-participation' imposed their stand just the day before the elections, which implies that positions were strongly divided until the very last minute.

41 In the words of Corrales's (2005) narrative, these years could be described as the escalation of 'extremist acts of politics' by the incumbent.

42 However, an opposition leader (Felipe Mujica) claims that the military reserves have the objective of dissuading opposition groups. Both statements are taken from BBC news at the website 'BBC Mundo'.

43 Obtained from an official pamphlet: 'The Chronology of the Bolivarian Process'.

44 The word 'latifundio' refers to a large unproductive state that typically has its origin in the concentration of the ownership of land.

45 Corrales (2005) argues that the cause for the lack of a stable coalition is the wide variety of ideological groups within the opposition. The composition of the opposition has varied through time but its current heterogeneity includes: traditional parties (such as AD and COPEI), some left-oriented parties (such as MAS, la Causa R, Bandera Roja), emerging parties (such as Primero Justicia), ex-managers of PDVSA, and representatives of the Catholic Church, mass media, labour unions and economic groups related to the ruling parties during the Punto Fijo regime.

46 The clearest examples are found in the evolution of his social programmes, as will be discussed in the next section, and in the versatility of his political discourse.

47 One could speculate that the perception of Chávez supporters about Chávez is that, despite his leadership, he is a principal that does not have any control over his agents, and that such agents consistently deceive Chávez. Furthermore, the high turnover of Chávez ministries might be considered an event that reinforces the above.

48 What could happen is that voters captured by the Chavismo with polarizing actions would probably stick permanently to the Chavismo.

49 We loosely refer to social goods as all types of goods (public, club or private) delivered to society and financed through public funding that intend to improve social welfare explicitly by generating a reallocation of resources among society members. The reallocation process can take several forms, such as: subsidizing or transferring resources to more vulnerable groups, enhancing productive capabilities of individuals (investing in human capital), or simply providing public goods.

50 First, the Banco Industrial de Venezuela (BIV), and then the Banco de Desarrollo Económico y Social de Venezuela (BANDES).

51 Such as Banco del Pueblo, Banco de la Mujer, and Banco de las Fuerzas Armadas.

52 In 2005, FONDEN also received $6 billion from the international reserves held at the Central Bank of Venezuela.

53 Some preliminary studies show that the coverage of the educational 'misiones', i.e. Robinson I and II, Ribas, Sucre and Vuelvan Caras, fluctuates between 5 per cent and 8 per cent of the target population.

54 Although the 'misiones' were essentially an initiative of the executive branch, support in the National Assembly was crucial to increase the amount of oil revenues that were managed off the budget and to approve the bilateral agreement with Cuba to exchange oil for technical assistance. In addition, support from some municipal

governments in the Caracas' metropolitan area resulted instrumental in the implementation of the pilot project for Misión Barrio Adentro. Finally, the backing in the Supreme Court, allowed the government fending off the legal challenges that some professional associations introduced against the presence of Cuban doctors in the country.

55 Implicitly, we are assuming that the conditions of the bidding process are such that the state ends up paying higher prices than the monopoly prices. In particular, collusion of bidders, or a private bargaining process between some bidders and the bureaucrats in charge of the auctioning process might be alleged as possible mechanisms affecting auction prices.

56 Clearly, our definition of rent seeking is closely related to corruption, broadly defined as 'the misuse [by both public officials and private agents] of entrusted power for private gain' (Thomas and Meagher 2004). Nevertheless, corruption is a multidimensional phenomenon that implies violating, in some form or another, the 'rules of the game'. In our definition of rent seeking, we want to allow for instances where, although agents act within the law or social norms, part of the public resources are not being productively used according to the expected ends.

57 One could also argue that the contract between the politician and the rent seeker includes the understanding that not returning the adequate political favour may cause the retirement of the right to rent or any form of political retaliation.

58 An excludable good is one whose personal consumption can be avoided at a low cost, although the good is publicly available.

59 By definition, the positive utility that the rent seekers obtain is smaller than the losses borne by the rest of society.

60 Moreover, low levels of private investment might be the result of bad expectations about future growth, and not their cause.

61 According to Venezuela's National Nutrition Institute the country's average caloric intake for 2004 was 2,358 calories per day. This represents a 12.4 per cent increase over the 2002 figure, which is still barely above the minimum caloric intake of 2,200 calories per day set by the United Nations (FAO) for a tropical country like Venezuela.

References

Alvarado, N. (2004) 'Pobreza y Exclusión en Venezuela a la Luz de las Misiones Sociales'. *Fermentum*, 39, 181–232.

Álvarez, A. (2003) 'La Reforma del Estado Antes y Después de Chávez', in S. Ellner and D. Hellinger (eds), *La Política Venezolana en la Época de Chávez*. Caracas: Editorial Nueva Sociedad.

Betancourt, R. (1978) *Venezuela, Política y Petróleo*. Barcelona: Editorial Seix Barral.

Bhagwati, J. and T. Srinivasan (1982) 'The Welfare Consequences of Directly-Unproductive Profit Seeking Lobbying Activities: Prices versus Quantities Distortions'. *Journal of International Economics* 13, 33–44.

Bjorvatn, K. and K. Selvick (2005) 'Destructive Competition: Oil and Rent Seeking in Iran'. Mimeo.

Chávez, H. (2004) *El Nuevo Mapa Estratégico: Taller de Alto Nivel*. Transcript edited by Marta Harnecker. Caracas, November 12 and 13, 2004.

Corrales, J. (2003) 'Power Asymmetries and Post-Pact Stability: Revisiting and Updating the Venezuelan Case'. Amherst College. Mimeo.

Corrales J. (2005) 'In Search of a Theory of Polarization: Lessons from Venezuela , 1999–2005', *European Review of Latin American and Caribbean Studies* 79, 105–118.

Di John, J. (2005) 'The Political Economy of Anti-Politics and Social Polarisation in Venezuela, 1998–2004', Crisis States Research Centre. Working paper no. 76.

Ellner, S. (2003) 'El Sindicalismo frente al Desafío del Chavismo', in S. Ellner and D. Hellinger (eds), *La Política Venezolana en la Época de Chávez*. Caracas: Editorial Nueva Sociedad.

Ellner, S. and D. Hellinger (2003) 'Perspectiva Democrática y no Democrática del Chavismo', in S. Ellner and D. Hellinger (eds), *La Política Venezolana en la Época de Chávez*. Caracas: Editorial Nueva Sociedad.

Fuenmayor, J. (1979) *1928–1948: Veinte Años de Política*. Caracas: Editorial Migue Ángel García e Hijo.

García-Guadilla, M. (2003) 'Sociedad Civil: Institucionalización, Fragmentación, Autonomía', in S. Ellner and D. Hellinger (eds), *La Política Venezolana en la Época de Chávez*. Caracas: Editorial Nueva Sociedad.

Gutiérrez, A. (2005) 'Políticas Macroeconómicas que Impactan la Seguridad Alimentaria', *Anales Venezolanos de Nutrición*, 18(1), 18–30.

Hawkins, K. (2006) 'Dependent Civil Society: The Círculos Bolivarianos in Venezuela', *Latin American Research Review*, 41(1), 102–132.

Kingdon, J. (1984). *Agendas, Alternatives and Public Policies*. Boston, MA: Little, Brown & Co.

Krueger, A. (1974) 'The Political Economy of the Rent Seeking Society', *The American Economic Review*, 64(3), 291–303.

Lander, E. (2004) 'El Referéndum Revocatorio en Venezuela', *La Chronique des Amériques*, September, 28.

López-Maya, M. (2003) 'Hugo Chávez Frias, su Movimiento y Presidencia', in S. Ellner and D. Hellinger (eds), *La Política Venezolana en la Época de Chávez*. Caracas: Editorial Nueva Sociedad.

Machado, M. and N. Alvarado (2005) 'Marco General para una Estrategia de Superación de la Pobreza en Venezuela', *Revista Venezolana de Análisis de Coyuntura*, 11(2), 95–116.

Mendoza-Potellá, C. (2006) 'Vigencia del Nacionalismo Petrolero', Banco Central de Venezuela. Mimeo.

Mommer, B. (2003) 'Petróleo Subversivo', in S. Ellner and D. Hellinger (eds), *La Política Venezolana en la Época de Chávez*. Caracas: Editorial Nueva Sociedad.

Monaldi, F. (2001) 'Sunk Costs, Institutions and Commitment: Foreign Investment in the Venezuelan Oil Industry', Stanford University. Mimeo.

Monaldi, F., R. González, R. Obuchi, M. Penfold, and E. Zambrano (2004) 'Political Institutions, Policymaking Process, and Policy Outcomes in Venezuela', Latin American Research Network, IADB. Mimeo.

Mora-Contreras, J. (2004) 'Política Petrolera y Estado Rentista bajo el Gobierno de Hugo Chávez', Universidad de Los Andes. Mimeo.

Norden, D. (2003) 'La Democracia en Uniforme: Chávez y las Fuerzas Armadas', in S. Ellner and D. Hellinger (eds), *La Política Venezolana en la Época de Chávez*. Caracas: Editorial Nueva Sociedad.

Luhnow, D. and J. Córdoba (2006) 'Chávez Aprieta a las Petroleras Extranjeras, pero Estaría Lejos de Romper Relaciones', *The Wall Street Journal*, April.

Palacios, L., A. Puentes and F. Gómez (2005) 'Venezuela, Crecimiento y Petróleo', Banco Central de Venezuela. Mimeo.

Penfold-Becerra, M. (2005) 'Social Funds, Clientelism and Redistribution: Chávez's *Misiones* Programmes in Comparative Perspective', Instituto de Estudios Superiores de Administración (IESA). Mimeo.

Proyecto de Reglamento del Decreto con Fuerza de Ley Orgánica de Hidrocarburos.

Roberts, K. (2003) 'Polarización Social y Resurgimiento del Populismo en Venezuela', in S. Ellner and D. Hellinger (eds), *La Política Venezolana en la Época de Chávez*. Caracas: Editorial Nueva Sociedad.

Robinson, J., R. Torvik and T. Verdier (2006) 'Political Foundations of the Resource Curse', *Journal of Development Economics*, 79, 447–468.

Rodriguez, F. (2003) 'Las Consecuencias Económicas de la Revolución Bolivariana', *Revista Nueva Economía*, 19, 85–142.

Rodríguez, F. (2004) 'Inequality, Redistribution and Rent Seeking',. *Economics and Politics*, 16(3), 284–320.

Sáez, F. and H. Zavarce (2005) 'Growth and Rent Seeking Behavior'. Banco Central de Venezuela. Mimeo.

Shucksmith, M. (2000) 'Endogenous Development, Social Capital and Social Inclusion: Perspectives from Leaders in the UK', *Sociologia Ruralis*, 40(2), 208.

Stein, E., M. Tomassi, K. Echebarría, E. Lora and M. Payne (2005) 'The Politics of Policies. Economic and Social Progress in Latin America: 2006 Report'. Washington, DC: Inter-American Development Bank.

Thomas, M. and P. Meagher (2004) 'A Corruption Primer: An Overview of Concepts in the Corruption Literature', IRIS Discussion Papers No. 04/03.

Tullock, G. (1967) 'The Welfare Costs of Tariffs, Monopolies and Theft', *Economic Inquiry* 5, 224–232.

Tullock, G. (1980) 'Efficient Rent Seeking', in J. Buchanan, R. Tollison and G. Tullock (eds), *Toward a Theory of the Rent Seeking Society*. College Station, TX: Texas A&M University Press.

6

Does Political Stability Matter?: The Economic Impact of Political Unrest in Ecuador

Guillaume Long
Institute for the Study of the Americas, University of London

Danilo Igliori
Department of Land Economy, University of Cambridge;
Department of Economics, University of São Paulo

Abstract

The theoretical and empirical economics literature suggests that political stability is crucial for growth and development. Ecuador is perhaps one of the most interesting countries in which to investigate this proposition. Since 1996 Ecuador has had six presidents, three coups and has experienced periods of dramatic political instability. However, it is not clear whether this situation has impacted substantially on the country's economic structure and performance. This paper attempts to assess and discuss the channels connecting the political scene with the economic reality in Ecuador by confronting the arguments put forward by recent research on political economy with the evolution of economic indicators and the respective contemporary political events.

Keywords: Political economy, Political instability, Latin America, Ecuador

JEL Classification: O10, O43, O54, P16

6.1 Introduction

The connections between the political and economic dimensions of society have been a subject of ongoing debate. John Stuart Mill, in his well-known methodological article, defined Political Economy as 'not the science of speculative politics, but a branch of this science' (Mill 1844)[1]. But the case for the indivisibility and concurrent nature of political and economic development has not been free of controversies. General equilibrium theory ignores the connections between political and economic systems and, until recently, political factors have had minimal impact in formal modelling developed by mainstream economics authors. However, in the last few decades, there has been a surge of interest in politically motivated economic behaviour in economic theory. Krueger (1974) acknowledged that political constraints on economic activities were pervasive in market economies and Nordhaus (1975) developed a model where government decisions regarding inflation and unemployment were made within a political framework. Ever since, authors have greatly intensified their efforts towards merging economics and political science. On the one hand, voting mechanisms and the role of democracy have become central in explaining economic policies and their consequences. On the other, the principal–agent model has defended the relevance of incentive mechanisms in a world with self-interested politicians (for an early study see Romer and Rosenthal 1979; for surveys on political economics, see Person and Tabellini 2000 and Laffont 2001).

Within this analytical framework, many economists and political scientists have suggested that the mutual dependency between political and economic progress is particularly evident in the study of the stable or unstable character of polities. In particular, the theoretical and empirical literature suggests that political stability is crucial for growth and development.

It is this contention, applied to the case of politically unstable Ecuador, which is explored by this paper. Since 1996, Ecuador has had three elected presidents, three interim presidents, a president for a day and an overnight three-member presidential junta. In 1997, 2000 and 2005, there were popular uprisings followed by military-parliamentary coups, which successfully toppled, in turn, the presidencies of Abdalá Bucaram, Jamil Mahuad and Lucio Gutierrez. Since 1996, no elected president has successfully completed his term of office. Furthermore, a number of presidents have fled prosecution at home and sought asylum abroad, in the midst of large-scale corruption scandals. At present, two ex-presidents, one ex-vice president and a long list of ex-government ministers are fugitives from Ecuador's justice system. Until recently, three more ex-presidents were, under arrest (two in prison, one under house arrest). The consequence of this political instability has been the 'judicialization of politics', which came to its peak in the last few months of Gutierrez's presidency in 2005, when the country's High Courts were the stage of incessant battles and takeovers on behalf of Ecuador's main political parties, attempting to both protect their leaders from prosecution and unleash the judicial apparatus onto their political enemies. It is striking that since 1997, no president has been spared, whether momentarily or permanently, from trial, arrest or exile.

Ecuador therefore offers a useful case study of the linkages between political and economic instability. In order to qualify this relationship, this paper needs to examine whether political instability has hindered economic performance. If the correlation between political instability and economic outcomes is less important than mainstream political economy has advocated, then it will be necessary to account for why this is the case.

After this introduction we provide a definition of political instability and a framework for understanding its links with economic outcomes. We then turn our attention to Ecuador's recent history of political instability and economic collapse. This will be followed by an analysis of economic growth, and its relationship with political instability and other variables in Ecuador. Similarly, we look at the role of political instability in shaping investor confidence and foreign direct investment in Ecuador. Our main discussion will examine our findings by returning to our definition of political instability. Finally, we will explore reverse causality, the impact of economic crisis on political stability in Ecuador. We conclude by presenting some of the principal challenges we believe lie ahead.

This chapter suggests that:

1. In Ecuador, political instability has not hindered economic growth to the extent expected by mainstream political economic theorists. On the contrary, the figures we present show relatively little effect of the former over the latter.
2. In Ecuador, the impact of political instability on investor confidence and on foreign direct investment is lower than what mainstream political economic theorists would normally anticipate.
3. The reasons for this lie in the type of political instability in Ecuador. First, we argue that 'elite' rivalries have not materialized in shifting changes in economic policy from one Ecuadorian government to the next. Every administration in power from August 1996 to April 2005 has been committed to *limited, non-predatory* economic policies. Secondly, we argue that the kind of instability in Ecuador, which we define as *institutional political instability*, has not significantly shaken the structural foundations of society. This is a consequence of the gradual retreat of state institutions, the weakening of the rule of law and the rise, as a compensation measure, of paralegal channels of negotiation between individuals, including negotiation between the State and the various economic actors in Ecuador. These channels, the 'real rules of the game', transcend Ecuador's political instability and enable informal conciliation and agreement.

In other words, frequent changes of government may occur but they have not, as yet, resulted in fundamental systemic change. Neither have these transitions led to significant reforms potentially threatening investment. Actors may change, but agendas can remain the same. This has given the entrepreneurial class, both foreign and national, the security that, despite a convoluted political reality, Ecuador offers the right conditions for 'business-as-usual'.

Three further qualifications should be made at this point. The first wishes to avoid the construction of an undesirable syllogism. Recognising that growth is not necessarily affected by political instability, because of the retreat of the state and its institutions, does not equate with making growth conditional on the retreat of the state and its institutions. If the state becomes less important in framing economic outcomes, then it is natural that what happens at its helm will bear less impact on the country's economic performance. It must be emphasized that we do not necessarily believe that *non-predatory* economic policies are a prerequisite for economic growth. Our argument is simply that political instability does not significantly affect growth, neither positively nor negatively, in the context of economic *laissez faire*. This note of caution does not apply to the links between *non-predatory* economic policies and Ecuador's financial risk factor, investor confidence and foreign direct investment, where the correlation is more straightforward.

Secondly, it is important to point to the data analysed in this chapter. We focus on the effects of political instability on economic growth and investor confidence and foreign direct investment. The impact of political instability on other economic factors is not explored in any depth. Nevertheless, we believe that these economic variables are particularly relevant in this context.

Lastly, we emphasize that the aim is not to downplay the negative effects of political instability on Ecuador, notably its impact on good governance, but merely to suggest that political instability is one of a long list of less important factors affecting the Ecuadorian economy. The data analysed below will suggest that the variables bearing the greatest and gravest consequences on the Ecuadorian economy are fundamentally linked to its export-led development model (as argued by Hentschel 1994; Acosta 2002; Correa 2004), and much less with its erratic political reality. Blame should therefore be assigned to the various factors responsible for bad economic outcomes in a hierarchical and proportionate manner, and the commonsensical assumptions about the ravages of political instability, when misleading, should be corrected. Indeed, we argue that attributing most economic misfortunes to 'political chaos', can be a highly deceptive scapegoat for what are more fundamental structural deficiencies in Ecuador's economic model.

6.2 Contending perspectives on political instability and economic development

6.2.1 Defining political stability

The first wave of academic essays on political instability (PI) attempted to define political instability by focussing on government longevity. This definition, however, is arguably insufficient as it equates greater amounts of government change, to higher levels of political instability regardless of the nature of the transitions. Alternative definitions and approaches were soon proposed. Feierbend and Feierbend (1966) explored violence, particularly aggression between political groups and actors or against the political system at large, as intrinsic characteristics of political instability. Lipset (1960) examined political stability in terms of political legitimacy and the respect of the constitutional order, regardless of longevity. Eventually, a more all-encompassing theoretical approach for political instability was born in what Hurwitz (1973) called a 'multifaceted societal attribute', which considered a wide range of factors and avoided the 'monomeasures' which, for Hurwitz, bring 'great precision in quantification' but are 'intuitively [less] acceptable' (p. 461). These included frequency, legitimacy, violence and effective decision making, but also gave importance to structural factors such as the need to have a resemblance between a polity's patterns of social authority and government.

Adopting a structural approach, Ake (1975) argued that political stability (PS) should be measured by the extent of 'regularity of political exchanges'. According to Ake (1975), PS occurs when 'members of society restrict themselves to the behaviour patterns that fall within the limits imposed by political role expectations' (p. 273). He saw the compatibility between 'law and custom' as an important element of political stability. As such, he argued that what typifies political stability in a specific polity and in a given time frame might well be a characteristic of political instability in a different setting. This is because different behaviour can be seen as either stabilizing or destabilizing depending on both the structural attributes of society and the period studied. Ake (1975) also distinguished *nonadaptive deviance*, defined as a political behavioural irregularity which remains throughout time, from *adaptive deviance*, an irregularity which through time 'becomes legitimate, modifying the system of political exchanges and the rules of the polity so that the next time it occurs it is no longer regarded as an irregularity, but as a regular pattern of political exchange' (p. 276). Following this argument, *coup d'états* or frequent changes of the executive of the state are not intrinsically or universally destabilising.

Using simple indicators of political stability/instability such as government longevity or constitutional/unconstitutional transitions certainly facilitates the establishment of mathematical models. These precise definitions lead to a highly quantifiable political instability. A polity is either stable or unstable, or can be graded on a scale of stability. Ake's broader and more complex definition is less quantifiable. It nevertheless remains more profound and clearly identifies the pitfalls of oversimplified concepts of political stability/ instability. We refer to the strictly political-institutional, government-centred definition as IPS/IPI (institutional political stability/instability) and to Ake's structural definition as SPS/SPI (structural political stability/instability).

6.2.2   Political instability and economic development

Lack of rigour in defining political stability/instability has not restrained political economists from engaging in the debate about its economic consequences. It seems reasonable to believe that wars, civil conflicts and high degrees of politically motivated violence are contrary to the provision of foundations for economic performance (although even this assumption has been challenged by Colombia's relatively successful economic record). However, the most recurrent recommendation takes the above argument to a more debatable step. This is perhaps best expressed by Holt and Turner (1966): 'one of the prerequisites of economic growth. . . is that government must maintain law, order and a modicum of security' (pp. 313–14). Admittedly, this argument has since gained in sophistication, but Holt and Turner's recommendation is still strongly imbedded in contemporary political economics.

Alesina *et al.* (1996) define political instability 'as the propensity of a change in the executive power, either by constitutional or unconstitutional means' (p. 205). Based on cross-country empirical evidence, Alesina *et al.* (1996) conclude that political instability reduces growth. Their results are particularly strong with regards to unconstitutional executive changes and less conclusive for the regular and frequent turnover of industrial democracies. Their argument relies on the links between political instability and political uncertainty 'which has negative effects on productive economic decisions such as investment and savings' (p. 190).

A similar argument is put forward by Darby *et al.* (1998) in their study of political instability in the context of the OECD. They conclude that even in the context of 'regular democracies' (where executive changes are regular and constitutional), political *uncertainty* rather than political instability hampers economic growth. Feng's (1997) study of the triangular relationship between democracy, political stability and economic growth also supports the above conclusions. His argument relies on the stabilising effect of democracy which 'provides a stable political environment', which in turn 'tends to have a positive effect on economic growth' (Feng 1997, p. 414).

Despite widespread agreement on the correlation outlined above, there is still some controversy with regards to attempts at generalizing them. Olson (1982), for example, warns that moderate instability can actually have positive effects on growth. Whilst recognising that beyond a certain threshold, instability is detrimental to economic growth, he also signals that consistently stable polities may lack the dynamism essential to growth. Others have questioned the causal relation between political instability and economic growth. In their work on political instability and economic growth in Mexico, Haber *et al.* (2001) insist on the importance of commitment to property rights, more crucial in their view than political stability. They distinguish *limited governments* ('governments that are bound by self-enforcing institutions to respect their own laws', pp. 1–2) from *predatory governments* (governments who 'levy high and arbitrary taxes, confiscate and redistribute property, and dramatically alter economic policies', p. 2).

Following this argument, we suggest that in Ecuador the *institutional political instability* (IPI) characteristic of a number of successive *limited* or *non-predatory* governments has not been the overarching cause of economic stagnation. The evidence discussed below allows us to speculate that IPI is of lesser importance than other variables in determining economic performance.

6.3   From incipient democracy to political chaos

After a prolonged period of military dictatorship, democratization was reintroduced in 1979. The newly democratically elected president, Jaime Roldós Aguilera, a young, charismatic social democrat from Guayaquil, certainly boasted unprecedented levels of popularity at the start of his mandate in 1980, but the economic panorama and renewed conflict with Peru reined in his goodwill. Roldós' premature death in a plane crash, which many have since doubted was accidental, resulted in Vice-President Osvaldo Hurtado, a young Christian Democrat and an academic, acquiring interim power. Under Hurtado, Ecuador was hit full blast by the debt crisis. It joined the group of nations negotiating with international creditors, and was forced to adopt, with increasing zeal, the recommendations of multilateral financial organizations. The 1982–83 *El Niño* floods were an additional hindrance to the economy. Under Hurtado, the transition from a developmentalist to a neo-liberal economic model was initiated.

Hurtado was followed by the more radical-conservative regime of León Febres Cordero (1984–88) and his Social Christian Party (PSC). Politically, Febres Cordero's rule was marred by constant squabbling and constitutional battles with Congress, a return to authoritarian practices, the appearance and subsequent defeat of a small guerrilla nucleus and two army rebellions. The second military mutiny successfully held Febres Cordero hostage to secure the release of the imprisoned actors of the first rebellion.

Rodrigo Borja's presidency (1988–92) was more moderate and conciliatory than that of his predecessor. It succeeded in securing a reasonable degree of macroeconomic stability, but failed to live up to the redistributive expectations associated with the social democratic credentials of the president and his party, the Democratic Left (ID). Social indicators deteriorated. Partly because of this, by the end of Borja's mandate a new group of actors had gained prominence on the domestic political arena: the indigenous movement, which in years to come would play a crucial role in the unfolding of political events in Ecuador.

Conservative Sixto Durán Ballén (1992–96) was the last elected Ecuadorian president to complete his mandate. Durán Ballén's administration was marked by the most ambitious privatization plan to date, a brief but successful war against Peru (the Cenepa Conflict), and a number of corruption scandals. Sixteen years of relatively orderly presidential succession had come to an end.

In 1996, Abdalá Bucaram was elected president, only to be toppled seven months into his mandate. Brother of Marta Bucaram de Roldós, the first lady who perished alongside her husband in the aviation tragedy of 1981, and nephew of populist leader and ex-mayor of Guayaquil Assad Bucaram, whose presidential ambitions the army had thwarted in 1972, Abdalá Bucaram had come to prominence when he was elected mayor of Guayaquil in the 1980s. He became famous for his dramatic escapes and theatrical returns to Ecuador, the first of which was orchestrated because of drug-trafficking charges made against him. After usurping his deceased brother in law's name for the creation of his party (the Ecuadorian Roldosist Party, PRE), Bucaram set up to run for the presidency, finally succeeding in his venture in 1996.

Rather than confront the elites on specific policy grounds, he relied on the use of cultural symbolism. For Bucaram, the oligarchy did not represent the nation. Rather, the 'poor' were presented as the true essence of Ecuadorian identity. To this strategy, Bucaram added a singular vein of vulgarity and obscenity as tools to ridicule his opponents. Under his presidency, Ecuador became the scene of a constant verbal battlefield, where Bucaram would imitate his opponents, mimicking their voices, often putting on an effeminate tone to delegitimize members of the technocratic classes. Perhaps the most noteworthy characteristic of the Bucaram administration was widespread corruption. In February 1997, after a national civic strike, demonstrations and roadblocks, Bucaram and his family finally fled the country.

The battle for succession raged between Vice-President Rosalía Arteaga and Fabián Alarcón, the president of Congress, and for a while it was unclear who was the actual president. Eventually Fabián Alarcón, backed by Congress, had the upper hand and took office as interim president, in the first of three military-parliamentary coups. Alarcón's presidency complied with the popular clamour for a Constituent Assembly, which effectively assembled in 1998, amended the Constitution, but failed to live up to the expectations of many Ecuadorians who yearned for profound political and institutional reforms.

The elections of 1998 saw the triumph of Jamil Mahuad, the mayor of Quito and Christian Democrat pupil and protégé of ex-President Osvaldo Hurtado. The technocratic rule of Jamil Mahuad sought to distance itself from the aggressive populism of coastal parties typical of Febres Cordero's PSC and Bucaram's PRE, as well as the shady wheeling and dealing political ruse of his predecessor, Fabián Alarcón. Mahuad's government also aligned itself to the orthodox economic policies of market liberalization and quickly became associated with endemic corruption. Under his government Ecuador experienced one of the most serious economic crises of the twentieth century.

When the Mahuad government was finally toppled in January 2000, Ecuador was in an economic shambles. With the worst real GDP decrease ever recorded (−7.3 per cent in *sucres*, −30 per cent in dollar terms), and the total collapse of the *sucre*, the year 1999 was regarded as a total disaster. In the background of the crisis, there were the *El Niño* floods, which decimated agricultural exports, cut off road networks and had repercussions both on food production and the people's vulnerability to infectious diseases. The gradual fall of oil prices, which reached an all-time low of close to $9/barrel in 1998 and only started a slow recuperation in 1999 (around $15/barrel), also crippled the Ecuadorian economy. Finally, the Asian crisis, with its global effect on Russia, then Brazil and Argentina, severely affected Ecuador's trade balance.

Ecuador's vulnerability to the international crisis was made worse by the deregulation and liberalization of financial markets initiated under the Durán Ballén presidency, which allowed Ecuadorian financial institutions to open off-shore agencies. This, it was argued, would stimulate foreign deposits and savings in Ecuadorian institutions, but it never materialized. Instead, deregulation led to Ecuadorian banks establishing dollar accounts and making important profits from the devaluation of the *sucre*, which in turn fomented the process of natural or *de facto* dollarization of the Ecuadorian economy, a stepping stone for the institutional dollarization of the economy decreed by Mahuad in early 2000.

If financial *laissez-faire* increased profits, it also unfortunately increased risks. When the banks finally crumbled, Mahuad came to their rescue. In 1998, the state bailed out *Solbanco, Banco de Préstamos, Filanbanco* and *Banco de Tungurahua*. In 1999, it salvaged *Filancorp, Finagro, Banco del Azuay, Banco del Occidente, Banco del Progreso, Bancomex, Crediticio, Bancounión, Banco Popular, Banco de la Previsora* and *Banco del Pacífico* (Acosta 2002, pp. 213–14).

To prevent capital flight, Mahuad, with the backing of the DP and the PSC majority in Congress, enforced a 1 per cent tax on all domestic and international banking transactions, whilst simultaneously eradicating income tax. The result was an unprecedented speculative wave of capital flight before Congress ratified the new law. The Ecuadorian government then decreed the total freezing of all bank accounts and deposits in both *sucres* and dollars owned by individual citizens. This amounted to a total of $3.8 billion, most of which was eventually paid back, but with no regard to interest rates and the loss of purchasing power as a product of inflation and devaluation (Acosta 2002, p. 213). The result was a wave of panic amongst the population. The news started reporting frequent suicides, evidently linked to the confiscation of savings. Soon, Ecuadorians were once again protesting in the streets. The taxi drivers' strike and roadblocks and, over a longer time period, the tenacious resistance of the CONAIE (Ecuadorian Indigenous Confederation) proved particularly destabilizing for the regime. From March to July 1999, Ecuador was the scene of incessant paralyses, roadblocks, marches and strikes. Meanwhile, the Ecuadorian currency continued its downward spiral. The annual average exchange rate of 5,438 *sucres*/dollar in 1998, went to 11,803 *sucres*/dollar in 1999 (Acosta 2002, p. 356), reaching 30,000 *sucres*/dollar in early 2000, before dollarization fixed it at 25,000 *sucres*/ dollar, in so doing greatly impoverishing the holders of accounts in *sucres* and debtors in dollars.

Over Christmas and New Year 1999–2000, the main indigenous organization, CONAIE, and its members migrated in huge numbers from their native villages and occupied the parks, plazas and public spaces of Quito. On the morning of 21 January 2000, troops led by Colonel Lucio Gutierrez and Colonel Mauricio Cobo, opened the doors of Congress to the indigenous masses camped outside who proceeded to occupy it. From inside the parliament building, they declared the formation of a popular government and read a ten-point communiqué to the nation. Mahuad, who initially refused to step down, lost the support of the generals of the Armed Forces' High Command, and fled. The same generals invited the rebel colonels for talks in the presidential palace. On the night of the 21st/22nd, a triumvirate was formed. Lucio Gutierrez, unacceptable to the generals because of his rank, was dropped. Instead, General Carlos Mendoza, CONAIE president Antonio Vargas and Guayaquil lawyer and politician Carlos Solórzano assumed full powers. Within hours, Mendoza dissolved the junta and the mid-ranking military actors of the coup, including Gutierrez, were arrested. Mahuad's vice-president, Gustavo Noboa Bejarano, was sworn in as interim president.

Noboa ratified the dollarization process and accelerated structural reform. A main focus of his administration was privatization since, it was argued, Ecuador trailed behind other Latin American nations in this regard. Claims that if Ecuador had privatized less than some of its neighbours it was because in Ecuador there were no big state-owned companies in the first place (unlike Chile, Mexico, Bolivia, Peru, etc.) were ignored by the Noboa administration. The Ecuadorian economy started recovering by itself, in exactly the same way it would have, had Mahuad remained in power. The gradual rise in oil prices during the remaining two years of Noboa's interim presidential term and the stabilisation of the global crisis, avoided a worsening of macro-economic conditions. Cyclical exogenous factors and not Ecuadorian government policies contributed to economic stabilisation if not to prosperity.

Lucio Gutierrez was elected to the presidency in 2002. Granted an amnesty by Noboa after the coup, Gutierrez created a party (the Patriotic Society Party-21st of January) and was elected with the support of the indigenous movement CONAIE, its political wing Movimiento Pachakútik, and a number of minor left-wing parties and social movements. Gutierrez was of the generation of officers who had earned the respect of civil society for their victory in the Cenepa Conflict against Peru (1995), whilst some of the higher-ranking officers enriched themselves personally through the illegal sale of weapons (mainly to Argentina). In addition, Gutierrez pretended to be an Ecuadorian emulation of the radical-nationalist military leaders of other Latin American countries, such as Velasco Alvarado and Torrijos, and more resolutely of Hugo Chávez, even if from the outset it was obvious that he demonstrated few of Chávez's rhetorical or political skills, and lacked both his charisma and popularity. Many on the Left were never convinced by Gutierrez's ideological credentials and sided with candidate León Roldós instead.

By July 2003, Gutierrez had secured friendly ties with the ultra-conservative PSC and its traditional and ageing leader León Febres Cordero and had steered the government's economic policy towards orthodoxy. The result was the indigenous leadership's resignation *en masse* from the ministries they had been attributed for their role in Gutierrez's presidential victory. Support for his administration soon plummeted as voters felt betrayed by his campaign promises. Corporatist nepotism and corruption rocketed. Gutierrez's friends and family, many with insufficient experience and/or qualifications, were positioned in the highest echelons of Ecuadorian public and private enterprises. In many ways, the Gutierrez administration reproduced the criminal practices of the Bucaram administration. Differences between the two kleptocratic regimes were essentially regional and cultural. Instead of encouraging the typically extrovert and exhibitionist coastal corruption, Gutierrez and his entourage empowered a markedly Andean and Amazonian cultural hybrid of the same practices, more entrenched in state institutions, in Quito's bureaucracy, as well as the police and the Armed Forces.

Nevertheless, the weakness of his party made him reliant on makeshift alliances with the different political forces in Congress. First allied to Pachakútik and the Left, then for a much longer spell with the conservative PSC, Gutierrez's luck ran out when he finally faced the possibility of congressional impeachment. In order to survive the attempt, he courted the PRE, steered by Bucaram from his exile in Panama, and the PRIAN, the party of banana magnate Alvaro Noboa. In order to gain their support, Gutierrez decided to assault the high courts of justice, traditionally dominated by judges sympathetic to the mainstream PSC and ID. Ecuador's judicial system was certainly in need of urgent reform. Unfortunately, Gutierrez decided to replace the hegemony of the PSC and ID by another hegemonic system, dominated by Alvaro Noboa and Abdalá Bucaram. (For more on the judicial crisis, see de la Torre, 2006.)

The courts were dissolved with no real attempt to disguise the *coup d'état* with pseudo-constitutional jargon. A close ally of Bucaram was appointed president of the Supreme Court and the long list of charges against Bucaram for corruption and embezzlement of public funds were immediately annulled. Within a few days, Abdalá Bucaram was able to stage one of his many theatrical comebacks. The return of an ever more arrogant Bucaram, eight years after his popular overthrow, was difficult for many Ecuadorians to accept. The middle classes in Quito, which had played an important role in the 1997 uprising, erupted in a spontaneous burst of anger against all symbols of executive, legislative and judicial power. Demonstrations started anew. On 20 April 2005, after a night of battles of stones against tear gas, with one foreign victim, Gutierrez further aggravated the anger of Quito's inhabitants by transporting buses of personal supporters from lowland villages to come to the city in order to disrupt the marches. As a result, even more people took to the streets. After some gunfire from the windows of the Ministry of Social Welfare, the Military High Command finally withdrew its support from the president. Within minutes, Congress had sworn in Vice-President Alfredo Palacio.

However, this time demonstrators expressed their dissatisfaction with the political transition. Saturated with the same congressional dance of replacing presidents by their second in command, thousands of people demanded the revocation of the mandates of all congressmen and -women and the creation of a Constituent Assembly. Quickly, congress was stormed by the populace. Many MPs were forced to resign. Alfredo Palacio himself was unable to leave the premises and was kept under popular siege for several hours. The slogan *que se vayan todos* ('away with all of them') echoed throughout Quito. After publicly promising to call for a Constituent Assembly and not to let the *forajidos* down (the name adopted by the demonstrators of April 2005), Palacio was finally allowed to leave the premises. However, the Constituent Assembly has not yet materialized

After a promising start, Alfredo Palacio disappointed the *forajidos* by not pressing on with his promised reforms. His government steered away from orthodox economic policies, but there has been no convincing effort at restructuring Ecuador's political or constitutional order and at fighting corruption. It is also true that the limited political mandate afforded to an interim regime limits the scope and ambition of potential reform. It is in this context that the November 2006 election of left-winger Rafael Correa, one of the standard bearers of the *forajidos*, is significant.

6.4   Political instability, exogenous factors and economic growth

The data presented here provide evidence that, despite the importance of a wide range of variables in determining Ecuador's economic growth, IPI does not feature amongst the most prominent ones. The data will demonstrate that IPI is outweighed by more determinant exogenous factors. Of particular significance on economic growth are: (1) the impact of natural disasters; (2) the impact of international financial crises/recessions; and (3) the impact of the international terms of trade and Ecuador's export revenues.

6.4.1   The absence of regional patterns linking stability to growth

Table 6.1 shows the number of years with negative GDP growth for a number of Latin American countries. For the period 1981–2003, Ecuador's has significantly fewer years of negative growth (seven years) than many other more stable Latin American countries, and less than the Latin American average of 8.5 years. These figures show no pattern relating growth with instability. Bolivia, for example, a highly unstable country (a coup in 1981, transition to military rule in 1983, flight of president in 2003, resignation of president in 2005), shares the same number of years of negative growth (ten) with Brazil, a relatively stable country (transition to democracy in 1985 and impeachment of president for corruption in 1992). Both Mexico and Uruguay, stable countries from 1981 to 2003, have more years of negative growth (nine years) than Ecuador. Colombia with no irregular government change over this period, but in the throws of a civil war and large portions of territory not directly controlled by the central government, shows the same number of years of negative growth as Ecuador (seven years). Costa Rica, heralded by

Table 6.1 Number of years with negative growth rates
in various Latin American countries

	Number of years with negative growth rates	
	1960–1980	*1981–2003*
Argentina	6	11
Bolivia	4	10
Brazil	3	10
Chile	6	3
Colombia	0	7
Costa Rica	2	8
Dominican Republic	4	5
Ecuador	3	7
Mexico	0	9
Peru	5	10
Uruguay	6	9
Venezuela	7	13
Average	**3.8**	**8.5**

Source: Solimano (2005), p. 10.

the international community as a model of political stability in Latin
America, shows more years of negative growth (eight years).

A number of countries that have been through more instability during
1960–81 than over the period 1981–2003 nevertheless show fewer years of
negative growth in the former. This is clearly the case for Argentina, Brazil,
Bolivia, the Dominican Republic, Ecuador, Peru and Uruguay. Venezuela is
the only country which may fit the pattern of a correlation between stability
and growth (no coups from 1960 to 1981, but two unsuccessful coups in 1992,
the impeachment of the president in 1993 and an unsuccessful coup in 2002).
On the other hand, Venezuela's high dependence on oil revenues would suggest that the real reason for its high number of years with negative growth from
1981 to 2003 lies in the drop of international oil prices from 1981 onwards.

Figure 6.1 shows the average annual GDP growth rate of several Latin
American countries for 1997–2005, a period that was marked in Ecuador by
acute IPI. Ecuador is just above the average Latin American annual GDP
growth rate.

Both extremes on this graph seem to confirm the hypothesis of a correlation between political stability and economic growth. Chile's high growth
matches its very stable nature, and Haiti's political collapse corresponds to
negative economic growth. But Argentina's relatively high growth does not
coincide with political stability, whilst Brazil and Mexico, politically stable
during this period, exhibit poor growth rates.

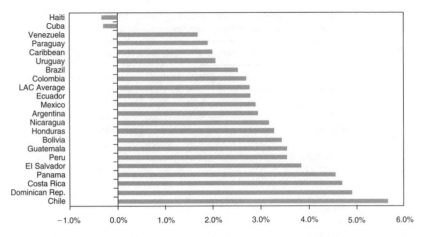

Figure 6.1   Average growth rates of Latin American countries, 1997–2005
Source: Solimano (2005), p. 6.

6.4.2   The absence of patterns linking stability and growth in Ecuador

Table 6.2 presents data compiled by Weisbrot *et al.* (2006) in their calculation of the percentage of real per capita GDP growth in Ecuador. Their figures show a marked difference between the high growth over the period 1960–1980 and the negative growth during 1980–2000.

The 1960s were nevertheless institutionally unstable. The 1970s were relatively stable, if not democratic (the military ruled from 1972 to 1979). The 1960s and 1970s were marked by bouts of authoritarian rule, both military and civilian. The 1980s, on the other hand, were relatively stable and the 1990s chronically unstable. Both the 1980s and the 1990s showed a high degree of commitment to some procedural form of representative democracy. This graph thus shows that patterns based on the linking of economic growth with either political stability or representative democracy are difficult to sustain in the case of Ecuador.

6.4.3   The impact of natural disasters on economic growth

Figure 6.2 shows the evolution of GDP from 1966 to 2005. A close look at GDP growth over this period suggests that the impact of natural disasters on economic growth has been of prime importance. Three principal dips stand out from Figure 6.2. The first dip coincides with the 1982–83 *El Niño* phenomenon. The second dip coincides with the 1987 earthquake. Finally, the third dip coincides with the 1998–99 *El Niño* phenomenon.

The *El Niño* phenomenon is a warming of surface ocean waters and changes in atmospheric conditions in the eastern tropical Pacific. In

Table 6.2 Real per capita GDP growth (%) in Ecuador

	1960–1980	1980–2000	2000–2005
Real per capita GDP growth (%)	110	−14	8

Source: Weisbrot *et al.* (2006), p. 2.

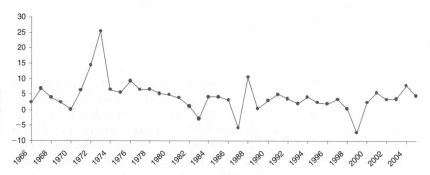

Figure 6.2 GDP growth (%), 1966–2005
Source: Banco Central del Ecuador.

Ecuador, it leads to intense rains, flooding and mudslides. Both the 1982–83 and the 1998–99 phenomena led to important disruptions in agricultural, infrastructure, road networks, bridges, housing (especially on river banks) and a rise in epidemics and public health emergencies. CEPAL estimated the costs of the 1998 *El Niño* phenomenon at $2.8 billion (Acosta 2002, p. 198). Weisbrot *et al.* (2006) have estimated the damage caused by the 1998 *El Niño* phenomenon to be as high as 13 per cent of GDP (p. 6). Similarly, the March 1987 earthquake was devastating for the Ecuadorian economy. Forty kilometres of the *Trans-Ecuadorian* oil pipeline were completely destroyed, causing oil output to be interrupted over a period of six months. 1987 was also marked by a particularly prolonged period of drought. None of the 'dips' in growth on Figure 6.2 coincide with the coup years of 1997, 2000, and 2005.

6.4.4 The impact of international financial crises on Ecuador's economic growth

In order to understand growth patterns in Ecuador it is crucial to consider the impact of international financial crises. Figure 6.2 shows that the decline in the growth rates of the early 1980s corresponds to the onset of the international and Latin American debt crisis, which Ecuador was particularly affected by. Table 6.3 is particularly illustrative of how Ecuadorian growth fits into the greater regional picture and the extent to which Ecuador's GDP growth has conformed to the regional trend.

Table 6.3   Real GDP per capita annual growth in comparative perspective: Ecuador and Latin America (percentages)

	1973–1980	1980–1989
Ecuador	3.3	−0.7
Latin America*	2.3	−0.6

Note: *Latin American countries included in this estimate are Argentina, Brazil, Colombia, Chile, Mexico and Venezuela.
Source: Acosta (2002), p. 382.

The increase in the price of oil from $3.83 per barrel in 1973 to $13.4 per barrel in 1974 facilitated Ecuador's access to abundant credit lines in the international capital market in the 1970s. Ecuador's foreign debt leaped from $260.8 million in 1971 to $5.8 billion in 1981 (Acosta, 2005, pp. 121–2). It is in this context that the dramatic rise of interest rates in 1981 precipitated the Ecuadorian slump. By 1983, Ecuador's indebtedness became unmanageable and the economy came to a standstill.

As in 1983, the international financial crisis of 1997–1999 led to low, even negative, GDP growth in Ecuador. Weisbrot *et al.* (2006) have argued that Ecuador's crisis in 1999 was primarily a consequence of 'external factors', such as the impact of the Mexican 'Tequila Crisis' and the 'increase of US short term interest rates (from 3 to 6 per cent for 1994–1995)', so that Ecuador was forced to raise interest rates to 50 per cent (almost 30 per cent real interest rates) in order to keep its currency afloat (p. 5). This situation was later aggravated by the high financial costs of the Cenepa Conflict against Peru (1995) and the *El Niño* phenomenon (1998). The 1997 Asian crisis, which spread first to Russia, then to Brazil and Argentina, finally hit Ecuador in 1999. Ecuador faced an increase in debt interest costs, which rose from 4.2 per cent of GDP in 1998 to 7.1 per cent in 1999 (Weisbrot *et al.* 2006, p. 6).

6.4.5   The impact of exports and terms of trade on Ecuador's economic growth

A common explanation for Ecuador's high growth rates in the 1970s and the low growth rates in both the 1980s and 1990s is that the 1970s coincided with the boom in oil prices. Accordingly, the poor growth rates of the 1980s–90s coincide with the decline in oil prices from 1981 onwards, and the total collapse of international oil prices in 1986. Hence, improvements in oil prices since 1999, and more decisively since 2002, have coincided with an overall improvement in GDP growth in the new millennium.

Table 6.4 illustrates Ecuador's export dependence on oil and traditional agriculture and fishing (bananas, cocoa, shrimp, coffee and tuna). It illustrates how events affecting Ecuador's agriculture make export earnings more

Table 6.4 Ecuador's exports per sector

Year	% of exports of oil and oil derivatives	% of exports of traditional agriculture and fishing	% of exports of non-traditionals and other	Total exports in '000 US$	GDP growth %	Background
1980	63.31	26.20	10.49	2,506,242	4.9	
1981	67.90	22.14	9.95	2,541,368	3.9	fall of price of oil
1982	68.25	22.98	8.76	2,237,416	1.2	
1983	74.25	22.32	3.43	2,225,646	−2.8	el niño phenomenon
1984	70.01	24.55	5.44	2,620,419	4.2	
1985	66.33	27.96	5.72	2,904,736	4.3	
1986	44.95	48.16	6.89	2,185,849	3.1	fall of price of oil
1987	37.61	53.76	8.63	1,929,194	−6.0	earthquake and drought
1988	44.53	46.26	9.21	2,193,501	10.5	
1989	48.75	43.21	8.05	2,353,883	0.3	
1990	52.07	41.10	6.83	2,724,134	3.0	
1991	40.40	51.94	7.66	2,851,012	5.0	
1992	43.38	46.38	10.25	3,101,526	3.6	
1993	40.99	42.19	16.82	3,065,615	2.0	
1994	33.96	48.09	17.96	3,842,682	4.3	
1995	34.92	45.56	19.51	4,380,707	2.3	
1996	35.89	41.30	22.81	4,872,648	2.0	
1997	29.58	48.73	21.69	5,264,364	3.4	Bucaram overthrow
1998	21.96	51.80	26.24	4,203,052	0.4	fall of price of oil + el niño
1999	33.24	40.78	25.97	4,451,087	7.3	
2000	49.58	26.43	24.00	4,926,627	2.3	Mahuad overthrow

Sources: Acosta (2002), pp. 361–3 and Banco Central del Ecuador.

dependent upon oil income. Likewise, events affecting Ecuador's oil income make export earnings highly dependent on agriculture. The rise of non-traditional exports from the mid-1990s onwards can be explained by the cut-flower export boom. When both oil and agricultural exports are affected by adverse effects, the result is an exports crisis. Clear examples of exports crises are 1983, 1987 and 1999, which have corresponded to negative growth. Here, the years particularly associated with IPI, such as 1997 and 2000, do not coincide with a reduction in export earnings.

6.4.6 Ecuador's vulnerability to external shock

Hentschel (1994) has argued that 'low trade elasticities on the import side' and 'an undiversified export base' are crucial to understanding Ecuador's poor economic growth. He explains much of Ecuador's growth crisis in the 1980s as a product of 'deteriorating terms of trade' (p. 15). Hentschel (1994) sees Ecuador's lack of economic diversification as crucial to under-standing Ecuador's vulnerability to external shock. Correa (2004) agrees and argues that Ecuador's unsatisfactory growth has been a product of its vulner-ability to external shocks. He identifies positive supply shocks (such as the reconstruction of the pipeline in 1988 after the 1987 earthquake) as the pri-mary stimulators of growth (10.5 per cent for 1988). Correspondingly, for Correa (2004), negative supply shocks have had dire consequences on growth (pp. 46–7). This illustrates a highly dependent economic structure where the changes in the political actors in government play a small part in determining growth.

6.5 Institutional political instability, investor confidence and foreign direct investment

One of the principal arguments for the debilitating impact of political instabil-ity on economic outcomes is linked to *uncertainty*, which creates an adverse climate for investment. In order to qualify this hypothesis in the case of Ecuador, it is necessary to investigate whether political instability has truly resulted in unstable, irregular or volatile economic policies. A brief overlook of past policies is thus necessary.

6.5.1 Economic policies, 1981–1996

From a macrohistorical perspective, Ecuador's economic policies reveal a grad-ual move from developmentalist economic policies in the late 1970s to the entrenchment of much more orthodox economic policies in the mid-1990s. Osvaldo Hurtado (1981–84) was the first Ecuadorian president to show any serious commitment to liberalizing the Ecuadorian economy. The first steps in Ecuador's adjustment process were aimed at the flexibilization of labour, cuts in public spending to curb inflation and the so-called *sucretización*, a mechanism by which private Ecuadorian debts held in dollars were converted into *sucres* (the local currency), whilst the state assumed the responsibility for paying foreign creditors in dollars. Its detractors called it the 'socialisation of private debt' (see Acosta 2002, p. 310). León Febres Cordero (1984–88) was elected on an ultra-liberal platform. However, despite a more aggressive, some might add neo-populist right-wing rhetoric, Febres Cordero's administration did little to intensify the structural adjustment programme undertaken by Hurtado. The *sucretización* initiated by Hurtado was continued and even extended. Similarly, the government allowed the flotation of currencies and interest rates, but the terrible 1987 earthquake which stopped oil production for almost half a year, reined in much of Febrers Cordero's ultra-liberal agenda. In addition, electoral incentives, corruption and mismanagement led to an increase in public spending in the period 1984–88. In January 1987, the right-wing Febres Cordero administration was even forced to default on debt servicing. His successor, Rodrigo Borja (1988–92), carried out what were regarded as 'symbolical payments' to show goodwill on resolving Ecuador's moratoria. Following liberal guidelines, left-of-centre President Borja signed the *ley de reforma arancelaria* (1990) which significantly reduced import duties. This was followed by the Maquila Law, which established the legality of free trade zones and furthered the legal framework for the flexibilisation of labour. Sixto Durán Ballén (1992–96), who was elected in 1992 on a conservative platform, accelerated the adjustment, which both Febres Cordero and Borja had failed or hesitated to hasten. After reducing inflation to 25 per cent, Durán Ballén then orchestrated a series of dramatic fuel price hikes and, as part of a negotiated loan agreement with the International Monetary Fund, proposed the privatization of a number of strategic state companies, including telecommunications, electricity and oil. Durán Ballén inaugurated the Macroeconomic Stabilization Plan and privatized the influential national cement companies *Cemento Nacional* and *Cemento Selva Alegre*. He also privatized the state sugar company AZTRA, the agricultural supplies, services and fertilizers company FERTISA and the state-run airline *Ecuatoriana de Aviación*. Political pressures meant that Durán Ballén was unable to fully privatize the state-run telecommunications company EMETEL and the electrical company INECEL. Instead 49 per cent of their shares were transferred to private hands. The oil sector was significantly reformed by the Oil Law of 1993, which regulated new participation contracts between the state and international oil consortiums. In 1995, Ecuador was officially integrated into the World Trade Organization. In many regards Durán Ballén's administration marked Ecuador's most ser-ious efforts to introduce structural reforms.

The period 1981 to 1996 was marked by a gradual shift from a state-centred approach to a more liberal approach based on the recommendations of the Washington Consensus. It is also important to recognise that during this period structural adjustment was not a linear, ongoing process. The period 1986–92 was marked by a high degree of stagnation in the pace of neo-liberal reforms.

6.5.2 Economic policies 1996–2005

Abdalá Bucaram, elected in 1996, presented himself as the candidate of the poor and constantly attacked the oligarchy. He was nonetheless a staunch defender of structural adjustment and economic *laissez-faire*. Bucaram's economic programme was based on monetary convertibility and pegging the Ecuadorian *sucre* to the US dollar. Lack of time, however, prevented Bucaram from carrying out his monetary plan or, indeed, any significant economic policy. He did, however, enforce a package of price hikes for public services, eliminated gas subsidies (before reinstating them a few days before his overthrow), raised petrol costs, and even implemented fees in previously free popular hospitals. Despite his rhetoric, Bucaram never endangered the structural reforms carried out by his predecessors, nor can he be described as having carried out *predatory* economic policies. His successor, interim president Fabián Alarcón, made no substantial amendments to Ecuador's economic status quo. Nevertheless a degree of compliance with the International Monetary Fund's orthodox recipes earned the Alarcón administration a new credit line. In 1998, Mahuad made bolder moves towards accelerating reforms aimed at enhancing fiscal discipline. He eliminated state subsidies for electrical consumption and state subsidies for natural gas consumption. Under Noboa, and greatly encouraged by the International Monetary Fund, the Congress' ratification of the *Trole 1* Law legalized dollarization and its corresponding monetary reforms. The *Trole* law also took specific measures for the further flexibilization of the labour market, allowed private consortiums to build pipelines and approved the *full* privatization of telecommunications and the production/distribution of electricity which Durán Ballén had failed to pass. Money continued to be channelled into *Filanbanco*, but no real efforts were made at recuperating the funds lent to the old owners or to big debtors of the banks now in the hands of the state. President Gutierrez was fortunate that rising oil prices enabled him to avoid much of the unpopular price hikes.

The period 1996–2005 shows no fundamental shift in economic policies. President Durán Ballén's adjustment laws were not reversed, and neither were privatized assets re-nationalized. The pace of the Mahuad reforms slowed down after the total collapse of the economy in 1999 and a number of banks were bailed out by the state, with the sole intention to re-privatize them in due course.

6.5.3 The importance of non-predatory economic policies on foreign direct investment and investor confidence

The above shows that recent Ecuadorian administrations have all followed what Haber *et al.* (2001) have called *limited*, non-*predatory* economic policies with regards to private property, and have all shown some degree of commitment to the Washington Consensus. Whilst some administrations have not accelerated structural reform with the same zeal as others, no Ecuadorian administration since 1981 has moved away from the hegemonic development model favoured by multilateral lenders. The reason for the stability of economic policies, despite rampant instability in the political arena, is that political instability in Ecuador has largely been a product of 'elite rivalries'. These 'elite rivalries' have fundamentally been over the control of Ecuador's national and sub-national institutions and have not put in question Ecuador's hegemonic development model. Pro-business *laissez-faire* has been Ecuador's economic trademark, regardless of whether neo-populist Abdalá Bucaram or technocratic Jamil Mahuad has been in power.

The servicing of the state's foreign debt is a good example of this phenomenon. Just as Ecuador is expected to respect private property, it is similarly held to account for its financial obligations and commitments. In this sense a *non-predatory* economic policy must include the imperatives of debt servicing.

Figure 6.3 appears to confirm the arguments of Alesina *et al.* (1996) and Darby *et al.* (1998) that political uncertainty creates a climate that is adverse to foreign direct investment. It illustrates the high level of financial risk assigned to Ecuador at the time of the collapse of its financial system in 1998–2000. However, Figure 6.3 also shows that by 2002, Ecuador's financial risk factor had returned to normality: slightly higher than the Latin American average and lower than Brazil's.

The question is thus to account for the sudden normalization of Ecuador's financial risk factor from 2000 onwards, given the country's recent history of political instability. A closer look at Figure 6.3 demonstrates the importance of Ecuador's moratoria on the servicing of its foreign debt and its effect on its financial risk factor. The decision to dollarize, which was taken without consultation with the IMF (Fisher 2000), and the end of Ecuador's monetary devaluation did not reduce Ecuador's financial risk factor, although admittedly it may have played a role in the longer term. More surprising still is that the

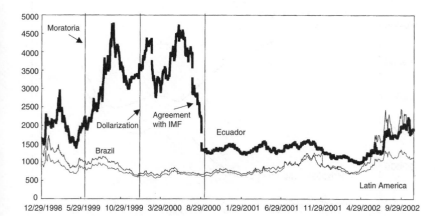

Figure 6.3   Ecuador's financial risk factor (December 1998–September 2002).
Sources: JP Morgan; Lopez-Calix (2003), p. 18.

coming to power of Gustavo Noboa, the subsequent decrease in political tensions, the disbanding of mass popular mobilizations, indeed, the return to a more 'normalized' or 'stable' political climate, failed to reduce Ecuador's financial risk factor. Only the agreement with the International Monetary Fund, which ended Ecuador's moratoria on debt servicing, was successful in significantly reducing its financial risk factor.

The first stage in solving Ecuador's moratoria was agreed with the IMF on 19 April 2000, in which a 12-month standby credit of $304 million was approved. Other multilateral lenders contributed another $600 million (Fisher 2000). Ecuador was, however, still in arrears to private holders of Brady and Eurobonds (with altogether a face value of $6.5 billion). Over the next few months, Ecuador negotiated a debt exchange with 97 per cent of all bondholders. By September 2000, Ecuador concluded its negotiation with Paris Club creditors and successfully deferred arrears and maturities due in 2000 (Fisher 2000). Figure 6.3 shows that from April 2000 to September 2000 there was a dramatic drop in Ecuador's financial risk factor.

What the financial risk factor ultimately shows is whether or not it is safe to invest in a country. Figure 6.3 illustrates that the real consideration in determining whether or not it is safe to invest in Ecuador, is whether the Ecuadorian state abides by its international agreements and pays its debts, much more than whether it is embroiled in bitter political infighting amongst its elites.

Figure 6.4 illustrates some of the transformations in the oil industry. It shows the decline of state exports and the rise of private exports of oil. The increase of private investment in oil exports is most significant from 1996

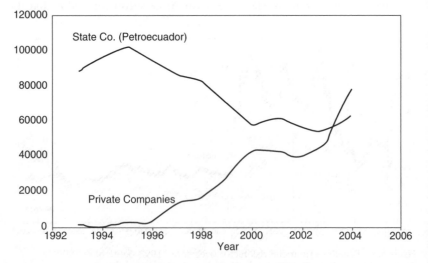

Figure 6.4   Oil exports by public and private sector (in 000s barrels)
Source: Larrea (2006), p. 67.

onwards – the year of Bucaram's election and the start of a period of acute IPI. This figure thus provides evidence which questions the assumption that IPI necessarily prevents foreign direct investment. It is also significant that the rise of private exports and the decline of state imports of oil coincide generally with the initial rise of oil prices. Accordingly, the 1998 collapse of world oil prices corresponds to a slow down in the growth of private oil exports. Similarly, the momentary decrease of international oil prices in 2001 matches the significant drop in the private exports of oil. This graph also encourages a hypothesis worth investigating: have the international oil prices played a greater role than Ecuador's IPI in fostering or undermining investor confidence?

6.5.4 The importance of 'predatory' economic policies: the case of the Palacio government and the 2006 election of Correa

The coming to power of Alfredo Palacio in 2005 frustrated some of the hopes of some of the more radical actors involved in Gutierrez's downfall. As his vice-president, Palacio had consistently criticized President Gutierrez for not fulfilling his electoral pledge and steering away from a left-of-centre economic agenda. Palacio's immediate nomination of a relatively unknown young radical economist, Rafael Correa, suggested a strong commitment to a more heterodox running of the Ecuadorian economy. This was the first time since the debt crisis in the early 1980s that Ecuador had a Minister of Economy who openly questioned the precepts of the neo-liberal agenda.

Correa lasted less than four months in the government, before business, congressional and US pressures forced his exit from the Ministry of Economy. During this time, however, Correa successfully mobilized a part of the population against a free trade agreement with the United States, warning against possible repercussions on Ecuador's agricultural sector. He openly criticized the World Bank and International Monetary Fund and defended a greater participation of the state in the oil industry. He successfully eliminated the FEIREP, an Oil Stabilization Fund, 70 per cent of which went towards debt servicing (see Weisbrot *et al.* 2006, p. 5), which Correa saw as artificially bolstering the value of Ecuadorian bonds and channelling money away from more pressing social needs (for more on Correa's critique of the FEIREP, see Correa 2005). In addition, Correa sought closer relations with Venezuela, whose government offered to refine Ecuadorian oil at cost prices. Whilst Ecuador has been an important exporter of crude, it is also an importer of many oil derivatives, which Correa has denounced as one of the reasons why Ecuador has not been able to fully benefit from the rise in the international price of oil. The deal with Venezuela, which was afforded strong political 'integrationist' connotations, both in Quito and Caracas, was aimed at curbing Ecuador's dependency on US imports whilst Ecuador constructed its own refinery. Correa was replaced before the agreement was sealed.

Table 6.5 shows the annual quantity of foreign direct investment in the context of political and economic events in Ecuador. It is clear that the 1997

Table 6.5   The impact of political and economic events on foreign direct investment, (1990–2005)

Year	Political events	Economic events	Foreign direct investment ($US million)
1990			126.18
1991			160.14
1992	Durán Ballén elected	Oil Law opens sector to foreign investment. Wave of privatizations.	177.90
1993			469.17
1994			530.81
1995	War with Peru.		469.98
1996	Bucaram elected		491.42
1997	Fall of Bucaram. Alarcón becomes interim president.	Law of Promotion and Guarantees for Investment. Free circulation of dollars.	695.42
1998	Mahuad elected	Elimination of state subsidies. Alignment with IMF and Washington Consensus. Economic and financial collapse. 1997–98	831.11
1999		Asian crisis, El Niño climatic phenomenon and drop in oil prices.	635.88
2000	Fall of Mahuad. Noboa becomes interim President	Dollarisation. Gradual rise in oil prices. End of Asian Crisis. Agreement with IMF.	720.00
2001		New wave of privatisations. Oil contracts.	1009.62
2002	Gutierrez elected		1121.74
2003		Gutierrez steers away from radical nationalist discourse towards economic orthodoxy.	1218.69
2004	Fall of Gutierrez. Palacio becomes interim president.	Rise of oil prices.	1351.90
2005		Correa named minister of economy. Height of EnCana and Oxy tax disputes. Possible oil deal with Venezuela. Free Trade Agreement negotiations with US under threat.	839.22

Source: World Bank and Banco Central del Ecuador.

uprising and coup, which was followed by *limited* economic policies, does not coincide with a reduction in foreign direct investment in Ecuador. The same can be said of the 2000 uprising and coup. However, 2005 is marked by a sudden drop in foreign direct investment in Ecuador. The question is whether we attribute this drop to the IPI surrounding the destitution of Gutierrez or whether what the US government and others perceived as the *predatory* policies of the first few months of the Palacio administration, before Correa was sacked as Minister of the Economy, played a more important role in the reduction of foreign direct investment. In light of the absence of a drop in foreign direct investment in 1997 and 2000, we believe that investors' fears of Correa's policies were much more decisive in shaping the drop in foreign direct investment in Ecuador in 2005.

Another important break with the past under the Palacio government has been the escalation of tensions between the Ecuadorian State and a number of international oil companies in Ecuador. Of significant importance and gravity were the clashes between Ecuador, the US company Occidental Petroleum (Oxy) on the one hand, and the Canadian company EnCana on the other. Both companies claimed that under an agreement previously reached with Ecuador, they were owed VAT rebates on their crude oil exports. The SRI (Ecuador's tax authority) refused to pay, arguing that the 12 per cent rebate had already been settled at the time of the contracts for drilling. In 2002, the Ecuadorian courts defended the SRI's claim, rejecting EnCana's $70 million lawsuit (See Business News Americas, online version, 31 December 2002). Ecuador's victory was later ratified by international arbitration. EnCana refused to take the matter further and sold its assets in Ecuador to a Chinese consortium. Oxy, on the other hand, was more successful in defending its claim when an arbitration tribunal ruled in its favour (for details on the ruling see Franck 2005). Ecuador appealed but the ongoing dispute with Oxy soon revealed a number of irregularities on behalf of the multinational, which Ecuador was quickly able to capitalise on. It soon emerged that Oxy, Ecuador's biggest tax contributor, had violated Ecuador's Oil Law and the contract it had signed with the Ecuadorian State. First, Oxy had transferred 40 per cent of its rights and obligations to the Canadian company EnCana without previous authorization from the Ecuadorian Ministry of Energy and Mines. Second, Oxy had not fulfilled the minimum investments required by the contract. Finally, Oxy was late in its payments of the percentage of participation to the state and by August 2005 it owed more than 1.5 million barrels. To end the legal dispute, Oxy offered the Ecuadorian government $1 billion in overdue investments, disputed taxes and 'informal' compensation, which some Ecuadorian sectors described as little more than a sophisticated bribe (see Acosta 2005).

In May 2006, President Palacio finally decided to comply with the law by cancelling Oxy's operating contract. The US Trade Representative's Office condemned Ecuador: 'we are very disappointed with the decision of Ecuador, which appears to constitute a seizure of assets of a US company' (Neena

Table 6.6   The Emerging Markets Bond Index (EMBI)
and the 2006 Presidential Elections in Ecuador

Date	EMBI*
29 November 2006	595.00
28 November 2006	598.00
27 November 2006	*604.00*
24 November 2006	536.00
22 November 2006	528.00
21 November 2006	518.00
20 November 2006	525.00
17November 2006	531.00
16 November 2006	519.00
15 November 2006	508.00
14 November 2006	507.00
13 November 2006	500.00
10 November 2006	501.00
9 November 2006	498.00
8 November 2006	495.00
7 November 2006	495.00
6 November 2006	493.00
3 November 2006	498.00
2 November 2006	510.00
1 November 2006	523.00

Source: Banco Central del Ecuador.
Note: *The Emerging Markets Bond Index (EMBI) is an index
which reflects the changes in bond prices in foreign currency.

Moorjani, Spokeswoman for the US Trade Representative, as cited in BBC news, online 17 May 2006). Washington, in the midst of negotiating a free trade agreement with Quito, immediately cancelled all negotiations. The message bore no ambiguity as to the correlation of events or the nature of the blackmail: 'at this time no further [free-trade agreement] discussions are scheduled'. According to Washington, countries were expected to 'obey the rule of law, with respect to foreign investors' in order for negotiations regarding free trade to be fruitful (Moorjani, as cited in BBC news, online, 17 May 2006). It is thus clear that the US government viewed the Palacio government's policy towards Oxy as *predatory*. It is also clear that a policy does not necessarily have to be inherently *predatory* in order to be regarded as such by some governments or actors in the international business community.

The election of Rafael Correa to the presidency in November 2006 has been unsettling for international money lenders and investors. Correa's promise to increase state presence in the petroleum industry, negotiate the deferral of Ecuador's debt servicing and, more generally, to follow a more radical-nationalist economic policy, sent shockwaves through the international financial capitals of the world. Table 6.6 shows the fluctuations in Ecuador's risk level (EMBI) during the second round of presidential elections in 2006. As long as the opinion polls favoured right-wing candidate, banana magnate Alvaro Noboa, Ecuador's risk factor remained relatively low. However when, around 15 November, it emerged that Correa was rising in the polls, Ecuador's risk level rose sharply. It finally shot up upon the news of Correa's electoral victory on 27 November 2006.

It is clear from the above that the *non-predatory* policies associated to economic *laissez-faire* favour investor confidence and foreign direct investment. Correa's upcoming presidency (starting on 15 January 2007) may provide further evidence as to what effects greater state participation in the economy has on investor confidence and foreign direct investment.

6.6   The case for Ecuador's structural political stability

6.6.1   The role of corruption

In 2000, the UNDP declared Ecuador to be the most corrupt country in Latin America (Acosta 2002, p. 342). World Bank data indicate that Ecuador is still in the bottom quartile in Latin America for the 'rule of law' and the worst performer in Latin America in the 'control of corruption' (Seligson and Recanatini 2003, pp. 413–15). It is important to emphasize that corruption is not just a problem affecting specific administrations, but that it is deeply embedded and structurally rooted in Ecuador's political and institutional make-up. Indeed, high levels of sleaze have played a major role in every Ecuadorian government of the last decade. Sixto Durán Ballén's vice-president, Alberto Dahik, escaped from Ecuador's judicial system after his misuse of public funds in 1995. Bucaram's corruption reached unprecedented levels, eventually leading to his overthrow. Interim President Fabián Alarcón was jailed for six months on charges of misuse of public funds. Alarcón's Minister of Interior, César Verduga, fled the country because of accusations against him for misuse of public funds and documents. Mahuad is still fugitive from Ecuador's judiciary (but gives courses on ethics and politics across US universities, including Harvard). Gustavo Noboa was also accused of corruption, this time in the renegotiation of foreign debt. He claimed he was the victim of persecution on behalf of ex-President León Febres Cordero, and fled to the Dominican Republic. He returned to Ecuador, at the same time as Dahik and Bucaram, following the Gutierrez–Supreme Court amnesties of 2005. After the fall of Gutierrez, Noboa was put under house arrest until the charges against him were finally dropped. Gustavo Noboa's Minister of Economy, Carlos Julio Emanuel, also ran away from Ecuador after allegedly receiving bribes in exchange for ministerial money transfers to municipalities.

This level of corruption in the upper echelons of public office has understandably resulted in Ecuadorians' complete loss of faith in their politicians, representatives and institutions. Corruption resulted in people taking to the streets in 1997, 2000 and 2005 and ultimately in more IPI. It is also often argued that corruption, a major source of political instability and judicial insecurity, hinders investor confidence in Ecuador. It is clearly not our purpose to explore the extensive debate surrounding the economic consequences of corruption. It will be sufficient to note that there has been a general paradigmatic shift towards the current consensus, which stipulates that the costs of corruption significantly outweigh its benefits. Nye (1967) had identified a number of potential economic benefits of corruption, such as 'capital formation', 'cutting red tape' and promoting 'entrepreneurship and incentives' (p. 5), as well as highlighting many of its significant costs. More recent research (North 1990; Alesina *et al.* 1996; Kaufmann 1997; Mauro 1995, 1998; Persson and Tabellini 2000 and others) has argued against such benefits and suggested that the rent-seeking of public officials stands in the way of a country's economic performance. Using sources from the World Bank Institute Seligson and Recanatini's study of Ecuador (2003) suggest that companies see public sector corruption and the cost of bribes as the biggest obstacles to the development of their business (pp. 418–19). However, the same findings also identify taxes and regulatory costs amongst the least important concerns for the development of business (p. 417). In light of this, and using Nye's argument (1967), corrupt states may enable companies to cut through red tape bureaucracy and open doors that legal routes, state control and constitutional rigour might otherwise close to companies, and ultimately play the role of what is commonly called 'speed money'. Corruption may thus become an alternative, albeit uneven and unfair, form of taxation.

Within the scope of this analysis, the importance of corruption is strictly limited to an analysis of its role within the context of political instability. We do not seek to assess whether corruption either hinders or favours economic development in Ecuador, but merely whether corruption contributes to the establishment of a more stable polity. The fundamental dilemma is whether we can consider corruption as establishing alternative 'rules of the game' in the absence of a functioning political system. If corruption does materialize in new 'rules', then these in turn become associated to what Ake (1975) calls 'behaviour patterns that fall within ... role expectations' (p. 273). By becoming a regular pattern of exchange, corruption becomes 'custom' and therefore offers a safety valve for the regulation of investment, hence re-creating a degree of stability. It is easy to see, as some authors have argued (North 1990; Kaufmann 1997), how corruption can cause institutional weakening. However, if institutional collapse is already entrenched, if there is an absence of credible state institutions, if there is a context of acute IPI, corruption may play a stabilizing role for investment. The payment of a bribe may ensure it safeguards the interests of a business, in a context which otherwise would prove too chaotic to invest.

6.2   Decentralization or atomization?

Another important factor to understand contemporary Ecuador is the role increasingly played by decentralization, which, we believe, has exacerbated the retreat of the state and its institutional 'rules of the game'. Undoubtedly decentralization, when it is associated with good governance and participation, may have positive impacts on development, democratization and legitimate popular aspirations (on the positive impacts of decentralization in Latin America, see Tendler 1997, Abers 2000). Unfortunately, in Ecuador, decentralization has further contributed to institutional breakdown and the collapse of the rule of law. However, the reverse is also true, in a sort of vicious spiral. The collapse of the rule of law and the breakdown of the central state and its institutions has paradoxically fortified the popular clamour for decentralization. In Ecuador, the difficulties associated with decentralization are based on organizational and jurisdictional problems, which were never directly tackled by the 1998 legislation on decentralization. In recent years, for example, there has been a rise in the creation of illegal municipalities. Close to 80 per cent of Ecuador's 220 municipalities have less than the required 50,000 inhabitants, many of which have been artificially created for the purpose of receiving decentralization funds (Sánchez 2004a, p. 88; Ojeda 2004, p. 104; van Cott 2002, p. 62). Border conflicts between provinces and cantons have further aggravated tensions previously restrained by centralization. Ongoing conflict for the control of funds has resulted in never-ending feuding amongst regional political actors. The result is an ever-weaker state.

Paradoxically, whereas decentralization was, in part, aimed at curbing clientelistic ties with the central government, clientelism has instead gained in importance. Indeed, the importance of the political ambitions of sub-national elites has been a major force behind the drive towards a decentralized political framework. As a consequence, *caciquismo*, a term which refers to the preeminence of local strongmen, has become a crucial feature of contemporary Ecuador. Bustamante prefers the expression Mafia patriarchs and equates this model of political interaction to a corporatist system based on family ties, regional loyalties and sectoral allegiance (Bustamante 2005, pp. 12–14). The result of decentralization has been the atomization of society, the multiplication and fractioning of polities and the proliferation of local leaderships and patron–client relationships. The result is a weak, atomized but peaceful polity.

6.6.3   A Lockean State of Nature?

Bustamante (2005) argues that Ecuador is facing a virtual Lockean State of Nature. Unlike Hobbes, who equated State of Nature with state of war, Locke believed human beings could overcome what Hobbes perceived as their original individualism and self-regulate in the absence of a sovereign arbiter, in a state of 'uncertain peace' (Simmons 1989, p. 458). Locke believed conflict resolution could take place outside the premises of an effective political system because of the existence of a 'natural law' where 'moral' merged with 'legal' (Ashcraft 1968, p. 901). War was for Locke, unlike for Hobbes, only *one* of the many possible outcomes of a State of Nature.

Equating Locke's (1988[1698]) State of Nature with the absence of government is a common misconception. Locke saw a State of Nature wherever the government was either absent or illegitimate – that is, when the collective refused to submit voluntarily to the arbitration of the sovereign. The weakness, often absence and frequent illegitimacy of the Ecuadorian government's arbitration, in a context of lack of widespread political violence, certainly if Ecuador is compared to neighbouring Colombia, means that Bustamante's (2005) argument seems to fit Ecuador's peaceful, yet anarchic political reality. In Ecuador, the rise of lynching as a paralegal form of justice, the demand on behalf of indigenous groups for the acknowledgement of customary law in indigenous villages (see van Cott 2002), provide examples of the popular rejection of what is perceived as either an absent or an illegitimate sovereign.

Admittedly, Locke's useful, all-encompassing definition may be somewhat imprecise and prone to subjective interpretation. Since Locke's 'political system' is based on the people's *voluntary* submission to the law of the collective, one might argue that any kind of political mutiny, demonstration or non-parliamentary mechanism of resistance against the government implies that the polity in question fails to escape the boundaries of the State of Nature. Nevertheless, for theoretical purposes, Locke's definition is highly accommodating, since it helps explain how paralegal forms of conflict resolution arise as alternative solutions to the institutional rule of law. It is in this context that Ecuador fits the Lockean model. Whilst the Ecuadorian central state and its institutions recede, the state is less and less likely to be the primary arbiter for the people's exchanges and disputes. Ecuadorians thus move towards a State of Nature and 'remain so, till by their own Consents they make themselves Members of some Politick Society' (Locke, 1988[1698], p. 278). In practical terms, Locke's State of Nature helps us to understand Ecuadorians' effective day-to-day social, political and economic interactions. People do not resort to the judicial courts, if they can avoid it, because the winner of a case is likely to be one who provides the highest bribe.

Another aspect that seems to strengthen the Lockean analysis is the increasing role played by migrants' remittances in the livelihoods of Ecuadorians. By 2005, they had reached $1.8 billion per year (Diario Hoy, online version, 3 March 2006). The most recent wave of Ecuadorian migration, primarily to Spain and Italy, was a direct consequence of the 1998–1999 economic collapse. Table 6.7 illustrates the growth of remittances over this period and compares it to oil income, Ecuador's traditional money earner, a sector where the state, either through the direct exploitation of mines or through the collection of royalties, still plays an important role. It is striking that in 2001, the total amount of remittances distributed in Ecuador was

Table 6.7 Growth of remittances in the Ecuadorian economy, 1995–2000

Year	Oil exports (in US$ millions)	Remittances from migrants (in US$ millions)
1995	1,529.90	382.00
1996	1,748.70	505.00
1997	1,557.30	644.00
1998	922.90	794.00
1999	1,479.70	1,084.00
2000	2,442.40	1,330.00

Source: Acosta (2002), p. 377.

equivalent to three times the public spending of local government: both provincial and municipal governments (Sánchez 2004b, p. 56).

The economic importance of remittances, which are neither taxed nor regulated by Ecuador's central state, has further fragmented the precarious relationship between the state, 'the arbiter', and the collective. The Inter-American Development Bank has claimed that only 17 per cent of remittances sent to Ecuador are channelled through the banking system (Diario Hoy, online version, 3 March 2006). The economic importance of remittances seems to go hand in hand with Ecuador's increasing institutional vacuum.

6.6.4 Structural political stability and business-as-usual

Lockean paradigms in the analysis of Ecuador's political reality suggest two central questions. First, does the absence of rule of law, the existence of paralegal forms of conflict arbitration, and a weak state described above constitute structural political instability (SPI) in contemporary Ecuador? Secondly, has this situation affected economic performance? In what follows we suggest a possible way of addressing these questions.

After ten years of political turmoil, many uprisings, three successful coups and a succession of weak corrupt governments, Ecuadorians have come to expect the fall of presidents before the completion of their electoral mandate. During the last two uprisings and coups, there seemed to be no real surprise or nervousness amongst the population as to what changes a *coup d'état* would bring. The uprising and coup against Bucaram may have been a first since 1972. But the uprising and coup against Mahuad in January 2000 was seen as a mere repetition. Likewise, the 2005 uprising and *coup d'état* was perceived as a replication of the events of 1997 and 2000. The fact that Gutierrez had been the actor of the 2000 uprising became immaterial to many Ecuadorians who felt that if he too was incapable of being honest, he too had to go. Many Ecuadorians simply saw the 1997, 2000 and 2005 coups as fair punishments for presidents that had been elected on a platform and had not respected their election promises or had indulged in acts of corruption.

Furthermore, whereas the 1997 uprising was boisterous and difficult to miss, the calm surrounding the 2000 coup was disarming. At the same time that the Congress was being stormed by an indigenous-military alliance, a few blocks away, the streets of Quito seemed unaffected. The banks, shops and street vendors were still working as if nothing was happening. No deaths were reported either in the storming of Congress or during the evening's march to the presidential palace. The 2005 coup repeated a similar scenario. The level of violence, if higher than during the anti-Bucaram and anti-Mahuad uprisings, was still low compared with much of the political violence associated with irregular regime change in other Latin American contexts. In Ecuador, The successive *coups d'état* were therefore relatively smooth political transitions. Many Ecuadorians found out about the coup the next day and shrugged their shoulders at the news, as if the political transition had been obvious, expected and inevitable from the start.

The 1997 coup undoubtedly began a period of institutional political instability (IPI). However, the relatively peaceful nature of instability in a context of continued weakening of the central state meant that neither the 2000 nor the 2005 uprisings showed mounting signs of structural political instability (SPI). Rather, the 2000 and 2005 coups did not disturb Ecuador's structural political stability (SPS). From 1997 onwards, the political transition based on the modality of the *coup d'état* became an example of *adaptive deviance*, an irregularity which through time 'becomes legitimate, modifying the system of political exchanges and the rules of the polity so that the next time it occurs it is no longer regarded as an irregularity, but as a regular pattern of political exchange' (Ake, 1975, p. 276). Here, the economic dimension clearly mirrors the social dynamics. In Ecuador, the *coups d'état* did not disrupt any economic activity. The coups were often welcomed by the business elite, since they put an end to the threat posed by popular discontent. In reality, the transitions were so smooth that none of Ecuador's export activities were significantly affected.

6.7   Reverse causality: effects of economic performance on political instability

We have argued that political instability is an overrated tool to evaluate economic performance in Ecuador. But we have not yet considered the reverse – namely, what the effect of economic stagnation and instability might be on politics. Whereas Huntington (1968) explains political instability from an institution-centred analysis, and as resulting from the incapacity of a political system to meet the new popular demands which arise from the transition to modernity, the approaches of Cardoso and Faletto (1979) see political instability as a product of material and economic hardship and of path-dependent development. In principle, it is fairly straightforward to anticipate how economic stagnation may lead to IPI. Prosperity rarely goes hand in hand with revolution. Tables 6.8 and 6.9 show the evolution of poverty from 1995 to 2000. Poverty and extreme poverty more than doubled between 1995 and 2000. In addition, Figure 6.5 shows that income distribution has worsened as the Gini coefficient increased by 0.10, from 0.46 to 0.56 over a

Table 6.8 Evolution of poverty in Ecuador (absolute numbers and percentage)

Years	Poverty		Extreme Poverty	
	Millions	*Percentage*	*Millions*	*Percentage*
1995	3.9	34	2.1	12
2000	9.1	71	4.5	31

Source: Acosta (2002), p. 379.

Table 6.9 Richest vs poorest quintile of the population (percentages)

Year	Poorest 20% (%)	Richest 20% (%)
1990	4.60	52.0
1995	4.10	54.9
2000	2.46	61.2

Source: Acosta (2002), p. 379.

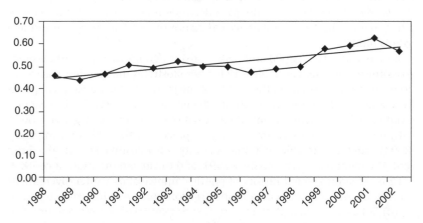

Figure 6.5 Evolution of Gini coefficient (1988–2002)
Source: Correa (2004), p. 33.

Table 6.10 Percentages of unemployment and underemployment, 1988–2002

Year	Unemployment (%)	Underemployment (%)
1988	6.5	45.5
1990	6.1	49.7
1992	8.9	47.8
1994	7.1	45.1
1996	10.4	43.3
1998	11.5	42.3
2000	9.0	60.4
2002	9.2	53.7

Source: Correa (2004), p. 91.

period of 14 years. Table 6.10 shows that both unemployment and underemployment have risen.

These figures support the view that worsening social indicators, related to poor economic performance, may be destabilizing and at the root of much political instability. However, based on this descriptive evidence we are not in a position to identify the actual mechanisms connecting economic performance with political instability. Therefore, we accept that the ultimate causality direction remains to be understood and deserves further investigation.

On the other hand, even this direct causal link between economic prosperity, social progress and political stability has its limitations. Indeed, Table 6.11 shows that a number of irregular regime changes have taken place against a backdrop of relative economic stability or in a setting where economic indicators were not immediate triggering factors of the unrest, even if they must be taken into account as core long-term causalities. Thus, whereas the 1925 *Revolución Juliana* clearly fits the path-dependent approach of political instability, neither the 1944 *Revolución Gloriosa* nor the 1972 military coup adhere to this model.

Similarly, the 1997, 2000 and 2005 uprisings/coups each present different economic circumstances. Table 6.12 further illustrates the manifest macroeconomic differences between the setting of the January 2000 uprising/coup and the conditions surrounding the April 2005 uprising/coup. While, the year preceding the 2000 uprising/coup (1999) was a year of dramatic negative growth with high inflation, by contrast, the year preceding the 2005 uprising/coup (2004) shows remarkable economic stability, with positive growth at 4.5 per cent, the highest growth rate since 1991, and the lowest inflation since 1972.

Thus, Ecuador's recent history of political upheaval may offer diverging or somewhat contradictory conclusions: (i) economic crisis has contributed to PI; (ii) PI has also taken place in a context of relative economic stability. The latter has also provided some renewed legitimacy to the theory of weak states and/or governments. According to this theory, certain governments may be

Table 6.11 Economic context and reasons for radical/irregular political transitions of 1925, 1944 and 1972

Date	Rebellion	Economic context	Reasons for collapse of ancien régime
1925	*Revolución Juliana*	Collapse of cocoa bonanza. Economic crisis.	Economic collapse and popular anger with plutocracy, opulence and corruption of banking elite.
1944	*Revolución Gloriosa*	Economic growth and renewal of exports because of increased demand during Second World War.	No trickle-down from economic improvement. Unpopular peace signed with Peru ceding most of the Amazon region. Corruption and dictatorial practices of Arroyo del Río's administration.
1972	Military coup	Discovery of large quantities of oil suggests promising economic future and is hailed as an end to underdevelopment.	Unpopularity of the last Velasco Ibarra presidency. Fear of the elite of the victory of populist mayor Assad Bucaram in the upcoming presidential elections. Discovery of oil and fear of 'civilian mismanagement' of natural resources.

Table 6.12 GDP growth and inflation, 1997–2005 (in percentage)

Year	GDP growth (%)	Inflation (%)
1997	2.4	30.6
1998	0.6	36.1
1999	−7.6	52.2
2000	1.3	96.1
2001	3.6	37.7
2002	1.9	12.5
2003	1.2	7.9
2004	4.5	2.7

Source: de la Torre (2006), p. 39.

more vulnerable to overthrows, irrespective of the economic context, because of certain structural and institutional factors.

In this regard, Conaghan and Espinal (1990) offer arguments which help to explain Ecuador's political instability. Published long before the recent bout of acute IPI in Ecuador, their article on democracy without compromise anticipated what they called the emergence of a 'crisis-prone' democracy. With hindsight, their accurate predictions enhance the credibility of their arguments today. They explained the fragility of Ecuador's democracy as a product of the domination of an extremely disorganized civil society by a conservative elite; a dependence on agricultural exports; a 'socio-cultural differentiation . . . retarded by industrialisation that was late, even by Latin American standards' and the weakness or absence of 'reformist middle classes, militant working classes, and a politically flexible bourgeoisie'. The weakness of Ecuador's democracy thus hinges on the fact that it 'did not emerge as a political arrangement to negotiate the relations between labour and capital' or as a 'product of class compromise', but rather as a 'vehicle for restructuring domination by economic and political elites in a context in which lower classes were not highly mobilised or threatening' (pp. 554–5).

Isaacs (1991) follows a similar analysis and stresses a transition based solely on a 'procedural definition of democracy' (p. 221). For Isaacs, the remarkable growth rates of the 1970s meant that the '[Ecuadorian military] government did not need to secure significant compromises either from labour or the private sector.' She agrees that the 'delayed character of Ecuadorian industrialisation, explain[s] the absence of a strong working class or industrial bourgeoisie likely to challenge the economic and political influence of the agricultural export elite' (pp. 222–3). Again, Ecuador's agro-export model may prove crucial to understanding the fragility of its political system. The development model may explain not just Ecuador's economic vulnerability to external shocks but also the dynamics of its domestic sociopolitical construction and institutional instability.

This structural approach should not distract us, however, from the importance of agency. In Ecuador, the unpopularity of a government, and therefore the likelihood of the prompt and premature termination of its mandate, is often a product of certain sociocultural responses. The last three uprisings were grounded in strong ethical and moralistic ideals, which revolved around the popular rejection of the corruption of the political elite and its impunity.

6.8   Summary and conclusions

Our findings lead us to believe that the argument blaming political instability for economic woes has been excessively used in both academic and non-academic contexts, and has become a scapegoat for more fundamental systemic flaws. Blaming Ecuador's poor economic record on political instability, for example, has meant that there has been insufficient focus on Ecuador's development model, and the inherent risks of economic *laissez-faire*, which, we believe, resulted in the financial collapse of 1999. Thus, if structural political stability has contributed to the maintenance of Ecuador's main economic activities in the short term, it has not helped to change Ecuador's economic structure towards a situation that is more conducive to development. For those of us who believe nation-building, institutional consolidation, coherent efforts against corruption and robust long-term heterodox economic policies are the key to the development of a sustainable democratic polity, the current status quo offers Ecuador an uncertain future. If institutional consolidation is really the key to long-term sustainable development, then the present syncretism between structural stability and institutional disintegration, will not act pro-development.

It is thus important to distinguish the short-term sustainability of the Ecuadorian political and economic model developed in this chapter, from the longer-term implications of the semi-anarchic framework presented here. It remains clear that there is an urgent need for the Ecuadorian state to finally assume its role as the sole, legitimate and sovereign arbiter of Ecuadorian interactions and exchanges. Equally, paralegal forms of conflict resolution, which are inherently forms of adaptation to a quasi-'state-less' vacuum, should disappear or be replaced by a working political system in order for Ecuador to move away from its current situation towards the institutional fold of an *état de droit*.

There will therefore emerge a crisis-point where a transition to a new political regime will necessarily materialize. In the long term, failure to steer Ecuador away from its current State of Nature could have dire consequences. Recent voting patterns and the rise of messianic leaderships (Bucaram, Gutierrez, A. Noboa) should draw our attention to the desperate popular appeals conjuring the Leviathan. Ultimately, Correa's great test will be to channel this popular aspiration into the creation of effective and stable institutions. Failure to do so may result in the popular clamour for a transition towards the formation of *any* strong regime, regardless of how authoritarian or undemocratic it may be.

Note

1 A shorter version, and the source of this quotation, has been published in Hausman (1994). The quote is on page 52.

References

Abers, N. R. (2000) *Inventing Local Democracy*. Boulder, CO: Lynne Rienner.

Acosta, A. (2002) *Breve Historia Económica del Ecuador*. Quito: Corporación Editora Nacional.

Acosta, A. (2005) 'Oxy y el Cuento de la Seguridad Jurídica' *La Insignia*. Accessed at http://www.lainsignia.org/2005/agosto/econ_011.htm.

Ake, C. (1975) 'A Definition of Political Stability', *Comparative Politics*, 7(2), 271–83.

Alesina, A., Ozler, S., Roubini, N. and Swagel, P. (1996) 'Political Stability and Economic Growth', *Journal of Economic Growth*, 1(2), 189–211.

Ashcraft, R. (1968) 'Locke's State of Nature: Historical Fact of Moral Fiction?, *American Political Science Review*, 62(3), 898–915.

BBC news, online version, 17 May 2006. Accessed at http://news.bbc.co.uk/hi/americas/4988624.stm.

Bustamante, F. (2005) 'En los Arrabales del Estado de Naturaleza', *Ecuador Debate*, 64, 7–20.

Cardoso, F. H. and Faletto, E. (1979) *Dependency and Development in Latin America.* Berkeley: University of California Press.

Conaghan, C. M. and Espinal, R. (1990) 'Unlikely Transitions to Uncertain Regimes? Democracy without Compromise in the Dominican Republic and Ecuador', *Journal of Latin American Studies*. 22(3), 553–74.

Correa, R. (2004) *La Vulnerabilidad de la Economía Ecuatoriana.* Quito: United Nations Development Program.

Correa, R. (2005) 'Canje de Deuda: Todo en Función de los Acreedores'. *La Insignia.* Accessed at http://www.lainsignia.org/2005/junio/econ_008.htm.

Darby, J., Li, C. and Muscatelli, A. (1998) 'Political Uncertainty, Public Expenditure and Growth', University of Glasgow, Working Paper No. 9822.

de la Torre, C. (2006) 'Populismo, Democracia, Protestas y Crisis Políticas Recurrentes en Ecuador', *Europa América Latina: Análisis e Informaciones*, Centro de Estudos Fundação Konrad Adenauer, No. 21, 5–43.

Diario Hoy, online version, 3 March 2006. 'Costo por el Envío de las Remesas'. Accessed at http://www.hoy.com.ec/NoticiaNue.asp?row_id=228293.

Feierabend, I. K. and Feierabend, R. 1966. 'Aggressive Behaviors Within Polities, 1948–1962: A Cross-National Study', *Journal of Conflict Resolution*, 10, 249–71.

Feng, Y. (1997) 'Democracy, Political Stability and Economic Growth', *British Journal of Political Science*, 27(3), 391–418.

Fisher, S. (2000) 'Ecuador and the IMF'. Hoover Institution Conference on Currency Unions. Accessed at http://www.imf.org/external/np/speeches/2000/051900.htm.

Franck, S. D. (2005) 'Occidental Exploration & Production Co. v. Republic of Ecuador. Final Award. London Court of International Arbitration Administered Case No. UN 3467'. *The American Journal of International Law*, 99(3), 675–81.

Haber, S., Razo, A. and Maurer, N. (2001) 'Economic Growth amidst Political Instability: Evidence from Revolutionary Mexico'. Accessed at http://wcfia.harvard.edu/seminars/pegroup/haberazomaurer.pdf.

Huntington, S. P. (1968) *Political Order in Changing Societies.* New Haven: Yale University Press.

Hausman, D. (ed.) (1994) *The Philosophy of Economics: An Anthology*, 2nd edition. Cambridge: Cambridge University Press.

Hentschel, J. (1994) 'Trade and Growth in Ecuador: A Partial Equilibrium View'. *Policy Research Working Paper Series* 1352. Washington DC: The World Bank.

Holt, R. T. and Turner, J. E. (1966) *The Political Basis of Economic Development.* Princeton: Van Nostrand.

Hurwitz, L. (1973) 'Contemporary Approaches to Political Stability', *Comparative Politics*, 5(3), 449–63.

Isaacs, A. (1991) 'Problems of Democratic Consolidation in Ecuador', *Bulletin of Latin American Research*, 10(2), 221–38.

Kaufmann, D. (1997), 'Corruption: The Facts', *Foreign Policy*, Summer, 114–31.

Krueger, A. O. (1974) 'The Political Economy of the Rent-Seeking Society', *American Economic Review*, 64(3), 291–303.

Laffont, J. J. 2001. *Incentives and Political Economy*. Oxford: Oxford University Press.

Larrea, C. (2006) 'Petróleo y Estrategias de Desarrollo en el Ecuador: 1972–2005', in G. Fontaine (ed.), *Petróleo y Desarrollo Sostenible en el Ecuador: 3. Las Ganancias y Pérdidas*. Quito: Facultad Latinoamericana de Ciencias Sociales.

López-Cálix, J. R. 2003. 'Maintaining Stability with Fiscal Discipline and Competitiveness', in V. Fretes Cibrils, M. M. Giugale and J. R. López-Cálix (eds), *Ecuador: An Economic and Social Agenda in the New Millenium*. Washington, DC: The World Bank, pp. 3–41.

Lipset, S. M. (1960) *Political Man: The Social Bases of Politics*. New York: Doubleday.

Locke, J. (1988[1689]) *Two Treatises of Government*. Cambridge: Cambridge University Press.

Mauro, P. (1995) 'Corruption and Economic Growth', *Quarterly Journal of Economics*, 110(3), 681–712.

Mauro, P. (1998) 'Corruption and the Composition of Government Expenditure', *Journal of Public Economics*, 69, 263–79.

Mill, J. S. (1844) *Essays on Some Unsettled Questions of Political Economy*, 3rd edition. London: Longmans Green & Co.

Nordhaus, W. D. 1975. 'The Political Business Cycle', *Review of Economic Studies*, 42(2), 169–90.

North, D. (1990) *Institutions, Institutional Change, and Economic Performance*. New York: Cambridge University Press.

Nye, J. S. (1967) 'Corruption and Political Development: A Cost–Benefit Analysis'. *The American Political Science Review*, 61(2), 417–27.

Ojeda, L. 2004. '¿Por qué la Decentralización no Avanza?', *Ecuador Debate*, No. 61: 95–116.

Olson, M. (1982) *The Rise and Decline of Nations: Economic Growth, Stagflation and Social Rigidities*. New Haven: Yale University Press.

Persson, T. and Tabellini, G. (2000) *Political Economics: Explaining Economic Policy*. Cambridge, MA: MIT Press.

Romer, T. and Rosenthal, H. (1979) 'Bureaucrats vs Voters: On the Political Economy of Resource Allocation by Direct Democracy, *Quarterly Journal of Economics*, 93(4), 563–87.

Sánchez, J. (2004a) 'Decentralización, Macroeconomía y Desarrollo Local', *Ecuador Debate*, 61, 77–94.

Sánchez, J. (2004b) 'Ensayo sobre la Economía de Migración en Ecuador', *Ecuador Debate*, 63, 47–62.

Seligson, M. A. and Recanatini, F. (2003) 'The Environment and Governance and Corruption', in V. Fretes Cibrils, M. M. Giugale and J. R. López-Cálix (eds), *Ecuador: An Economic and Social Agenda in the New Millenium*. Washington DC: The World Bank, pp. 411–43.

Simmons, A. J. (1989) 'Locke's State of Nature', *Political Theory*, 17(3), 449–70.

Solimano, A. (2005) 'Economic Growth and Macro Management in Latin America: Past, Present and Future Perspectives', in ECLAC, United Nations, REDIMA II. Accessed at http://www.comunidadandina.org/economia/redima2_cepal1.pdf.

Tendler, J. (1997) *Good Government in the Tropics*. Baltimore: John Hopkins University Press.

van Cott, D. L. (2002) 'Constitutional Reform in the Andes', in R. Sieder (ed.), *Multiculturalism in Latin America: Indigenous Rights, Diversity and Democracy*. London: Palgrave, pp. 45–72.

Weisbrot, M., Sandoval, L. and Cadena, B. (2006) Ecuador's Presidential Elections: Background on Economic Issues. Washington, DC: Centre for Economic and Policy Research. Accessed at http://www.cepr.net/documents/ecuador_elections_economic_issues.pdf.

Index